SHALL
NEVER PERISH
FOREVER

SHALL
NEVER PERISH
FOREVER

Dennis M. Rokser

Grace Gospel Press
Duluth, Minnesota

All Scripture quotations, unless otherwise indicated, are taken from the *New King James Version*®. Copyright © 1982 by Thomas Nelson, Inc. Used by permission. All rights reserved.

ISBN 978-0-9799637-8-0

Library of Congress Control Number: 2012946944

GGP◄
Grace Gospel Press
201 W. Saint Andrews St.
Duluth, MN 55803
U.S.A.
(218) 724-5914
www.gracegospelpress.com

Printed in the United States of America

I gratefully dedicate this book to my faithful and loving
wife, Nancy, who has been a gracious fellow-laborer
for the Gospel of grace through her prayers and support
over the twenty-five years that this book was very slowly
being written. She is a virtuous woman (Prov. 31) and
worthy of much praise now and at the Bema Seat
of Christ (1 Cor. 4:5).

And I give them eternal life, and they shall never perish [forever]; neither shall anyone snatch them out of My hand. My Father, who has given them to Me, is greater than all; and no one is able to snatch them out of My Father's hand. I and My Father are one.

John 10:28-30

ENDORSEMENTS

The clear message of the Gospel and eternal security is life's most vital and beautiful message. The Gospel is not God's exchange program where He says, "I will give you My salvation if you give me your life." Unsaved people are dead in trespasses and sins and have nothing to give God until they are born-again, and only then with great joy they can devote their lives to serve their wonderful Lord.

I am persuaded that no one clearly knows the Gospel until he knows what the Gospel is not, such as making a commitment to Christ; Lordship Salvation; surrendering all to the Lord; giving your heart to God; and other unbiblical sayings. These are not the Gospel. Nor does God place people on probation the moment they first believe in Christ as their Savior.

It gives us much joy to know our salvation is secure in Christ and not dependent on our loyalty and Christian living. Eternal security is such a vital, biblical message that every Christian should know it and rejoice in it.

I appreciate so much Pastor Dennis Rokser because he has such a heartbeat for God's Word. God has blessed him with an unusual ability to discern the truth from Scripture and to teach it clearly. The insights he writes about in *Shall Never Perish Forever* are not just his own personal theories and opinions but the true, biblical Gospel that radiates from his life as he keeps on keeping on and serving his wonderful Lord.

I encourage you to read this book. As you do, you will be thrilled once again with the many treasures we have in Christ.

Dr. Art Rorheim
Co-founder & President Emeritus
AWANA Clubs International

Christ's complete and final work of salvation has and will always be under attack. Dennis Rokser has written a very well-studied and documented support of the crucial doctrine of eternal security in *Shall Never Perish Forever*. I highly recommend *Shall Never Perish Forever* to young believers as well as to teachers and pastors. Rokser addresses the fundamental Biblical arguments, also going through those passages that are often used to undermine this precious assuring doctrine of eternal security in Christ. Dennis, thank you for this great contribution to the Bride of Christ.

Larry M. Brown
Chairman New Tribes Mission, USA

Dennis Rokser's book on eternal security is a book full of knowledge of Scripture. If anyone has a right to be an Arminian, it would be me. My father, a Methodist minister for 40 years, taught me never to accept the dangerous doctrine of "once saved, always saved." I remember asking Baptist friends, "Why do you believe once saved, always saved?" They could never give me any answer.

If they only could have had this book, it would have made all the difference in the world. This book answers all these questions and is a must read in order to know the Scriptures backing up the doctrine of eternal security.

As Dennis Rokser said, "If you can lose it, you have to work to keep it." He answers very clearly the wrong belief of yes God can't lose you but you can lose God by letting loose with your hand. I thought his response to that was very succinct, when Dennis Rokser said, sheep have hooves not hands.

You may be asking why it is so important to know this question. The answer is your salvation depends upon it. I would certainly recommend this book as a must read and recommend it to any family members to read to understand this important doctrine.

Usually books of this nature have a tendency to be boring but this book is anything but boring. I want to commend Dennis Rokser for the excellent job and scholarship in authoring this tremendous book.

> Dr. James A. Scudder
> Pastor, Bible Teacher, popular author,
> Host of Victory in Grace

This book is a valuable tool for counseling the many believers who have become confused about their assurance of salvation. Pastor Rokser gets the reader right into many specific Scripture passages including the so-called problem passages. He clarifies the difference between forensically perfect justification and subsequent variable sanctification; between objective security and subjective assurance. A loving pastoral spirit permeates the book with homey illustrations and helpful diagrams. Highly recommended especially for those believers struggling with life-dominating sins.

> Charles Clough
> Bible Teacher, Conference Speaker,
> founder of Bible Framework course

Pastor Dennis Rokser has given us a truly great book on the eternal security of the believer in Christ, and I heartily recommend it to anyone and everyone who is concerned about the certainty of salvation. He is thorough, gracious and right on target biblically. You'll not only want to read it for yourself, but it's the kind of book you'll want to have extra copies of to pass on to others. He not only clearly explains that the way of salvation is by grace alone through faith alone in Christ alone, he also gives great insights into passages that are sometimes wrongly used to "prove" one can lose salvation. One of the interesting characteristics of this particular book is that Pastor Rokser clearly explains why neither Arminians nor Calvinists can logically have absolute assurance of their salvation based on their respective doctrines of either losing salvation through sin (Arminiansim), or of not being certain of salvation until one has persevered to death (Calvinism). You will definitely want this book in your library.

Richard (Dick) Seymour
President, Clarity Ministries International,
Instructor, Frontier School of the Bible

Shall Never Perish Forever reflects a rare combination of prodigious research, thorough exegesis, sound theological synthesis, and matter-of-fact clarity. Crisply written and stylishly crafted, Rokser is a man on a mission. With a pastor's heart and a passion for grace, he engages the reader, engendering confidence and hope by pointing to the truth of God's Word. There is no shortage of books on the subject of eternal security, but Rokser's work is sure to become a tour de force on the topic. If you are looking for an authoritative doctrinal treatise on this important matter, or if you are struggling with your own eternal destiny, *Shall Never Perish Forever* belongs on your library shelf—but only after you've first read it and benefited from its enriching content!

Dr. J. B. Hixson
Professor of Systematic Theology
Grace School of Theology
www.notbyworks.org

New believers often wrestle with two questions. First, "Am I truly saved?" Second, "Do I truly remain saved regardless of what sin I commit or if I cease to believe?" Pastor Rokser's new work, *Shall Never Perish Forever*, focuses on answering the second question. This volume is one of the most extensive studies on the subject of eternal security I have ever read dealing with all the typical questions a new believer might ask or objections he or she might bring up. Rokser responds to issues raised both by Calvinists and Arminians and does not ignore any passage of Scripture dealing with the subject. If any biblical passage was ignored, I did not notice it. This work shows that while a believer can lose a number of things if he chooses to live in sin, salvation is not one of them. This work by Pastor Rokser is highly recommended.

Dr. Arnold Fruchtenbaum
Ariel Ministries, Bible teacher,
Conference Speaker

Pastor Dennis Rokser's book, *Shall Never Perish Forever*, is a crucial and timely encouragement for the Church today. Pastor Rokser concisely shows by a thorough and faithful exegesis of Scripture that the believer's salvation is absolutely and eternally secure, due to the work of the Father, the Son and the Holy Spirit. He clearly demonstrates that the believer's confidence in eternal security leads to the assurance of salvation which is foundational to the believer's enjoyment of spiritual rest and motivation to live godly in Christ Jesus. If you are unsure of your salvation or unsure that your salvation is secure, this book will help you understand the good news of the Gospel. Whether you are a new believer or have been a believer for many years, this book will encourage you in your walk with God and your spiritual growth.

Chet Plimpton
former General Secretary
New Tribes Mission

Dennis Rokser, in *Shall Never Perish Forever*, has provided an interesting and detailed series of biblical arguments defending the highly significant doctrine of eternal security. Its comprehensiveness is coupled with a readability that will help thoughtful Christians easily explore one of the most controversial and practical areas of theology. Eternal security is not some discussion in the intellectual realm alone but a doctrine with life-changing consequences. *Shall Never Perish Forever* properly leads the reader to appreciate and embrace eternal security without compromise. I recommend it without reservation.

Dr. Mike Stallard
Dean & Professor of Systematic Theology
Baptist Bible Seminary

CONTENTS

PREFACE

If you have put your trust in Jesus Christ and His finished work alone to save you, is your salvation eternal and secure? Or can eternal life be lost, given back, or forfeited? Are believers in Christ on divine probation with their destiny uncertain, or do God's grace and power keep them saved forever? These are crucial questions that God answers with absolute certainty in the only book He ever wrote—the Bible.

It is the purpose of this volume to spell out in clear and concise terms how GOD weighs in on these important issues. If you are unsure of your eternal salvation, this book should be helpful to you as it repeatedly explains and emphasizes God's grace-plan of eternal redemption, for God wants you to be assured and "know that you have eternal life" (1 John 5:13).

If you are a relatively new believer in Jesus Christ as Savior, it is imperative that you have absolute assurance of your eternal salvation so that you can properly "grow in grace" (2 Peter 3:18) and not be "tossed to and fro and carried about with every wind of doctrine" (Eph. 4:14). This book should assist you to that end.

If you've known and grown in Christ for a number of years, I trust that this book will still be exciting, enjoyable, and edifying to you as it will remind you of God's great and precious promises "though you know them and be established in the present truth" (2 Peter 1:12).

It has been my desire to avoid theological camps in writing this book and instead allow the verses of the Bible to speak for themselves. I have sought to carefully observe the *context* and *content* of each verse considered and then to *compare* the Scriptures with the Scriptures to arrive at an accurate biblical conclusion. I assure you that God has clearly spoken, and He has not stuttered regarding the believer's assurance and the security of eternal salvation.

But since these matters are confusing to some and controversial to others, I implore you to read the entirety of this book *before* you disregard or reject its content. I encourage you to seriously consider and apply James's exhortation: "So then, my beloved brethren, let every man be swift to hear, slow to speak, slow to wrath" (James 1:19).

Why the Title, *Shall Never Perish Forever*?

Jesus Christ boldly declared regarding those who had trusted in Him alone, "And I give them eternal life and they *shall never perish*." As I will explain in chapter 11, there are three words in the Greek text that remain untranslated in this verse in almost all English Bibles. They are the words *eis ton aiōna*. Though the literal rendering of this Greek phrase could be "into the age," the concept being communicated is that of "forever" and is translated as such in several verses in the New Testament. In this pregnant verse, Christ gives a triple guarantee of the duration of the believer's salvation by God's grace, stating in essence, "I give to them eternal life, and they *shall never perish forever*." Thus, the title of this book: *Shall Never Perish Forever*.

May God use this book for His glory by pointing its readers to the supremacy and sufficiency of Jesus Christ's person and finished work resulting in "full assurance" (Col. 2:2) of knowing their eternal salvation is safe and secure forever!

Part I

Identifying the Issue
of
Eternal Security

CHAPTER 1

Laying the Groundwork

During His earthly life, Jesus Christ's message and ministry received severe opposition on several occasions from various groups. In one particular situation, the Sadducees, who were the theological liberals of Jesus' day, questioned Him about man's future resurrection (which they denied) in order to attempt to trap Him. They asked Him,

> Teacher, Moses said that if a man dies, having no children, his brother shall marry his wife and raise up offspring for his brother. Now there were with us seven brothers. The first died after he had married, and having no offspring, left his wife to his brother. Likewise the second also, and the third, even to the seventh. Last of all the woman died also. Therefore, in the resurrection, whose wife of the seven will she be? For they all had her. (Matt. 22:24-28)

In answer to their hypothetical situation and foolish question, the Lord Jesus Christ gave this straightforward reply:

> *You are mistaken, not knowing the Scriptures nor the power of God.* For in the resurrection they neither marry nor are given in marriage, but are like angels of God in heaven. But concerning the resurrection of the dead, have you not read what was spoken to you by God, saying, "I am the God of Abraham, the God of Isaac, and the God of

Jacob"? God is not the God of the dead, but of the living.
(vv. 29-32)

What a precise and powerful answer! What a serious and scathing
indictment Jesus Christ made when He pointedly said, "You are
mistaken, not knowing the Scriptures nor the power of God" (v. 29).

Our Lord called a spade, a spade! He pulled no punches! He
told it like it was. He went for the Sadducees' spiritual jugular and
leveled their self-righteous pride when he said, "You are mistaken."
In effect, Christ was saying, "You Sadducees, you religious people,
you who think you have it all together, *you are mistaken*." This could
essentially be rendered, "You are repeatedly mistaken. You are
perpetually going astray. You are over and over again missing the
beaten path of truth." Why was this so? What were the root causes
for their erring? And what specific reasons did Jesus Christ offer
regarding their sad spiritual state?

THE ROOT PROBLEMS

Jesus Christ identified two failures which reveal the reasons for the
Sadducees erring from the truth.

1.   They were ignorant of the Word of God.

"You are mistaken, *not knowing the Scriptures*." Christ pointed out
that though they prided themselves in being followers of Moses,
they did not really understand what Moses taught. They did not
perceive the true meaning of Scripture. What condemnation! Unlike
some things in life, biblical ignorance is not bliss; it is a serious
blunder. Throngs of people today are biblically illiterate. Sad to say,
many couldn't care less. Few theological seminaries today believe or
teach that the Bible is the inspired, inerrant, infallible Word of the
living God. Church-goers are fed a steady diet of "sermonettes for
Christianettes," preached from Hallmark cards and dosed with social
reform and pop psychology instead of clear, accurate, and practical
Bible teaching. Church tradition, quasi-sanctified entertainment,
rote-ritual, religious Madison Avenue techniques—*ad infinitum, ad
nauseum*—dominate too many church services in our land.

The prophet Hosea's cry is still very applicable today: "My
people are destroyed for *lack of knowledge*" (Hos. 4:6a). What a sad
spiritual condition exists when so few know the truth about God,

His grace provision of salvation, His plan and purpose for man, and more. How tragic and how unnecessary when we have access to a completed Bible, the teaching ministry of the Holy Spirit, and the promise of Jesus Christ which states, "If anyone wants to do His will, *he shall know concerning the doctrine,* whether it is from God or whether I speak on My own authority" (John 7:17).

Everyone needs to know God's truth. There is no value in sticking one's head in the spiritual sand. God wants you to know His revealed truth. This is why He has given you His word. No wonder the Scriptures tell us,

> But He answered and said, "It is written, 'Man shall not live by bread alone, but by every word that proceeds from the mouth of God.'" (Matt. 4:4)

> As newborn babes, desire the pure milk of the word, that you may grow thereby. (1 Peter 2:2)

> Your word is a lamp to my feet and a light to my path. (Ps. 119:105)

Should it surprise us that in 2 Timothy 2:15 the apostle Paul says, "Be diligent to present yourself approved to God, a worker who does not need to be ashamed, rightly dividing the word of truth"? Because of the authority and sufficiency of the Scriptures, Paul instructs young pastor Timothy to,

> *Preach the Word;* be instant in season, out of season; reprove, rebuke, exhort with all long-suffering and doctrine. *For the time will come when they will not endure sound doctrine;* but after their own lusts shall they heap to themselves teachers, having itching ears; and they shall turn away their ears from the truth, and shall be turned unto fables. (2 Tim. 4:2-4)

Practicing what he preached, Paul explains to the Ephesian elders at Miletus regarding his own teaching ministry, "For I have not shunned *to declare to you the whole counsel of God"* (Acts 20:27).

From this sampling of verses, one thing is quite clear. A true understanding and steady diet of the Word of God is essential in our lives. Why were the Sadducees mistaken? Like many in pulpit and pew today, they went astray because *they were ignorant of the Word of God*. This is the first reason for the Sadducees' error, which leads us to the second reason Jesus Christ gave for their ignorance.

2.   They were ignorant of the power of God.

"You are mistaken, not knowing the Scriptures, *nor the power of God*." Their ignorance of Scripture resulted in an underestimation of God's power. They could not comprehend the power of God Almighty which could raise the dead in a future bodily resurrection. This did not fit their theological system which gave naturalistic answers and denied supernatural explanations. God is omnipotent or all-powerful. He has the power to do *anything* within the parameters of His nature and will. In fact, Romans 1:20 tells us that through the medium of His created universe, every day God reveals to us His "eternal power and Godhead; so that [we] are without excuse."

Ironically, God further displayed His supernatural power in the midst of the Sadducees' dark unbelief through the numerous miracles Christ performed, climaxed by His own resurrection from the dead. It is essential that we understand the power of God, especially since the saving message of the Gospel unleashes *"the power of God unto salvation* to everyone that believes" (Rom. 1:16).

The indictment of the Lord Jesus Christ to these Sadducees is very clear: "You are mistaken, not knowing the Scriptures, nor the power of God."

A PERSONAL APPLICATION

Could this be said of you? Do you know what you believe? Is your belief rooted and grounded in the Scriptures? Do your convictions have the biblical stamp of approval consisting of "thus says the Lord"? Have you taken into full consideration the supernatural power of God? I ask these questions of you because these two biblical essentials (the Word of God and the power of God) have everything to do with a correct understanding of the subject in this book, *Shall Never Perish Forever: Is Salvation Forever or Can It Be Lost?*

SOME PERTINENT QUESTIONS

Have you ever wondered, "Can a genuine believer in Jesus Christ ever be lost again?" Perhaps someone has asked you, "Can people who are truly saved ever commit a sin or sin to such a degree that they would lose their salvation and be condemned forever?" Approaching it from another angle, "Can a believer in the Lord Jesus Christ later fall away from salvation?" And "Can people know with 100-percent assurance they will be saved in one, five, or ten years from now? Or forever?" Or "Must one wait till he dies to see if he has persevered in faith and godliness, proving he is one of God's elect?" Good questions, wouldn't you say? Essential questions, for they address issues that lie right at the heart of understanding people's eternal destiny. I assure you that the Bible speaks very directly and clearly regarding these crucial issues.

FOUR COMMON RESPONSES

When the important issue of the security of salvation or these kinds of legitimate questions arise, people generally respond in one of four ways. To some individuals, the issue of the security of salvation is a . . .

Dilemma

Some people are honestly uncertain about what the Bible teaches regarding this. This is sometimes true of new believers or of churches where the Bible is not clearly taught. Others use the cop-out, "Bible scholars have debated and disagreed on these issues for many years." Dear friends, that is nothing less than skirting the issue. Though it seems hard to believe, I have even heard of those who seek to walk the middle of the road by saying, "Both sides are right! Salvation is eternal and secure, but you can lose it." That is theological double-talk. It's like having white blacktop, which is an oxymoronic impossibility. Still others are tossed to and fro on this issue, being blown around like spiritual tumbleweed depending on whom they are talking to or associating with that day. In each of these cases, the reaction or response to the issue of eternal security is one of *dilemma*. However, though some people view the eternal security of salvation as an unresolved dilemma, there is a substantial group of people who vehemently oppose and reject this teaching, calling it a . . .

Damnable Doctrine

Some folks in pulpit and pew conclude that to know you are saved forever and can never lose it is "satanic" and "straight from the pit of Hell." They further conclude that this teaching is a "license to sin," producing careless living among believers. Their concern is an understandable one, for God saves a sinner "from" sin, not "to" sin. Furthermore, we know that God hates sin and calls believers to "Be holy, for I am holy" (1 Peter 1:16). Oddly enough, some people reject this so-called "doctrine of the devil" while claiming that they personally have assurance that Heaven is *their* future home and that they shall never lose *their* salvation. Doesn't this sound contradictory and arrogant? If others can lose it, why can't they? So while some view the issue of eternal security as a *damnable doctrine*, a growing number of evangelicals have concluded that what you believe about eternal security . . .

Doesn't Matter

These individuals, even many who are pastors, view this issue as secondary and non-essential at best, and controversial and divisive at worst. While they may discuss it privately, they avoid teaching it publicly, not wanting to rock the boat of their numerically growing evangelical church. Oftentimes, people who attend this kind of church reflect a mixed bag of beliefs, consisting of those who embrace eternal security, those who deny eternal security, and those who just don't know or care. Unfortunately, the truths of the Word of God regarding this important issue are not taught, leaving people with the impression that it really *doesn't matter* what you believe about the security of salvation. Don't you think it is important to know for sure whether or not you are saved from Hell forever? How sad! And how unnecessary, when the Scriptures are replete with numerous verses specifically addressing this subject. The fourth prevalent response to the issue of the security of salvation is one of . . .

Delight

Many have found the eternal security of salvation to be one of the most comforting, assuring, and uplifting of all Christian truths. Those who understand and believe in the true nature of salvation by God's grace and the sufficiency of Christ's finished payment for all of our sins enjoy the assurance of an everlasting salvation. To them, the verses of Scripture we will examine in the chapters to follow are a *delight*. Like the prophet Jeremiah, they exclaim, "Your words were found, and I ate them, and Your word was to me the joy and rejoicing of my heart; for I am called by Your name, O LORD God of hosts" (Jer. 15:16).

A PERSONAL CHALLENGE

What response to this important issue of the security of eternal salvation do you have? Is it an unresolved dilemma? If so, then make sure you carefully read this book with an open heart, paying close attention to the clear verses of Scripture. Remember, "The entrance of Your words gives light" (Ps. 119:130a)!

Perhaps your response to this issue has been to consider it a damnable doctrine of satanic or human origin. If this is true of you, let me ask you a very probing question that you need to honestly face. Do you reject this teaching based on an objective understanding of all the Scriptures regarding it? Why do you believe what you believe? Please consider and study the numerous Scripture verses which this book will give.

On the other hand, you may be of the opinion that the issue of the assurance of eternal salvation does not matter. But are you willing to search the Scriptures to see *if it matters to God*? And if it does, will you change your mind?

Lastly, you might be thinking, "I believe that my salvation is eternal and secure." Great! Could you support your beliefs from the Bible? And could you communicate your convictions clearly to someone else?

WHAT IS YOUR FINAL STANDARD OF AUTHORITY?

Whether you realize it or not, you base your beliefs on some authority, standard, or evidence which you hold to be valid or right. What is it? Take a moment to think it through. Evaluate. Consider the options. Is your conviction based on your *human experience* so that you reject this teaching as a fabrication of people's fantasies? Is it because you say to yourself, "I knew a person once who claimed to be saved, but later he did such and such a sin. I'm sure he lost his salvation"? I ask you, how do you know for sure he was genuinely saved to begin with? If he was saved by God's grace, how do you know he lost his salvation? What is your standard? What if someone else had just the opposite human evaluation or experience? Who is right?

The apostle Peter makes it clear to us that the Word of God alone, not human experience, is the final determiner of truth.

Moreover I will endeavour that ye may be able after my decease to have these things always in remembrance. For we have not followed cunningly devised fables, when we made known unto you the power and coming of our Lord Jesus Christ, but were eyewitnesses of His majesty. For he received from God the Father honour and glory, when there came such a voice to Him from the excellent glory, "This is my beloved Son, in whom I am well pleased." And this voice which came from heaven we heard, when we were with him in the holy mount. *We have also a more sure word of prophecy;* whereunto ye do well that ye take heed, as unto a light that shineth in a dark place, until the day dawn, and the day star arise in your hearts: *knowing this first, that no prophecy of the scripture is of any private interpretation.* For the prophecy came not in old time by the will of man: but holy men of God spake as they were moved by the Holy Ghost. (2 Peter 1:15-21, KJV)

The written Word of God is more sure than human experience. Your human experience is an unreliable final authority for God's truth, just as is *human emotion*. Listen closely when people discuss this issue. They will often say, "Well, I feel . . ." Realistically, the final determiner of truth is not what we feel but what God's Word says! I don't always feel very alive, but all the vital signs are still there.

Or perhaps you base your beliefs about these matters on *human opinion*. When this is the case, you will find yourself saying, "I had a friend once who told me I could lose my salvation. This must be right." Or perhaps this unreliable guide masquerades by prefacing statements with, "I personally think" or "I heard Mr. Evangelist once say." But all our human opinions fade into oblivion when we remember that *"All Scripture is given by inspiration of God, and is profitable* for doctrine, for reproof, for correction, for instruction in righteousness, that the man of God may be complete, thoroughly equipped for every good work" (2 Tim. 3:16-17).

Still others uphold *church tradition* as a reliable determiner of truth. Jesus Christ ripped this conclusion to shreds when He declared, "Thus *you have made the commandment of God of no effect by your tradition. . . .* And in vain they worship Me, teaching as doctrines the commandments of men" (Matt. 15:6, 9).

THE ONLY AUTHORITATIVE STANDARD OF TRUTH

Dear friend, the final determiner of truth is not one's *human experience*, no matter how real it may seem. Neither is it one's *human emotion*, regardless of how sincere it may be. Nor is it one's *human opinion*, no matter how credible it is. Neither is it *church tradition*, regardless of how enduring and popular it is. The only final court of appeal in determining God's truth is the *Holy Scriptures*. Remember what Jesus Christ said in Matthew 22:29? "You are mistaken, not knowing *the Scriptures*, nor the power of God." He also affirmed the absolute authority of Scripture in John 17:17 when He prayed, "Sanctify them through Your truth: *Your Word is truth.*"

We have in the Scriptures the inspired, infallible, and inerrant source and record of divine truth, so we can know with certainty what *God* has to say on these matters. And when *God* says it, that settles it, no matter what anyone feels or thinks about it. The gavel of truth stands or falls not on what some theologians have taught about the security of salvation but on what the Scriptures reveal and teach. In fact, I encourage and challenge you to put everything in this book to the acid test of Scripture. Be like those noble Bereans of Paul's day who "received the Word with all readiness, and *searched the Scriptures daily* to find out whether these things were so" (Acts 17:11). Did you notice again what is the final determiner of truth? They "searched the Scriptures." Will you be willing to follow their example on this crucial issue of the security of salvation? You will be glad you did!

How firm a foundation, ye saints of the Lord,
Is laid for your faith in His excellent word!
What more can He say than to you He hath said—
To you who for refuge to Jesus have fled.[1]

---

[1] Robert Keen, *How Firm a Foundation*. Observe how all the songs mentioned in this book have a ring of the absolute assurance of salvation in them.

CHAPTER 2

Defining Our Terms

Sad to say, insecurity plagues numerous lives in our world. Many people hurl themselves down various dead-end streets philosophically and practically in order to find real identity, unconditional love, personal acceptance, significant purpose, and genuine security in life, only to come up empty-handed and miserable. Even in Christian circles, some individuals profess to have trusted in Christ but believe that their salvation is neither eternal nor secure. They believe that if they don't "hang-in-there," God will boot them out of His family. Or they fear that if they seriously "slip up," salvation will "slip out" of their hands. Is this the message of the Scriptures? Is this the good news of the Gospel of Jesus Christ? Is God's gift of salvation to undeserving sinners eternal and secure or not?

WHAT IS ETERNAL SECURITY?

It would be well for us to define our terms at the outset. What do we mean by the theological phrase "eternal security"?

> **Eternal security means that those who have been genuinely saved by God's grace through faith alone in Jesus Christ alone shall never be in danger of God's condemnation or loss of their salvation, but God's grace and power keep them forever saved and secure.**

Please don't get sidetracked by the phrase "eternal security" itself. I realize that it is not in the Bible. But neither is the word "Bible," though I believe in it. Neither is the word "Trinity," though the Bible teaches it. All of these theological terms help us concisely explain particular truths that the Scriptures clearly declare. So let's not get hung up on the term itself.

OBSERVING THIS DEFINITION

Several components of this definition are worthy of noting. First, eternal security only applies to those "who have been genuinely saved by grace through faith in Jesus Christ alone." This eliminates any counterfeit "Christians" who think salvation is something they earn from God by way of their good works, instead of trusting in what God does for them because of Christ's finished work on the cross. 2 Timothy 1:9 clearly teaches us that it is God "*Who has saved us and called us with a holy calling, not according to our works, but according to His own purpose and grace* which was given to us in Christ Jesus."

Second, notice that this definition explains the quality or extent of salvation that undeserving sinners receive when they trust in Christ alone as Savior. Their salvation is eternal and secure so that they "shall never be in danger of God's condemnation or loss of their salvation, but God's grace and power keep them forever saved and secure." Regarding this, the Lord Jesus Christ clearly declared, "Most assuredly, I say to you, he who hears My word and believes in Him who sent Me *has everlasting life, and shall not come into judgment, but has passed from death into life*" (John 5:24).

Last, God wants you to recognize that one's eternal salvation and security are all by God's *grace* and *power*. No one can save himself or keep himself saved through his repentance from sin, holy life, commitment to Christ, or faithfulness to God. God's gift of salvation and eternal security are both spiritual realities that God alone provides and accomplishes for us to His own praise and glory. As the apostle Paul explains, "For by grace you have been saved through faith, and that not of yourselves; it is the gift of God, not of works, lest anyone should boast" (Eph. 2:8-9). Thus our definition ends with, "but *God's grace and power* keep them forever saved and secure."

CLARIFYING THE CONFUSION

In seeking to explain what something is, it is often helpful to explain what it is not. The result of this contrast is greater clarity and comprehension of the truth. Paul uses this teaching technique in the two verses you just read: Ephesians 2:8-9. The glaring contrast within these verses serves to clarify the truth of salvation by grace through faith apart from our works. By applying this teaching technique to the issue of the security of salvation, I will clarify what eternal security does *not* mean.

1. Eternal security does not mean that all who *profess* Christ actally *possess* eternal salvation.

A classic passage of Scripture expressing this truth occurs in Matthew 7:21-23. From the lips of the Lord Jesus we read,

> Not everyone who says to Me, "Lord, Lord," shall enter the kingdom of heaven, but he who does the will of My Father in heaven. Many will say to Me in that day, "Lord, Lord, have we not prophesied in Your name, cast out demons in Your name, and done many wonders in Your name?" And then I will declare to them, *"I never knew you;* depart from Me, you who practice lawlessness!"

The individuals in this passage *profess* Christ, but do *not* actually *possess* eternal salvation. They accurately call Him "Lord, Lord," and indeed, Christ is Lord. They apparently had "prophesied," "cast out devils," and "done many wonders" all in His "name." Surprisingly, Christ does not deny the reality of these claims; He just denies the reality of their salvation. While they profess to Him their own faithfulness and good works at this time of judgment, He professes to them, "I never knew you." Christ does not reply, "I used to know you, but you lost your salvation." Instead He replies to these religious but lost individuals, "I *never* knew you." Christ never had a personal saving relationship with them. Like so many people who claim to be "Christians" today, they profess Christ but do not actually possess salvation, for they trust in themselves and their goods works to save them. They fail to do the will of God, which is not an issue of their surrender and submission to Christ's mastery over their lives but instead is stated so simply in John 3:16: "For God so loved the world that He gave His only begotten Son, that *whoever believes in Him* should not perish but have everlasting life."

Salvation is not a reward for good people or good works (Eph. 2:8-9; Rom. 3:28); it is a gift for undeserving sinners who trust in Christ alone. *"And if by grace, then it is no longer of works; otherwise grace is no longer grace.* But if it is of works, it is no longer grace; otherwise work is no longer work" (Rom. 11:6). God is not impressed with our good works, wrought from sinful hands: "But we are all like an unclean thing, *and all our righteousnesses are like filthy rags*" (Isa. 64:6). If you add just one work to God's plan of grace, it destroys the truth of grace, for it is then earned favor. Grace is God's unmerited favor. Grace is God giving to you something you don't deserve and cannot earn by your good works, commitment, surrender, or faithfulness. This is why the only right response to God's message of salvation is not faith in Christ *plus*, but faith in Christ *period*.

> Not by works of righteousness which we have done, but according to His mercy He saved us, through the washing of regeneration and renewing of the Holy Spirit. (Titus 3:5)

> But to him who does not work but believes on Him who justifies the ungodly, his faith is accounted for righteousness. (Rom. 4:5)

> Knowing that a man is not justified by the works of the law but by faith in Jesus Christ, even we have believed in Christ Jesus, that we might be justified by faith in Christ and not by the works of the law; for by the works of the law no flesh shall be justified. (Gal. 2:16)

The Bible makes it abundantly clear that we are all born sinners and part of Satan's "4-H" club: we are helpless, hopeless, hell-bound, and horrible sinners before the eyes of a thrice holy God. This provides the dark background for God's wonderful, thrilling plan of salvation. Being helpless and hopeless, we can do nothing to save ourselves from sin's penalty. Therefore, God says, "I will do it all for you." As long as we think we can do anything to save ourselves, we don't perceive ourselves as helpless. As long as we think there is hope in our own efforts and works to save ourselves, we don't see ourselves as hopeless. For Jonah 2:9 tells us, "Salvation is of the Lord"!

I emphasize this because you will never get a true picture of God's grace until you see the helplessness of man because of sin and that his only hope is found in Christ. Thus, the good news of the Gospel is that God determined to make a perfect salvation possible for unworthy sinners like you and me! In order to accomplish this, God sent His Son to the cross of Calvary to lay all our sins on Him, to punish Him for our guilt, and then to offer this completed salvation freely as a gift to "whoever believes."

> All we like sheep have gone astray; we have turned, every one, to his own way; *and the LORD has laid on Him the iniquity of us all.* (Isa. 53:6)

> *For Christ also suffered once for sins, the just for the unjust,* that He might bring us to God, being put to death in the flesh but made alive by the Spirit. (1 Peter 3:18)

> For God so loved the world *that He gave His only begotten Son,* that *whoever believes in Him* should not perish but have everlasting life. (John 3:16)

The one condition on our part in order to receive God's gift of eternal life is to believe in Jesus Christ alone, trusting in Christ and His finished work *alone* to save us and not our own religious or moral works. Faith alone in Christ alone is the only means of receiving God's gift of grace.

2. Eternal security does *not* mean that all who trust Christ *plus* their good works are eternally saved or secure.

As we've already noted, salvation is not a reward for good people or good works; it is a gift for undeserving sinners who trust in Christ alone. The hymn writer of the past was right on target when he wrote, "Nothing in my hand I bring, simply to Thy cross I cling."

Do you see the simplicity of God's grace plan of salvation for you? Salvation is not a matter of putting your trust in Jesus Christ *plus* being baptized (though baptism has a place of testimony for believers). Salvation is not a matter of trusting Christ *plus* going to church (though Bible study can help believers to grow). Salvation is not a matter of asking Jesus into your heart (though He comes in when you believe).[1] Salvation is not a matter of making Christ "Lord of your life" (though He is Lord).[2] Can you see that it is not a matter of trusting in Christ *plus* good works (though good works should be the result of salvation)? Of

[1] Dennis M. Rokser, *Seven Reasons NOT to Ask Jesus into Your Heart* (Duluth, MN: Grace Gospel Press, 2012).
[2] Michael D. Halsey, *Truthspeak: The True Meaning of Five Key Christian Words Distorted through Religious Newspeak* (Milwaukee: Grace Gospel Press, 2010), 52-53.

the three approaches to God illustrated below, which one describes you?[3]

> Therefore we conclude that a man is justified by faith apart from the deeds of the law. (Rom. 3:28)

> So they said, "Believe on the Lord Jesus Christ, and you will be saved." (Acts 16:31)

> These things I have written to you who believe in the name of the Son of God, that you may know that you have eternal life, and that you may continue to believe in the name of the Son of God. (1 John 5:13)

John Newton, former slave-trader and converted preacher and songwriter, said it so well when he insightfully wrote,

> Amazing grace, how sweet the sound, that saved a wretch like me. I once was lost, but now am found, was blind, but now I see.

> T'was grace, that taught my heart to fear, t'was grace, my fears relieved. How precious did that grace appear, the hour I first believed.

3. Eternal security does *not* mean that knowing for sure that you are saved forever gives you license to sin; rather, it grants you liberty to serve Christ with full assurance of your eternal destiny.

Paul, the unequalled apostle of grace, clarifies this point in his great doctrinal dissertation of the Christian faith—the epistle of Romans. In Romans 6:1-2, he states, "What shall we say then? Shall we continue

---

[3] Diagrams adapted from R. Larry Moyer, *Free and Clear: Understanding and Communicating God's Offer of Eternal Life* (Grand Rapids: Kregel, 1997), 81.

in sin that grace may abound? *Certainly not!* How shall we who died to sin live any longer in it?" Prior to these verses, Paul had previously explained in Romans several key truths about justification.

- Justification is received by faith alone in Christ alone (Rom. 3),
- Justification before God is not by works, law, or ritual (Rom. 4),
- The blessings of justification include the eternal security of salvation (Rom. 5).

Anticipating the objection that God's plan of eternal salvation by grace would lead to careless or sinful living, Paul emphatically exclaims, "God forbid!" Christ came to set us free from the guilt of our sins and the bondage of our sin natures. Every believer in Christ has "died to sin" because of his/her identification with Jesus Christ in His death, burial, and resurrection (Rom. 6:3-5). Christ has provided a new life in Himself so that "we also should walk in newness of life" (Rom. 6:4) by means of the Holy Spirit who indwells us (Rom. 8:1-4). Galatians 5:13 reiterates this truth saying, "For you, brethren, have been called to liberty; only do not use liberty as an opportunity for the flesh, but through love serve one another."

The objection that eternal security leads to sinful living is a "straw man" at best, as it would be very difficult to prove that those who reject this teaching actually sin *less* than those who accept it. In fact, let me affirm personally that being saved by God's grace alone through faith alone in Christ alone, coupled with the full assurance of eternal security, has not encouraged sin in my life but instead has produced an attitude of gratitude that has motivated me to devote my life to serving Jesus Christ: *"For the love of Christ compels us, because we judge thus: that if One died for all, then all died; and He died for all, that those who live should live no longer for themselves, but for Him who died for them and rose again"* (2 Cor. 5:14-15).

AN ILLUSTRATION TO REMEMBER

When engineers constructed the Golden Gate Bridge in San Francisco, they anticipated that a number of lives would be lost during the dangerous construction that would transpire. The construction crews proceeded slowly and carefully; nevertheless, a few workers fell to their death. Consequently, the engineers stretched a safety net below the bridge and above the water in order to catch any falling men, thus saving lives. This strategic invention resulted in tremendous personal security and greater production among the construction crews. Do you see the analogy? Instead of the eternal security of salvation being a license to sin, it grants believers in Christ tremendous personal security and the motivation to serve Christ all the days of their lives because of God's grace and love.

> The steps of a good man are ordered by the LORD, and He delights in his way. *Though he fall, he shall not be utterly cast down; for the LORD upholds him with His hand.* (Ps. 37:23-24)

SOME IMPORTANT QUESTIONS

Dear reader, who or what have you trusted to save you from the wrath and judgment of God? If you were to die and stand before the infinitely holy God today, what would you say? Would it be, "Lord, Lord, I've done this and I've done that for my salvation"? Or would it be the glad refrain, "Jesus paid it all, all to Him I owe; Sin had left a crimson stain, He washed it white as snow. And when before the throne, I stand in Him complete; 'Jesus died my soul to save' my lips shall still repeat."[4]

If you have never personally trusted the Lord Jesus Christ *alone* to be your Savior, today can be *your* day of salvation. He died for your sins and rose again to provide salvation as a gift of God's grace for you. Isn't it time to accept His free gift by faith in Jesus Christ alone? It is a matter of eternal significance. "For He says: 'In an acceptable time I have heard you, and in the day of salvation I have helped you.' *Behold, now is the accepted time; behold, now is the day of salvation*" (2 Cor. 6:2).[5]

> If you could see and know
> Just what the future holds
> You'd never take the chance
> and lose your soul

---

[4] Elvina M. Hall, *Jesus Paid It All.*
[5] For further reading on settling your eternal destiny, see Dennis M. Rokser, *Let's Preach the Gospel* (Duluth, MN: Duluth Bible Church, n.d.) and Ron Shea, *The Gospel* (Duluth, MN: Duluth Bible Church, n.d.).

But God above can see
From here to eternity
So give it a thought my friend
Meet the Lord.

Time is a precious thing
It can't be recalled again,
Those years you waste in sin
Are gone evermore
So start today anew
Let Jesus walk with you
And when the journey's through
You'll meet the Lord.

Before you die
meet the Lord
Reach out by faith in Him,
Heed His Word.
Be certain you're not wrong
Eternity is long
Before you die
Meet the Lord.[6]

---

[6] Dottie Rambo, *Before You Die.*

CHAPTER 3

Does It Really Matter What You Believe about Eternal Security?

One day, I had an interesting conversation with a man who professed to be "born again" but who thought that he could somehow lose his salvation. I asked him, "Fred, do you know for sure that you are saved?" His immediate reply was, "Yes, I believe that I'm saved today." Having learned over the years of the need to probe deeper to find out exactly who or what someone is trusting for salvation, I inquired further, "But do you know beyond the shadow of a doubt that you will be saved *five years from now*?" This time he answered in less than certain terms. While still considering my last inquiry, he asked, "But what does it matter so long as I know that I'm saved today?" Seeking to be biblical and discerning, I responded by stating, "Well Fred, here is why it is so important. If you don't know for sure that you'll be saved five years from now, then you don't ultimately know that you'll go to Heaven when you die. And if that is not enough to cause concern, let me add that if *you're* not even certain that you're going to Heaven, then how can anyone else know that about you? In fact, are *you* sure that you are truly saved?" Ultimately, Fred was uncertain of his eternal destiny and ignorant of the importance of assurance.

Still others reason along these lines: "The doctrine of eternal security doesn't matter; for if a professing believer is living in sin, either he was never saved (Calvinistic view) or he has lost his salvation (Arminian view). In both cases, he is on his way to Hell. Therefore, it doesn't really matter what you believe about eternal security." But what about the carnal Corinthians (1 Cor. 3:1-4), worldly Lot (2 Peter 2:7-8), the Christian involved in ongoing incest

(1 Cor. 5:1-5), or King David who committed adultery and murder (Ps. 51:12)? While their sins carried serious consequences in their daily walk, were they not saved by God's grace and eternally secure? And what about *you*, with your daily sins and spiritual failures, both known and unknown?

Fred's reply is a typical answer among many evangelicals today because they view the doctrine of eternal security either with rejection, suspicion, neglect, or, in many cases, as optional. Does it really matter what the Bible teaches about eternal security? Let me give seven reasons why this wonderful biblical truth is not optional. Instead, it is an essential, biblical doctrine for the absolute assurance of salvation, for spiritual growth, for grace motivation to serve your Savior, for biblical understanding of future rewards, and for the assurance of your participation in the Rapture or blessed hope.

1. To deny eternal security diminishes the "good news" of the Gospel.

> For I am not ashamed of the gospel of Christ, for it is the power of God to salvation for everyone who believes, for the Jew first and also for the Greek. (Rom. 1:16)

The Greek word translated "gospel" (*euangelion*) literally means "good news." The Gospel is good news from God to man regarding Jesus Christ and His substitutionary death on the cross and bodily resurrection from the grave (1 Cor. 15:3-4).[1] This is extremely good news because God is now offering eternal "salvation" to undeserving, helpless sinners who trust in Christ alone because of the cross-work and accomplishment of the Lord Jesus.

Regarding God's wonderful gift of salvation, we previously defined eternal security by stating,

Eternal security means that those who have been genuinely saved by God's grace through faith alone in Jesus Christ alone shall never be in danger of God's condemnation or loss of their salvation, but God's grace and power keep them forever saved and secure.

---

[1] For further explanation of this key passage, see Thomas L. Stegall, *The Gospel of the Christ: A Biblical Reply to the Crossless Gospel Regarding the Content of Saving Faith* (Milwaukee: Grace Gospel Press, 2009), 529-89.

Dear friends, if you could lose or forfeit God's gift of salvation by your sin, backsliding, unfaithfulness, or other means, the Gospel would become something less than fully "good news." Instead of eternal security, God would offer you "temporal insecurity" through Christ. Does that sound like good news? Instead of the message of salvation bringing glad tidings, it would offer bad tidings. And how then would the Gospel of grace really be different from the "hope-so" salvation that religion offers to lost souls? If you don't have *eternal* life, you *don't* have eternal life. Does this sound like something optional?

2. To deny eternal security is to garble the Gospel of grace.

It is my conviction that eternal security is not merely a nice benefit or add-on to the Gospel, but that this biblical truth strikes right at the heart of the Gospel's offer of salvation as a free gift. God does not owe salvation as a reward to those who keep the law; God offers salvation as a grace gift to those who place their faith in Christ's work. If our salvation depends on us doing something to earn it or keep it, then Christ's death is insufficient to save us. The apostle Paul explains it this way: "I do not set aside the grace of God; for if righteousness comes through the law, then Christ died in vain" (Gal. 2:21).

In my conversation with Fred, I went on to state, "Fred, if you can do something to lose your salvation, then you must do something to keep your salvation. If you must do something to keep your salvation, then salvation depends on your walk instead of solely on Christ's work. And if that is the case, then you are working for your salvation while you claim that salvation is not by your works." This is a critical truth to grasp! Can you see the confusion in all this?[2] If Jesus Christ died for all of our sins when He paid our sin debt in full on the cross, what sins are left to be removed by our good works or the sacraments of the church? None!

Those who believe they can lose, forfeit, or give back their salvation invariably contend that this can possibly happen because of a personal choice, a particular sin, or a pattern of sins in one's life. But why then did Jesus Christ die and what did it accomplish?

> Who being the brightness of His glory and the express
> image of His person, and upholding all things by the

---

[2] For further helpful reading on this point, see J. B. Hixson, *Getting the Gospel Wrong*, rev. ed. (Duluth, MN: Grace Gospel Press, 2012).

word of His power, *when He had by Himself purged our sins*, sat down at the right hand of the Majesty on high. (Heb. 1:3)

For *Christ also suffered once for sins*, the just for the unjust, that He might bring us to God. (1 Peter 3:18a)

To Him who loved us and *washed us from our sins in His own blood.* (Rev. 1:5b)

Clearly, Christ's death takes away all of our sins, even the sins we commit after we are saved. Though sin in the believer's life leads to serious consequences (a topic discussed in chapters 20-21), it cannot result in the loss of *eternal* life. Eternal life, by its very definition, must go on for how long? Forever! And if you could lose your salvation by your sins, you must then face the fact that to remain saved, you are required to live a holy life in order to keep it. Does this sound like salvation *by grace*? Are you trusting Christ *alone* for your salvation? Or are you trusting Christ *plus* your holy walk and faithfulness? This is *not* the same Gospel of salvation the Bible presents. Like the old hymn joyfully proclaims,

> My hope is built on nothing less
> Than Jesus' blood and righteousness.
> I dare not trust the sweetest frame,
> But wholly lean on Jesus name.
> On Christ, the solid Rock I stand;
> All other ground is sinking sand.
> All other ground is sinking sand.[3]

3. **To deny eternal security annihilates the absolute assurance of eternal salvation.**

These things I have written to you who believe in the name of the Son of God, *that you may know that you have eternal life,* and that you may continue to believe in the name of the Son of God. (1 John 5:13)

Most assuredly, I say to you, he who hears My word and believes in Him who sent Me *has everlasting life, and*

---

[3] Edward Mote, *The Solid Rock.*

shall not come into judgment, but has passed from death into life. (John 5:24)

Like my acquaintance, Fred, those who embrace a garbled gospel lack absolute assurance of going to Heaven when they die because their trust is not in Christ and His cross-work alone. Yet the Bible guarantees eternal life to every believer based on the finished work of Christ and the promises of God.

While attending Bible College in West Virginia, my wife and I commonly heard the older folk whom we saw during our nursing home visitations say, "I'm saved." But then when we asked, "Does that mean that you know for sure when you die that you are going to heaven?" a strange silence would pervade the room. Further conversations with these precious souls would often reveal that they lacked a clear understanding of the Gospel and often had never been saved at all.

On other occasions I have conversed with individuals who declared, "I believe you can lose your salvation, but I don't think *I* ever will. So I think [not know] I'll be saved five years from now." Dear friends, it is the epitome of arrogance and self-righteousness to think that while others can lose their salvation, you never will! In other words, either you have faith in your on-going faithfulness, or you believe that you will make the cut with your daily spiritual batting-average while others won't. Doesn't this remind you of Peter's self-confidence on the eve of our Lord's crucifixion?

> And when they had sung a hymn, they went out to the Mount of Olives. Then Jesus said to them, "All of you will be made to stumble because of Me this night, for it is written: 'I will strike the Shepherd, and the sheep will be scattered.' But after I have been raised, I will go before you to Galilee." Peter said to Him, "Even if all are made to stumble, yet I will not be." Jesus said to him, "Assuredly, I say to you that today, even this night, before the rooster crows twice, you will deny Me three times." But he spoke more vehemently, *"If I have to die with You, I will not deny You!"* And they all said likewise. (Mark 14:26-31)

To those of you who erroneously believe that while others can lose their salvation, you never will because of your faithfulness or godly walk, I say but one thing: "Cock-a-doodle-do, cock-a-doodle-do, cock-a-doodle-do!"

4. **To deny eternal security is to disregard the direct statements of Scripture.**

> All that the Father gives Me will come to Me, and the one who comes to Me *I will by no means cast out.* For I have come down from heaven, not to do My own will, but the will of Him who sent Me. This is the will of the Father who sent Me, that of all He has given Me *I should lose nothing,* but should raise it up at the last day. And this is the will of Him who sent Me, that everyone who sees the Son and believes in Him may *have everlasting life; and I will raise him up* at the last day. (John 6:37-40)

> My sheep hear My voice, and I know them, and they follow Me. And *I give them eternal life, and they shall never perish; neither shall anyone snatch them out of My hand.* My Father, who has given them to Me, is greater than all; and *no one is able to snatch them out of My Father's hand.* I and My Father are one. (John 10:27-30)

The Scriptures are replete with clear verses stating without reservation that eternal life is the present and permanent possession of those who have relied on the Lord Jesus Christ as Savior. How can one read or teach the Word of God and miss, neglect, or distort all of these clear verses?

Now you may be thinking, "Are people who reject the truth of eternal security not saved?" Not necessarily. They could be confused believers who heard the Gospel at one time, put their trust in Christ alone, and then later became confused because of poor teaching. However, if people do not know they have been saved forever, how could anyone else know if they are saved? And if their faith has been in Jesus Christ *plus* and not in Jesus Christ *period*, they are still unsaved and working for their salvation. In either case, they need to hear a clear presentation of the Gospel of grace. Does eternal security sound optional, or is it nonnegotiable?

5. **To deny eternal security means you will lack the right foundation for genuine spiritual growth.**

> As you have therefore received Christ Jesus the Lord, so walk in Him. (Col. 2:6)

This fifth reason why belief in eternal security matters assumes that a person has been genuinely saved. Colossians 2:6-7 states that believers should seek to live the Christian life in the very same manner in which they were saved—by grace alone through faith alone in Christ alone. Based on their blessings and position in Christ, they are to walk by faith and not by sight (2 Cor. 5:7), which results in spiritual fruitfulness (John 15:1-7) and Christ-honoring works (Col. 1:10) to the glory of God (Heb. 13:20-21). However, without a clear understanding of the eternal nature and security of salvation, they will never correctly understand their position in Christ, Christian carnality, the place of rewards, or other topics pertaining to the Christian life. This explains why the apostle Paul in his epistle and great doctrinal treatise to the Romans settles the issue of justification by faith (Rom. 3:21–4:25) and eternal security (Rom. 5) *before* he launches into the issue of sanctification by grace or being set apart to God from sin's power in the Christian life (Rom. 6–8). Does eternal security sound like something Paul thought was optional, or does he consider it non-negotiable? It forms the foundation or root system that is essential for every believer's establishment in the Christian life and spiritual growth.

> Rooted and built up in Him and established in the faith, as you have been taught, abounding in it with thanksgiving. (Col. 2:7)

6. To deny eternal security means that the fear of Hell, instead of the love of Christ, becomes the major motivator to live a fruitful Christian life.

> For *the love of Christ compels us,* because we judge thus: that if One died for all, then all died; and He died for all, that those who live should live no longer for themselves, *but for Him who died for them and rose again.* (2 Cor. 5:14-15)

When people deny eternal security, good works cease to be the fruit of their salvation (Eph. 2:10) and walk of faith in Christ (Titus 3:8); instead, good works become the means of maintaining salvation or necessary to prove they possess salvation. Instead of good works in believers' lives being a "thank you" note to Jesus Christ for saving them, those who reject eternal security make good works the I.O.U. note that they must pay in order to maintain salvation and ultimately make it to Heaven. God wants believers to enjoy the assurance of eternal salvation at the very moment of faith in Christ, but when they reject this wonderful truth, the Christian life becomes a form of spiritual probation to determine if they were ever truly saved (Calvinistic view) or whether they will lose their salvation or not (Arminian view). Thus, in either case, a failure to have a victorious Christian life will ultimately result in condemnation to the Lake of Fire.

Interestingly, in 2 Corinthians 5 (mentioned above), Paul wrote that he and the Corinthian believers had the absolute assurance that they would one day go to heaven: "So we are always confident, knowing that while we are at home in the body we are absent from the Lord. For we walk by faith, not by sight. We are confident, yes, well pleased rather *to be absent from the body and to be present with the Lord*" (vv. 6-8). Coupled with this absolute assurance of Heaven was the stark reality that their post-salvation works would be evaluated at the Judgment Seat of Christ to determine whether or not they would receive a reward. (Remember, salvation is a gift, not a reward.) "Therefore we make it our aim, whether present or absent, to be well pleasing to Him. For we must all appear before the judgment seat of Christ, that each one may receive the things done in the body, according to what he has done, whether good or bad" (vv. 9-10).

Though believers in Christ need a healthy "fear of the Lord" (a reverential attitude that takes God seriously) in their daily walk, no born again child of God should live with the unhealthy fear of Hell. And while the danger of eternal damnation is a great reason to trust Christ as Savior and be saved, Scripture never sets it forth as a motivator to live for Jesus Christ after salvation.

Discussing this very issue with a pastor a few years ago, I said, "Before I was saved, I trusted Christ *plus* my works for salvation. I felt like the church had me hanging over Hell by a thread, and that if I didn't fly right, it would have the scissors to snip the thread. Now, if you say that I have to do something to not lose my salvation, such as live a holy life or be faithful, aren't you really saying in essence the same thing that my church told me?" His reply was, "I wouldn't say believers are hanging over Hell by a thread. I think it is more like a rope." Instantly I responded with, "What does it matter if it's a thread or a rope *if it's over Hell?!*"

> Blessed be the God and Father of our Lord Jesus Christ, who according to His abundant mercy has begotten us again to a living hope through the resurrection of Jesus Christ from the dead, *to an inheritance incorruptible and undefiled and that does not fade away, reserved in heaven for you, who are kept by the power of God through faith for salvation* ready to be revealed in the last time. (1 Peter 1:3-5)

7. **To deny eternal security means that you will never be certain that the Rapture will involve you; therefore, you have no blessed hope personally.**

Believers in Jesus Christ are to be…

> Looking for the blessed hope and glorious appearing of our great God and Savior Jesus Christ. (Titus 2:13)

> But I do not want you to be ignorant, brethren, concerning those who have fallen asleep, lest you sorrow as others who have no hope. For if we believe that Jesus died and rose again, even so God will bring with Him those who sleep in Jesus. For this we say to you by the word of the Lord, that we who are alive and remain until the coming of the Lord will by no means precede those who are asleep. For the Lord Himself will descend from heaven with a shout, with the voice of an archangel, and with the trumpet of God. And the dead in Christ will rise first. Then we who are alive and remain shall be caught up together with them in the clouds to meet the Lord in the air. And thus we shall always be with the Lord. Therefore comfort one another with these words. (1 Thess. 4:13-18)

Paul wrote the latter passage both to inform (v. 13) and to comfort (v. 18) those who had personally believed "that Jesus died and rose again" (v. 14). He was assuring them that the "dead in Christ" as well as "we which are alive and remain" would not miss out on the Rapture of the Church, and that every believer in Christ "shall be caught up together with them in the clouds to meet the Lord in the air: and so shall we ever be with the Lord." Is there any sense of uncertainty or insecurity for any believer in this passage? Not at all! Why? "For God did not appoint us to wrath, but to obtain salvation through our Lord Jesus Christ, who died for us, that whether we wake or sleep, we should live together with Him" (1 Thess. 5:9-10).

A REAL-LIFE TESTIMONY

If you happen to be of the persuasion that this issue of eternal security only affects the classrooms of Bible colleges and seminaries, but doesn't relate to or touch the average person in the pew, read the following true testimony that was recently sent to me.

> "Oh, give thanks to the LORD, for He is good! For His mercy endures forever!" (Ps. 107:1). What a joy to read about salvation's permanence in such certain and irrefutable terms. To read this book is to revel in God's grace.
>
> Before I was saved, I was sincerely religious but worried about losing my "salvation." I professed to be a Christian, and I acted like a Christian, yet I struggled inwardly with doubt. The truth is, I was lost. Instead of trusting in Christ's work alone, I also trusted my own efforts for salvation. I was hung up on the idea that eternal life depended on the quality of my Christian life and the perseverance of my faith. As a result, troubling questions plagued my thinking: "What if I sin too much?" "What if my faith isn't strong enough?" "What if I die in a moment when I am not faithful?" I was constantly afraid that I wasn't measuring up to God's standard. At times, the fear was like torment.
>
> My religious friends encouraged me in my belief that salvation could be lost. We scorned anyone who believed salvation was forever, and we accused them of exploiting God's grace and promoting a sinful lifestyle. I remember hearing comments like, "They think you can just live any way you want to and still go to Heaven!"

My years at a Bible college only muddled my thinking. I remember a classroom debate about whether or not salvation could be lost. When it became too heated and uncomfortable, the professor put an end to the debate saying, "This issue is just too divisive, and no one can know for sure either way."

But my professor was wrong. God in his grace faithfully provided the information I needed in the form of sound expository Bible teaching. Praise the Lord that though I was confused, God's Word is clear. My religious blindfold began to come off as I realized that I wasn't saved because I had never put my faith in Christ alone. I learned that "he who hears My word and believes in Him who sent Me has everlasting life, and shall not come into judgment" (John 5:24). I learned that salvation is a gift for helpless sinners, not a reward for the good or the faithful. I learned that my belief that salvation depended on my performance had enslaved me under legalism and blinded me to God's grace. I learned that salvation is the present possession of every believer, not a future possible attainment. I learned that salvation had nothing to do with the quality of my faith, but it had everything to do with the quality of its object: Jesus Christ.

Perhaps the most encouraging thing I learned from the Scriptures was that it is not my own faithfulness keeping me saved; instead, God's faithfulness keeps me saved, for He, unlike me, is incapable of breaking His promises. Over time, as I was willing to reconsider verses that I thought proved I could lose my salvation, I saw that I was misinterpreting them by adding my own ideas and ignoring their context. I had to admit that I was wrong. I can take no credit for my eternal salvation, for God provided all that was necessary to save me and keep me saved. This humbles me and glorifies Him.

Understanding that salvation is eternal and cannot be lost brings believers to their knees in praise and gratitude and helps them "comprehend with all the saints what is the width and length and depth and height—to know the love of Christ which passes knowledge" (Eph. 3:18-19). It also motivates us to loving service out of thankfulness, not fear and obligation.

If you believe you can lose your salvation, or if this issue has confused you, I encourage you to read this book, study the verses it cites, keep a humble attitude, and seek God's guidance through prayer. For "Whoever is wise will observe these things, and they will understand the lovingkindness of the LORD" (Ps. 107:43).[4]

CLOSING QUESTIONS

Does it really matter what you believe about eternal security? Does the doctrine of eternal security still sound optional to you, or is it an essential biblical doctrine to be grasped, enjoyed, and taught? Does the church you attend teach eternal security? When was the last time you heard a sermon or Bible study regarding this wonderful and scriptural doctrine? Do you as a pastor, teacher, or missionary include it in your preaching? If the Bible clearly declares it, why don't you? Eternal security is a major, non-negotiable, essential biblical doctrine that has numerous ramifications related to the "good news" of the Gospel of Jesus Christ! And in the following chapters, you will have the opportunity to examine verse after verse after verse from the Scriptures that dogmatically teach this wonderful truth. Are you ready for the journey? I would suggest that you buckle up and enjoy the ride!

Redeemed, how I love to proclaim it!
Redeemed, by the blood of the Lamb!
Redeemed thro' His infinite mercy —
His child, and *forever*, I am.[5]

---

[4] Written by Kristin Warmanen. For more encouraging testimonies of God's saving grace showing the importance of a clear gospel and eternal security, see *Trophies of God's Grace* (Duluth, MN: Duluth Bible Church, 2006).

[5] Fanny J. Crosby, *Redeemed*.

Part II

The Scriptural Support
for
Eternal Security

CHAPTER 4

No Weak Links in God's Chain

You have probably heard someone say, "A chain is as strong as its weakest link." In this chapter, we'll apply this axiom to the scriptural truth of the believer's security of salvation. It may surprise you to know that over 50 verses of Scripture directly teach or relate to the eternal security of salvation. And as with creation or the resurrection of Jesus Christ from the dead, all three members of the triune Godhead (the Father, the Son, and the Holy Spirit) are not only involved in providing salvation to unworthy sinners, but they are faithfully responsible in keeping the believer's salvation eternally secure.

ETERNAL SECURITY BY GOD THE FATHER

Every believer in Christ is eternally secure because it's the PURPOSE of God the Father to glorify every believer in Christ (Rom. 8:28-30).

Three verses in Romans chapter 8 explain this wonderful truth and highlight what God is determined to accomplish in every believer's life.

1. God's PROMISE to us. (Rom. 8:28)

> And we know that *all things work together for good* to those who love God, to those who are the called according to His purpose. (Rom. 8:28)

This wonderful verse has been called a "soft pillow for a troubled heart." It promises that God, without violating our human volition and without cancelling negative consequences for bad choices, is determined to work all things together for our spiritual good and to His own glory.

2. God's PURPOSE with us. (Rom. 8:29)

> For whom He foreknew, He also predestined *to be conformed to the image of His Son, that He might be the firstborn among many brethren.* (Rom 8:29)

The conjunction "for" connects verses 28 and 29 together, while "whom" refers back to believers in Christ as described in the preceding verse. In God's omniscience and sovereignty, He foreknew and predestined every believer to a predetermined end. What exactly is it? It is important to note that this predestination is *not* for believers to be saved from sin's penalty (justification), but for believers "to be conformed to the image of His Son." And why does God do this? "That He [Jesus Christ] might be the first born among many brethren." God's purpose from eternity past is to bring believers to full spiritual maturity in order that the Lord Jesus Christ would have the preeminence and glory due His name. But what does all this entail?

3. God's PLAN for us. (Rom. 8:30)

> Moreover whom He predestined, these He also called; whom He called, these He also justified; and whom He justified, these He also glorified. (Rom. 8:30)

This verse addresses five links in God's unbroken chain for the believer from eternity past to eternity future.

The "whom" and "these" in these verses *always* refer to the *same* group. The same individuals whom God foreknew He predestinated, called, justified, and glorified. This allows for *no* drop-outs along the way. This means that 100 percent of those whom God "foreknew" (believers) are "predestinated." 100 percent of those whom God "predestinated" are "called"; 100 percent of those "called" are "justified"; and 100 percent of those who have been "justified" are "glorified."[1]

---

[1] Charles C. Ryrie, *Basic Theology* (Wheaton, IL: Victor, 1986), 330.

What part does man fulfill in this? Nothing, except *"Being justified by faith,* we have peace with God through our Lord Jesus Christ" (Rom. 5:1). Also, there are *no* "ifs" in God's plan. God guarantees it from beginning to end.

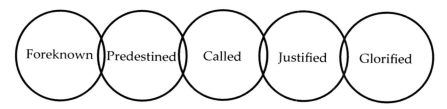

But let's be careful to note what is *not* mentioned in this verse. You would usually expect to find "sanctification" between justification and glorification. Why is it missing? Because while positional sanctification is true of all believers in Christ (1 Cor. 1:2; 6:11; Heb. 10:10; Jude 1), progressive or practical sanctification (a growing, holy life) is *not* absolutely guaranteed in time for every believer. Though God desires all believers to grow in holiness, progressive sanctification may not occur because of the possibility and reality of carnality, unfaithfulness, worldliness, and even the sin unto death (1 Cor. 3:1-4; 11:30; 1 John 2:15-17; 5:16).

Romans 8:30 deals with divine certainties and guarantees, not human possibilities or probabilities. It clearly explains that there is *no* slippage in God's plan for the believer in Christ. Our Lord will not be counting His sheep in heaven saying, "96, 97, 98, 99 . . . 99? 99? Where is that Rokser anyway?" Michael the Archangel will not reply, "Sorry, Lord, but he lost his salvation." If God foreknew that you would lose your salvation along the way because of sin, unfaithfulness, or carnality (if this was possible), why did He design this plan of glorification in the first place? Cannot His Word be believed at face value?

Please notice the word *"glorified,"* which is like a maraschino cherry on top of a hot fudge sundae. This Greek verb (*edoxasen*) indicates a completed action which God does and you receive. It is a fact or reality for every believer.[2] Now keep in mind that the

---

[2] The Greek word for "glorified" (*edoxasen*) is an aorist tense, active voice, indicative mood verb. The active voice indicates that God Himself, rather than the believer, accomplishes the act of glorifying. The aorist tense combined with the indicative mood normally speaks of a completed event in past time from the standpoint of the writer or speaker. Here the aorist indicative is used in a proleptic or futuristic sense "to describe an event that is not yet past as though it were already completed" (Daniel

believer's glorification is a *future* reality. God will not fully glorify you until you are with Him in Heaven with a new, resurrected body. Yet the word "glorified" is translated in our Bibles in the *past* tense. Why? This is theologically called a "prophetic past." The reason Paul could pen this as if the believer's glorification has already occurred is because in God's mind, the believer's future destiny is *absolutely certain* and *guaranteed*. As far as God is concerned, every believer is sure to be glorified. Isn't that great?

For any believer who was once justified by grace alone through faith alone in Christ alone[3] to be lost amounts to a failure in God's plan and purpose to glorify the believer. Why would He record for us in no uncertain terms that we will (without a doubt) be glorified if this is not absolutely guaranteed? Would this not then be inaccurate and misleading, perhaps even deceptive? What God starts, He finishes—praise the Lord! Because of this, there should be no room for past guilt but plenty of space filled with present gratitude in the heart of every believer. If a chain is as strong as its weakest link, and all five links in the chain depend on God, *all believers in Christ can know with absolute assurance that they are saved and secure forever!* Now that's eternal security!

> More secure is no one ever
> Than the loved ones of the Savior;
> Not yon star, on high abiding,
> Nor the bird in home-nest hiding.
>
> God His own doth tend and nourish,
> In His holy courts they flourish;
> Like a father kind He spares them,
> In His loving arms He bears them.
>
> Neither life nor death can ever
> From the Lord His children sever;
> For His love and deep compassion
> Comforts them in tribulation.

B. Wallace, *Greek Grammar beyond the Basics: An Exegetical Syntax of the New Testament* [Grand Rapids: Zondervan, 1996], 563-64).

[3] When I employ the phrase "by grace alone through faith alone in Christ alone," I am referring to personal trust in the *person* of Jesus Christ (God who became a man) and *work* of Jesus Christ (that He died for our sins and rose again) as presented in the Gospel (1 Cor. 15:3-4).

Little flock, to joy then yield thee!
Jacob's God will ever shield thee;
Rest secure with this Defender—
At His will all foes surrender.[4]

---

[4] Lina Sandell Berg, "More Secure is No One Ever" in Kenneth W. Osbeck, *101 More Hymn Stories* (Grand Rapids: Kregel, 1985), 186.

CHAPTER 5

The Final Verdict in God's Righteous Courtroom

Imagine for a moment being seated in a courtroom with God as the judge, Jesus Christ as the defense attorney, and you (the believer) as the defendant. This is the scene before us in Romans 8:31-34.

Every believer in Christ is eternally secure because of the PROVISION of God the Father involving His Son's death, resurrection, ascension, and present intercession.

> What then shall we say to these things? If God is for us, who can be against us? He who did not spare His own Son, but delivered Him up for us all, how shall He not with Him also freely give us all things? Who shall bring a charge against God's elect? It is God who justifies. Who is he who condemns? It is Christ who died, and furthermore is also risen, who is even at the right hand of God, who also makes intercession for us. (Rom. 8:31-34)

On the heels of Romans 8:28-30, we have a series of five questions that solidify even more the truth of the eternal security of salvation and God's guarantee of future glory for the believer.

1. "What shall we say to these things?"

What "things" does Paul have in mind? They are the truths of God's promise, God's purpose, and God's plan in verses 28-30. How about replying, "Amen!" and "Hallelujah!"?

And we know that all things work together for good
to those who love God, to those who are the called
according to His purpose. For whom He foreknew, He
also predestined to be conformed to the image of His Son,
that He might be the firstborn among many brethren.
Moreover whom He predestined, these He also called;
whom He called, these He also justified; and whom He
justified, these He also glorified. (Rom. 8:28-30)

2. "If God is for us, who can be against us?"

The word "if" is a first class conditional statement in the Greek text.[1]
It assumes a reality from the standpoint of the writer. "If God is for
us [and He is!] who can be [prevail] against us?" The anticipated
answer is, "No one!" Why?

3. "He who did not spare His own Son, but delivered Him up for us all, how shall He not with Him also freely give us all things?"

While the penalty of our sin is death, God did not spare His Son this
punishment when *He died* on Calvary as our substitute. Instead of
refraining from this, God "delivered Him up for us all." The Greek
verb translated "delivered up" communicates a completed event
which God did as a fact of history.[2] And whom did Christ do this
for? The passage says "for us *all*." What a gracious God! Since God
did this for us, "how shall He not with Him also freely give us all
things?"

For when we were still without strength, in due time
Christ died for the ungodly. (Rom. 5:6)

But God demonstrates His own love toward us, in that
while we were still sinners, Christ died for us. (Rom. 5:8)

Since God did this for us, "How shall He not with Him also
freely give us all things?" The prepositional phrase "with Him"

---

[1] The word "if" in the Greek has four class conditions: (1) if and it's assumed to be
true; (2) if and it's assumed not to be true; (3) if and it might or might not be true;
and (4) if and I wish it were true. The Greek words and grammar determine which
case is being used.

[2] The Greek word for "delivered . . . up" (*paredōken*) is an aorist tense, active voice,
indicative mood verb.

underscores the believer's positional identity with Jesus Christ. The very moment you trusted Jesus Christ alone to save you, God united you to His Son. This is your position and identity. You are now a new creation in Christ (2 Cor. 5:17). The words "freely give" (*charisetai*) are derived from the root word for God's "grace" (*charis*). When you have Jesus Christ, you have all the grace blessings that come with Him. Should not all this underserved blessing make every believer love Him more and more?

4. "Who shall bring a charge against God's elect?"

Again, the scene is a divine courtroom. The question is who shall bring a charge, accusation, or indictment in the future[3] against God's elect (a description for a believer). Answer? "It is God who justifies." Who can rightfully point a bony finger at you in the future when you sin, fall, or fail, since *God* is the one declaring you righteous (justified)? To charge you is to impeach the Judge who cleared you of every indictment and who declared you righteous in Christ the moment you put your trust in Him alone.

But you may wonder, "What if I'm unfaithful?" The issue is not *if*, but *when*. All believers in Christ still sin and fail the Lord in their daily walk with Him. But in His mercy God will never condemn you, for it is *God* who justifies you. "But what if I commit a terrible sin or a pattern of sins in the future?" While several practical consequences can occur should this happen,[4] the fact still remains: it is *God* who justifies you. Your salvation remains secure not based on your innocence or guilt, but on the facts of what *God* has done for you and declared about you in Christ.

C. I. Scofield summarized this truth of permanent justification well when he wrote,

> The law can nevermore condemn the believer who is "justified from all things" (Acts 13:39). He has already been tried, condemned and executed in Christ, his Substitute. Every claim of justice has been met in his behalf. Therefore, he is *safe*. . . . The justified believer is a *safe* man, never to be called in question for the guilt of his sins.[5]

---

[3] The Greek word for "shall bring" (*egkalesei*) is a future tense, indicative mood verb.
[4] See chapters 20-21.
[5] C. I. Scofield, *Twenty-Six Great Words of Scripture*, Scofield Bible Correspondence

5. "Who is he who condemns?"

Who can presently "condemn"[6] or pass sentence on the believer? No angel, man, devil, or demon can successfully do so. Why? Four remarkable truths give us God's reasons.

- "It is Christ who died"

Who can pass sentence upon the believer since it is Christ who voluntarily died as a payment for our sins? But Paul's explanation does not stop with Christ's sacrificial death.

- "and furthermore, also is risen"

Jesus Christ was raised[7] from the dead by God Himself as proof that He, God the Father, was completely satisfied with the payment of sin Christ made for us. The resurrection of Christ serves as the canceled check, proving that God accepted Christ's full payment for our sins. But the reasons do not stop with Christ's resurrection.

- "Who is even at the right hand of God"

This refers to our Lord's ascension to the place of honor—the right hand of God—which further indicates God the Father's acceptance of Jesus Christ's substitutionary death on the cross. But Paul's argument does not cease with Christ's death, resurrection, and ascension. For what is Jesus Christ presently doing at the Father's right hand?

- "Who also makes intercession for us."

Jesus Christ "makes intercession"[8] for us as He prays for believers and pleads their case as their defense attorney, thwarting every accusation of the past, present, and future against them. Why is this necessary? Revelation 12:9-10 indicates that the Devil accuses the brethren before God day and night. What is God's solution to the

---

Course, vol. 5 (Chicago: Moody Bible Institute), 1346.

[6] This is a present tense verb.

[7] The Greek word for "is . . . risen" (*egertheis*) is in the passive voice, indicating that God the Father raised Jesus Christ from the dead. Other passages speak of Christ raising Himself (John 2:19-21).

[8] The present tense expression, "makes intercession," emphasizes Christ's continual, current action in Heaven on behalf of believers.

Devil's repeated accusations against us?

> My little children, these things I write to you, so that you may not sin. *And if anyone sins, we have an Advocate with the Father, Jesus Christ the righteous. And He Himself is the propitiation for our sins, and not for ours only but also for the whole world.* (1 John 2:1-2)

> Therefore He is also able to save to the uttermost those who come to God through Him, *since He always lives to make intercession for them.* (Heb. 7:25)

What could someone accuse you of in this present time? You could be rightfully accused of some (perhaps many) personal sins. But what did Christ die for on the cross? He died for all of your sins—past, present, and future (Heb. 10:12). And what did God forgive the moment you trusted the Lord Jesus Christ? All of your sins—as far as the east is from the west, past, present and future!

> As far as the east is from the west, so far has He removed our transgressions from us. (Ps. 103:12)

> And you, being dead in your trespasses and the uncircumcision of your flesh, He has made alive together with Him, having forgiven you *all* trespasses. (Col. 2:13)

What does this mean to the believer in Christ? If God is for you (and He is); if Christ died for all your sins, and God raised Him from the dead as proof of His acceptance of Christ's substitutionary sacrifice on your behalf (and He did); if God is declaring you righteous in Christ (and He is); and if no one (even Satan) can properly bring an accusation in the future or rightly condemn you in the meantime (and this is true), *how could you ever lose your salvation?* Impossible! Now that's eternal security!

This means that God guarantees future glory to every believer. But is this guarantee of eternal salvation a result of your walk or Christ's work? *Christ's* work! Is this eternal security based on your ongoing faithfulness or Christ's finished work and ongoing faithfulness? *Christ's* work and His faithfulness! Dear readers, if you have trusted in Jesus Christ alone to save you, you are eternally secure because of the *provision* of God the Father which includes

Jesus Christ's past death, past resurrection, past ascension, and present intercession for you. Do you believe this? Are you resting by faith in Christ alone? Dear believer, God is for you! Can you rejoice with the songwriter who penned,

> Before the throne of God above
> I have a strong and perfect plea
> A great High Priest whose name is Love
> Who ever lives and pleads for me
> My name is graven on His hands
> My name is written on His heart
> I know that while in heaven He stands
> No tongue can bid me thence depart
> No tongue can bid me thence depart
>
> When Satan tempts me to despair
> And tells me of the guilt within
> Upward I look and see him there
> Who made an end of all my sin
> Because the sinless Savior died
> My sinful soul is counted free
> For God the judge is satisfied
> To look on Him and pardon me
> To look on Him and pardon me
>
> Behold Him there the Risen Lamb
> My perfect spotless righteousness
> The great unchangeable I Am
> The King of Glory and of grace
> One in Himself I cannot die
> My soul is purchased by His blood
> My life is hid with Christ on high
> With Christ my Savior and my God
> With Christ my Savior and my God.[9]

---

[9] Charitie Lees Bancroft, *Before the Throne of God Above.*

CHAPTER 6

Does God Have a Daisy Theology?

The scenario of a man who plucks petals off a daisy while telling himself, "She loves me; she loves me not; she loves me; she loves me not" is well known. His hope is that there will be an odd number of petals on the flower so that he can be assured that "she loves me." Unfortunately, some individuals perceive God as having a daisy theology and are only hopeful but not certain that when they die God will declare, "I love you." But does God love and save sinners based on their religious performance, faithfulness, and good works? And is there anything that can cause God to stop loving His own blood-bought children? We have previously seen how genuine believers in Christ are eternally secure because of God's *purpose* and *provision*, but Romans 8 provides even more assurance.

Every believer in Christ is eternally secure because of the PERPETUAL LOVE of God the Father, from which no one and nothing can ever separate the believer in Christ.

> Who shall separate us from the love of Christ? Shall tribulation, or distress, or persecution, or famine, or nakedness, or peril, or sword? As it is written, "For Your sake we are killed all the day long; we are accounted as sheep for the slaughter." Yet in all these things we are more than conquerors through Him who loved us. For I am persuaded that neither death nor life, nor angels, nor principalities nor powers, nor things present nor things to come, nor height nor depth, nor any other created thing, shall be able to separate us from the love of God which is in Christ Jesus our Lord. (Rom. 8:35-39)

This passage begins with the very question we are seeking to answer. Does this question not directly relate to the issue of eternal security and guaranteed future glory for the believer in Christ? Can believers under certain circumstances ever lose their salvation, be separated from God's love, and then face His righteous wrath instead of guaranteed future glory? Paul raises this question right on the heels of what we have previously examined in Romans 8:28-34.

Verse 35 underscores seven potential difficult circumstances that Christians face as it expands the question: "Who shall separate us from the love of Christ?" "Shall . . ."

- "tribulation" – difficulties and trials that create great stress in your life.

- "distress" – great anguish because of financial stress, relationship problems, or other serious troubles.

- "persecution" – to feel pursued like a wild beast in a hunt because of your faithfulness and testimony for Jesus Christ.

- "famine" – to be destitute and suffering from hunger.

- "nakedness" – to be without sufficient clothing.

- "peril" – to experience great danger.

- "sword" – to lack external peace due to violence.

Verse 36 then goes on to emphasize life's difficulties: "As it is written: 'For Your sake we are killed all day long; we are accounted as sheep for the slaughter.'" These are troubles that every believer can expect while living under the curse (Gen. 3) in the Devil's world. Our Lord taught, "In the world you will have tribulation; but be of good cheer, I have overcome the world" (John 16:33b). Is the fact that you are experiencing any or all of these circumstances proof that God has ceased loving you and forgotten you? Are these conditions in your life evidence that you are not saved and secure in God's hand? If you base the assurance of God's love and your eternal salvation upon your circumstances or walk, you may begin to wonder and doubt. Yet if you base the security of your eternal salvation on *Christ's work* on the cross for you, and if you base the assurance of your eternal redemption on the *promises of God* to you, then you can declare with the apostle Paul (who knew firsthand of these difficulties), "Yet in all these things we are more than conquerors through Him who loved us" (Rom. 8:37).

The definite and scriptural answer to the question of verse 35 is an emphatic *"No!"* Every believer is a special object of God's agape love and a super-conqueror through Christ. There is no tribulation too serious, no distress too great, no persecution too intense, no famine too severe, no nakedness too revealing, no peril too frightening, and no sword too sharp, to ever separate any believer from the love of Christ. Fantastic! But does this mean that believers have never failed the Lord under these circumstances? No, for the Scriptures are replete with even great and godly believers who failed the Lord miserably at times. However, though you and I may fail the Lord after we have been saved by His amazing grace, God's love never fails us! This is why Paul concludes this triumphant passage with the dogmatic affirmation: "For I am persuaded that neither death nor life, nor angels nor principalities nor powers, nor things present nor things to come, nor height nor depth, nor any other created thing, shall be able to separate us from the love of God which is in Christ Jesus our Lord" (Rom. 8:38-39).

To further expand the question of verse 35, the apostle of grace next examines five spheres or situations that are *not* able to separate the believer in Christ from being a specific object of God's perpetual love.

- Spheres of *existence*: "neither death, nor life"

Does God qualify the kind of death? No—whether it is an automobile accident, maximum divine discipline via the sin unto death,[1] or even suicide.[2] Can "death" ever separate the child of God from the love of

---

[1] Sometimes God in His love disciplines a hard-hearted believer by way of a premature death so as to take him home to heaven (1 Cor. 11:30; Acts 5:1-11; 1 John 5:16-17).

[2] Suicide is a horrific sin that is contrary to the will of God. It is never God's will for anyone to commit suicide, especially a believer in Jesus Christ. Yet because it is a sin before God, this means that Jesus Christ died for the sin of suicide like every other sin. And God accepted the payment His Son made for the sin of suicide as well as all other sins. Thus, when a sinner trusts in the Savior for the forgiveness of his sins, God forgives his sins totally and completely—past, present, and future—including the sin of suicide (Col. 2:13). This explains why "neither death" in Romans 8:38 is totally unqualified without an exception clause. Therefore, even the horrific sin of suicide can never separate the believer in Christ from the love of God, though it is a sad and tragic testimony for Jesus Christ. In fact, there are seven suicides recorded in the Bible in which three of them were committed by professed believers—Samson (Judg. 16:26-31), King Saul (1 Sam. 31:3-6), and Ahithophel (2 Sam. 17), while four

his Heavenly Father? No! Nor can any failure, trial, sin, or difficulty in "life." By the way, do you know of anything in between "death" and "life"? So if neither death nor life can ever separate the believer from the perpetual love of God, how could one ever lose his or her salvation?

- Spheres of *angelic created beings*: "nor angels, nor principalities, nor powers"

Scripture uses these three specific terms to refer to ranks of angelic beings, whether good or bad (Eph. 6:12; Col. 1:16, 2:15). These terms also include Satan, who is a fallen angel. If angels generally, and ruling angels specifically, including Satan, cannot separate the believer in Christ from the love of God, how could one ever lose his or her salvation?

- Spheres of *time*: "nor things present, nor things to come"

Nothing in the present (including your sin, your unbelief, or your carnality), nor anything in the future (including the future judgment of God) can create a chasm between the believer and God's agape-love. Since your past has not separated you from God's love, and because your present and future cannot separate you from the love of God, how could you ever lose your salvation?

- Spheres of *location*: "nor height, nor depth"

These are extremes of space. Wherever believers could travel in the universe, they would never arrive at a place where they can escape God's love. However, this is not true of the unsaved, as they will be separated from the blessings and love of God in eternal Hell because of their rejection of Jesus Christ (John 3:18, 36; 5:24; 8:24). Since "death" in the Bible involves *separation*, eternal separation from God is called "the second death" (Rev. 20:14). So how could one who has been born again into God's family, who now possesses "eternal life," and who *cannot* be separated from God's perpetual love, ever lose his or her salvation?

---

were committed by those whose faith we are uncertain of except for Judas (Matt. 27:4-5) who was never saved (John 13:10-11). They are Abimelech (Judg. 9:54), Zimri (1 Kings 16:18), and Saul's armor bearer (1 Sam. 31:5).

God declares without qualification that spheres and extremes of existence, angelic beings, time, and location cannot separate the believer from God's perpetual love. Can you think of anything not included in this list? It includes everything in Heaven and in Hell, now and in the future. And among them all, not a thing can be found that can separate one who has been saved by God's grace from the love God that is in Christ Jesus. Now that's eternal security!

AN ANTICIPATED OBJECTION

However, as if anticipating an objection, Paul is ready to answer the doubter or denier of eternal security who retorts, "All of this is true, but can't I personally separate myself from God's love and His eternal salvation by my conduct, will, choice, unbelief, unfaithfulness, or sin?" To oppose this, Paul adds an all-encompassing phrase to verse 39: "nor any other created thing." This includes *everybody* and nails the coffin of human objection closed. Every human being falls into this category, including you and me. You (believer) cannot separate yourself from the love of God and neither can I. And though believers in Christ can spurn the fellowship of God (1 John 1:5-10), grieve the Holy Spirit through sin (Eph. 4:30-32), lose their joy now (Ps. 51:12), and lose their rewards in heaven later (1 Cor. 3:11-15), the Scriptures dogmatically assert, "nor any other created being, shall be able to separate us from the love of God, which is in Christ Jesus our Lord."

Romans 8 begins with the liberating truth of "no condemnation" in Christ (8:1) and ends with the triumphant refrain of "no separation" from God's love in Christ Jesus our Lord (8:39). And between these wonderful bookends of God's grace is the wonderful promise that "all things work together for good." It doesn't get much better than that!

ARE YOU PERSUADED?

Perhaps you noticed that I purposefully omitted any comment on the first phrase of verse 38, "For I am persuaded." Can you say emphatically like Paul, "For I am persuaded"? Paul was not persuaded of this truth because he was emotionally swayed. The issue of eternal security does not rest on what you feel, what you heard someone say, or what a particular church affirms. Paul was persuaded and convinced of these truths because of what God's

Word taught.[3] God had thoroughly convinced him based on the His unfailing Word and Christ's finished work. There is no question in Paul's mind where he stands on the issue of God's perpetual love and the eternal security of salvation.

Let me ask you, dear reader: do you stand persuaded or convinced of God's perpetual love for you and your eternal security based on the Scriptures? Do you have a *hope-so*, temporal salvation or a *know-so*, eternal salvation? God rendered His verdict in His courtroom scene and it is clear: no one and nothing, at any time or place, whether angelic or human, can ever separate the born-again child of God from God's perpetual love. Now *that* is eternal security!

But remember that the promise of eternal security and God's perpetual love is only for those who have recognized their helpless, hopeless, and hell-bound condition as sinners before a holy God and decided to rely on Jesus Christ alone, who died for their sins and rose again to save them. If this describes you, you can confidently sing, without any daisies in hand,

> Jesus my Lord will love me forever;
> From Him no power of evil can sever.
> He gave His life to ransom my soul;
> Now I belong to Him.
>
> Once I was lost in sin's degradation;
> Jesus came down to bring me salvation—
> Lifted me up from sorrow and shame.
> Now I belong to Him.
>
> Joy floods my soul, for Jesus has saved me—
> Freed me from sin that long had enslaved me.
> His precious blood He gave to redeem;
> Now I belong to Him.
>
> Now I belong to Jesus; Jesus belongs to me—
> *Not for the years of time alone, but for eternity.*[4]

---

[3] The perfect tense and indicative mood is used for the word "persuaded" (*pepeis-mai*), indicating it was a historical fact that Paul stood completely convinced from the past to the present time that Romans was written (Robert P. Lightner, *Sin, the Savior, and Salvation* [Nashville: Thomas Nelson, 1991], 233). The passive voice shows that Paul did not convince himself of this but was convinced by God.

[4] Norma J. Clayton, *Now I Belong to Jesus*.

CHAPTER 7

Kept by the Power of God

The previous chapters have demonstrated from Scripture that every believer in Christ is eternally secure because of God the Father's *purpose* to bring every justified person to glorification (Rom. 8:28-30), because of His *provision* of His Son (Rom. 8:31-34), and because of His *perpetual love* for His children (Rom. 8:35-39). This chapter will present even more scriptural proof that God the Father keeps every child of God eternally secure.

Every believer in Christ is eternally secure because of the POWER of God the Father.

> Blessed be the God and Father of our Lord Jesus Christ, who according to His abundant mercy has begotten us again to a living hope through the resurrection of Jesus Christ from the dead, to an inheritance incorruptible and undefiled and that does not fade away, reserved in heaven for you, who are kept by the power of God through faith for salvation ready to be revealed in the last time. (1 Peter 1:3-5)

This passage conveys four wonderful truths relevant to every believer in Christ.

1. You have been born again according to God's mercy.

The phrase "has begotten" (*anagennesas*) means to "give new birth or life to" someone. If you have put your trust in Christ alone for your salvation, you have been *born again* (John 3:1-18). Who was the source of your new birth? *God the Father* (v. 3a). And how did God accomplish this? Peter answers this question later in this chapter where he writes:

> Having been born again, not of corruptible seed but incorruptible, *through the word of God* which lives and abides forever, because "All flesh is as grass, and all the glory of man as the flower of the grass. The grass withers, and its flower falls away, But the word of the LORD endures forever." *Now this is the word which by the gospel was preached to you.* (1 Peter 1:23-25)

God uses the instrument of His Word—and, in particular, the Gospel of Jesus Christ—to give spiritual birth and life to ungodly sinners who were spiritually dead in trespasses and sins (Eph. 2:1).

On what basis did God do this for you? Was it because you deserved it? Was it due to human merit, religious works, or church ritual? No, it was all "according to His mercy." This marvel of God's grace gives all the glory to Him and all of God's blessings to the believing sinner.

> But *God, who is rich in mercy,* because of His great love with which He loved us, even when we were dead in trespasses, made us alive together with Christ (*by grace you have been saved*), and raised us up together, and made us sit together in the heavenly places in Christ Jesus, that in the ages to come He might show *the exceeding riches of His grace* in His kindness toward us in Christ Jesus. (Eph. 2:4-7)

It is assuring to know that this new birth ("begotten again") is a completed and non-repeatable event from the very moment that you put your trust in Christ alone to save you. A believer in Christ is not born again and again and again. Like physical birth, a spiritual birth occurs only *once* at the very moment of time you trust in Jesus Christ, never to be repeated. So how then could you later be *unborn* through some sin or wrong choice? And if you could lose your salvation and need to regain it, would you not have to be repeatedly born again? This is clearly not what the Bible teaches.

2. You now have a living hope through the resurrection of Jesus Christ from the dead.

The new birth has given every believer the confident assurance of God's certain and future blessings. The word "hope" in the Bible does not involve anxious wishing or uncertainty; rather it means a confident assurance of something yet future. Unlike the empty and false hopes of this world-system, God has given believers a "living hope" of guaranteed future blessings "by the resurrection of Jesus Christ from the dead" (v. 3b). Lenski explains the significance of Christ's resurrection:

> His bodily resurrection from the dead (*ek nekron*) . . . was the demonstration that He is indeed the Son of God and the Savior of the world, and that his dying sacrifice is sufficient to cancel the sins of the world and to satisfy the righteousness of God.[1]

What certain "hope" does the believer in Christ have?

> Through whom also we have access by faith into this grace in which we stand, and rejoice *in hope of the glory of God.* (Rom. 5:2)

> Not only that, but we also who have the firstfruits of the Spirit, even we ourselves groan within ourselves, eagerly waiting for the adoption, *the redemption of our body. For we were saved in this hope,* but hope that is seen is not hope; for why does one still hope for what he sees? (Rom. 8:23-24)

> For we through the Spirit eagerly wait for *the hope of righteousness* by faith. (Gal. 5:5)

> To them God willed to make known what are the riches of the glory of this mystery among the Gentiles: which is Christ in you, *the hope of glory.* (Col. 1:27)

[1] R. C. H. Lenski, *The Interpretation of the Epistles of St. Peter, St. John, and Jude* (Columbus, OH: Lutheran Book Concern, 1938), 29-30, as quoted in D. Edmond Hiebert, *1 Peter* (Chicago: Moody Press, 1992), 56.

> But let us who are of the day be sober, putting on the breastplate of faith and love, and as a helmet *the hope of salvation*. (1 Thess. 5:8)

> Paul, a bondservant of God and an apostle of Jesus Christ, according to the faith of God's elect and the acknowledgment of the truth which accords with godliness, *in hope of eternal life* which God, who cannot lie, promised before time began. (Titus 1:1-2)

> Looking for the *blessed hope and glorious appearing of our great God and Savior Jesus Christ*. (Titus 2:13)

If you could lose your salvation, is your *hope* really a *certain* one? And if not, would it really be any different than the *iffy* hopes of this world?

3. You now have a reserved inheritance waiting in Heaven.

> To an inheritance incorruptible and undefiled and that does not fade away, reserved in heaven for you. (v. 4)

In this context, the believer's "living hope" is directly connected with his heavenly inheritance. Notice carefully the four-fold description of your inheritance.

- Your inheritance is *"incorruptible"* — not subject to decay (unlike your car).

- Your inheritance is *"undefiled"* — not subject to imperfection and impurity (unlike your body).

- Your inheritance *"does not fade"* — not subject to change (unlike bank rates).

- Your inheritance is *"reserved in heaven"* — the best place in the universe (unlike earth).

Believer, does this description of your heavenly inheritance sound like something that can be lost? One author says, "Nothing can destroy it, defile it, diminish it, or displace it!"[2] Another explains how

---

[2] Charles R. Swindoll, *Hope in Hurtful Times: A Study of 1 Peter* (Nashville: Thomas

these terms picture your inheritance as "death proof," "sin proof," and "time proof."[3] These conclusions are very fitting in light of the fact that our inheritance is described as "incorruptible" (*aphthartos*) in 1 Peter 1:4. This term is used elsewhere in the New Testament to describe the unchangeable and eternal nature of God (Rom. 1:23; 1 Tim. 1:17), the believer's future resurrected, glorified body (1 Cor. 15:52), and the permanent, eternal rewards given to believers at the future Judgment Seat of Christ for their faithful service to Him (1 Cor. 9:25).

In addition, the word translated "reserved" (*tetērēmenēn*) is a perfect tense participle in the Greek text, emphasizing that your inheritance has been and continues to be reserved, guarded, kept, or preserved under God's safekeeping from the day you received it until this present day. It indicates a permanent possession. It is also a passive voice verb, indicating that God, not the believer, keeps this inheritance preserved. And where does God keep it? "In heaven," a great and safe place. And for whom is it reserved? "For you" who have been born again, as the verse gives no other conditions. If you have been born again, this inheritance is neither probationary nor dependent upon your walk or works. God has permanently reserved it for you. If you could lose your salvation inheritance because of sin, apostasy, or continual carnality, then why does God keep it reserved in heaven for you with no conditions attached?

These specific truths would be very comforting to Peter's readers who had been displaced from their homeland and had suffered great physical and financial loss due to their faithfulness in serving Jesus Christ. Peter addresses them as *"The pilgrims of the Dispersion* in Pontus, Galatia, Cappadocia, Asia, and Bithynia" (1 Peter 1:1). While these believers may have experienced or been in danger of losing their earthly inheritances because of persecution, they were *never* in danger of losing the heavenly inheritance that God the Father had given them and was reserving for them.

4. **Not only is your heavenly inheritance eternally safe, but you (the inheritors) are eternally secure by the power of God.**

Who are kept by the power of God through faith for salvation ready to be revealed in the last time. (v. 5)

Nelson, 1996), 14.

[3] William M. MacDonald, *1 Peter: Faith Tested, Future Triumphant* (Wheaton, IL: H. Shaw Publishers, 1972), 16.

The word "who" refers back to those who had been born again because of the "blood" (v. 2) and "resurrection" of Jesus Christ (v. 3). The phrase "are kept" (*phrouroumenous*) is a military term for being guarded or protected.[4] This guarding of heavenly heirs is continual and on-going as the present tense indicates. It is also in the passive voice, showing that God does this keeping, not the believers, thus assuring their constant safekeeping. This divine protection is not an on-again, off-again guarding. God takes no coffee breaks when it comes to His perpetual guarding of His children and heirs.

How is the believer kept, protected, and guarded? "By the power of God." Is there any power greater? Can the power of man's will or of Satan's forces ever defeat it? *Never!*

Dear believer, why did God reserve this inheritance in heaven for you? Why would He constantly keep you secure if He knew that somewhere along the way you were going to lose it and go to Hell anyway? Why use such powerful adjectives and precise grammar to describe this inheritance and these inheritors if they could lose their salvation?

So how does a sinner obtain and enter into this heavenly inheritance and the keeping power of God? By being born again "through faith" (v. 5). The one condition is simply to put your trust in Jesus Christ alone as presented in the Gospel. The phrase "through faith" reminds us of Ephesians 2:8-9: "For by grace *you have been saved through faith*, and that not of yourselves; it is the gift of God, not of works, lest anyone should boast."

What does all of this eventually result in for the believer in Christ? Verse 5 ends, "For [resulting in] *salvation* ready to be revealed in the last time." This *future* salvation from sin's very *presence* encompasses this heavenly inheritance in its eschatological sense, including the glorification of our bodies. D. Edmond Hiebert explains, "Peter portrayed our future salvation as something ready to be revealed in the last time! 'Ready' indicates that all that was needed for the realization of salvation has been accomplished."[5] Edmund P. Clowney explains it this way: "Nothing need be added to God's preparation. The salvation that God has got ready does not need a few final touches from us . . . God's salvation, finished,

---

[4] Walter Bauer, William F. Arndt, and F. Wilbur Gingrich, *A Greek-English Lexicon of the New Testament and Other Early Christians Literature*, 3rd ed., rev. and ed. Frederick W. Danker (Chicago: University of Chicago Press, 2000), 1066-67; and J. H. Moulton and G. Milligan, *Vocabulary of the Greek Testament* (London: Hodder & Stoughton, 1930; reprint, Peabody, MA: Hendrickson, 1997), 677.
[5] Hiebert, *1 Peter*, 63.

perfect, and unchangeable is kept for us by God Himself."[6] Now that's eternal security!

Dear readers, this passage again underscores the eternal security of salvation for all believers in Christ. And how should this encourage every believer to respond?

- With great and continual praise to God for His mercy and grace.

  Blessed be the God and Father of our Lord Jesus Christ, who according to His abundant mercy has begotten us again to a living hope through the resurrection of Jesus Christ from the dead. (1 Peter 1:3)

- With great joy amidst the painful trials of this life.

  In this you greatly rejoice, though now for a little while, if need be, you have been grieved by various trials, that the genuineness of your faith, being much more precious than gold that perishes, though it is tested by fire, may be found to praise, honor, and glory at the revelation of Jesus Christ. (1 Peter 1:6-7)

- With a growing love for the Savior who shed His blood for you and rose again.

  Whom having not seen *you love.* (1 Peter 1:8a)

- With great expectation of going to Heaven someday.

  Though now you do not see Him, yet believing, you rejoice with joy inexpressible and full of glory, *receiving the end of your faith— the salvation of your souls.* (1 Peter 1:8b-9)

Like the popular Christian song articulates so well,

This world is not my home,
I'm just a passing through,
My treasures are laid up,
Somewhere beyond the blue;

---

[6] Edmund P. Clowney, *The Message of 1 Peter: The Way of the Cross* (Downers Grove, IL: InterVarsity, 1994), 49.

The angels beckon me from heaven's open door,
And I don't feel at home in this world anymore.[7]

---

[7] Albert E. Brumley, *This World Is Not My Home*.

CHAPTER 8

The Only True Promise-Keeper

W hile men and women make promises to one another, the reality remains that at times they break their promises. But this is *never* true of God. He *always* keeps His promises. He is the only true Promise-keeper!

> Indeed, *let God be true but every man a liar.* (Rom. 3:4a)

> In hope of eternal life *which God, who cannot lie,* promised before time began. (Titus 1:1-2)

> Let us hold fast the confession of our hope without wavering, *for He who promised is faithful.* (Heb. 10:23)

Does this apply to the believer's security of salvation? We have so far examined how God keeps us saved because of His *purpose,* His *provision,* His *perpetual love,* and His *power.* And as if that were not enough,

Every believer in Christ is eternally secure because of the unfailing PROMISES of God.

> Therefore, having been justified by faith, we have peace with God through our Lord Jesus Christ. (Rom. 5:1)

> But God demonstrates His own love toward us, in that while we were still sinners, Christ died for us. Much more then, having now been justified by His blood, we

shall be saved from wrath through Him. For if when we
were enemies we were reconciled to God through the
death of His Son, much more, having been reconciled,
we shall be saved by His life. (Rom. 5:8-10)

Romans 5:9-10 contain two tremendous promises from God that
every child of God should know and believe. The phrase, "Much
more then," reminds us that if Christ died for us when we were
sinners (v. 8), what will He do for us now that we are God's children?!
God has declared every believer righteous before Him ("justified")
from the moment of faith in Christ (5:1) on the basis of His Son's
substitutionary death on the cross ("His blood"). In light of this,
God's guaranteed promise is that "we shall be saved from wrath
through Him." As in 1 Peter 1:5, this *future* salvation from wrath
is accomplished solely by God and is a guaranteed fact through
Jesus Christ alone.[1] God requires no ongoing conditions for you to
fulfill in order to guarantee this *future* salvation, such as not sinning,
confessing your sins, or being faithful. He guarantees this promise
to every believer in Christ whom He "justified" by His grace. This is
eternal security!

If verse 9 is not thrilling enough, verse 10 comes along and
also guarantees "For if[2] when we were enemies we were reconciled[3]
to God through the death of His Son, much more, having been
reconciled, we shall be saved by His life." It is amazing to think
how God has reconciled every one of His former enemies who have
trusted in Christ alone. In light of this, verse 10 ends by declaring

---

[1] The word "saved" (*sōthēsometha*) occurs twice in verses 9-10 and is in the passive
voice, emphasizing that the act of saving is done by God to the believer rather than
something the believer accomplishes. Being in the future tense and indicative mood,
this verb expresses a guaranteed fact. It is not in the subjunctive mood like the term
"walk" in Romans 6:4, which deals with the Christian's sanctification, where the
subjunctive mood expresses intended purpose or desired result but without absolute guarantee. The context of Romans 5 (the blessings of justification) along with
the wording and grammar of this passage argue strongly for eternal security rather
than the potential practical sanctification of believers in Christ. For a fuller treatment
of this passage and explanation of why it is promising eternal security rather than
potential sanctification, see Thomas L. Stegall, *The Gospel of the Christ: A Biblical Response to the Crossless Gospel Regarding the Contents of Saving Faith* (Milwaukee: Grace
Gospel Press, 2009), 447-52.
[2] The word "if" is in the first class condition in the Greek text which is the condition
of assumed reality. It could be interpreted, "For if when we were enemies [before
our salvation and we were] we were reconciled to God by the death of His Son."
[3] "Reconciled" (*katēllagēmen*) is pregnant with meaning, indicating a completed act
(aorist tense) which God did for you (passive voice) resulting in a know-so salvation
(indicative mood) through the sacrificial death of Jesus Christ.

"much more, having been reconciled, *we shall be saved*[4] *by His* [resurrected] *life*." Does this guaranteed future salvation (indicative mood) sound questionable, uncertain, or doubtful? *Never!* Now that's eternal security!

But notice carefully that the doctrine normally found between justification and glorification is missing from these verses. The believer's sanctification is absent from Romans 5:8-10 just as it is missing from the five links of God's unbroken chain in Romans 8:30. Paul discusses sanctification in Romans chapters 6–8, which he begins by writing, "What shall we say then? Shall we continue in sin, that grace may abound? God forbid. How shall we, that are dead to sin, live any longer therein?" (Rom. 6:1-2). God did not direct Paul to discuss sanctification and how to live the Christian life until after completely settling the issues of justification by grace and eternal security in Romans 5. Why? Perhaps because your salvation and eternal security are not based on your Christian walk but upon Christ's finished work on the cross. Furthermore, while your daily walk with the Lord fluctuates, Christ's work on the cross is finished. Thus, your eternal salvation is not assured because of your faithfulness to Christ but because of His unfailing promises to you. May we never confuse this!

How should we then respond to these wonderful promises from God? Does He want believers to be faithful to Him? Without question. Does God want believers to faithfully serve Him enabled by the power of the Holy Spirit? Without debate. But the reality is too often we fail in these matters because of our unbelief and sin natures. And though God rewards the believer's faithfulness in time and eternity, God's guaranteed promises of salvation's security could never be iron-clad if they depended upon the believer in any measure. Charles Stanley puts it this way: "Can joy and insecurity really coexist? How realistic is it to expect us to rejoice over a relationship that is only as secure as our behavior is consistent?"[5] But instead of becoming discouraged by our inconsistent behavior, we can always *rejoice* in God's unfailing promises of permanent salvation. Thus, it should not surprise us that Paul ends this section stating triumphantly, "And not only that, but *we also rejoice in God*

---

[4] Future, passive, indicative verb. Again, the context of Romans 5 (the blessings of justification) along with the wording and grammar of this phrase argues for eternal security rather than the potential practical sanctification of the believer in Christ.
[5] Charles Stanley, *Eternal Security: Can You Be Sure?* (Nashville: Thomas Nelson, 1990), 188.

through our Lord Jesus Christ, through whom we have now received the reconciliation" (Rom. 5:11). Have you received the reconciliation?

> Great is Thy faithfulness, O God my Father;
> There is no shadow of turning with Thee;
> Thou changest not, Thy compassions, they fail not;
> As Thou hast been, Thou forever wilt be.
>
> Pardon for sin and a peace that endureth
> Thine own dear presence to cheer and to guide;
> Strength for today and bright hope for tomorrow,
> Blessings all mine, with ten thousand beside!
>
> Great is Thy Faithfulness!
> Great is Thy Faithfulness!
> Morning by morning new mercies I see.
> All I have needed Thy hand hath provided;
> Great is Thy faithfulness, Lord, unto me![6]

---

[6] Thomas Chisholm, *Great Is Thy Faithfulness*.

CHAPTER 9

It Is Finished!

Y es, that is exactly what Jesus Christ triumphantly declared while hanging on the cross (John 19:30). All of our sins were "paid in full." Commenting on this, John Cross in his excellent book, *The Stranger on the Road to Emmaus* writes,

> The phrase "It is finished" is translated from a single Greek word *tetelestai*. *Tetelestai* had many different usages, but the following three have significance to the story.
>
> 1. *Tetelestai* was used by a servant reporting to his or her master upon completing a task: "The job you gave me is finished."
>
> 2. *Tetelestai* was also a familiar term in Greek commercial life. It signified the completion of a transaction when a debt was paid in full. When the final payment was made, one could say "*tetelestai*," that is, "The debt is finished." Ancient receipts for taxes have been found with *tetelestai* — paid in full — written across them.
>
> 3. The selection of a lamb for sacrifice in the temple was always an important time. The flock would be searched and, upon finding an unblemished lamb, one would say *tetelestai* — the job was finished.
>
> Quite literally Jesus shouted: "The work you gave me is completed, the debt is paid, the sacrificial lamb is

found." The Scripture says Jesus cried out in a loud voice, "It is finished."

The centurion, seeing what had happened, praised God and said, "Surely this was a righteous man." (Luke 23:47)

It is noteworthy that it was the centurion, an officer in charge of 100 soldiers, who immediately commented upon Jesus' cry. Surely he, a military man, knew the difference between a gasp of defeat and a shout of victory.[1]

But how does this relate to the believer's eternal salvation? We have seen how God the Father keeps our salvation secure. Let's examine now . . .

ETERNAL SECURITY BY GOD THE SON

Every believer in Christ is eternally secure because of the PROPI-TIATORY SACRIFICE of Jesus Christ.

For the law, having a shadow of the good things to come, and not the very image of the things, can never with these same sacrifices, which they offer continu-ally year by year, make those who approach perfect. For then would they not have ceased to be offered? For the worshipers, once purified, would have had no more consciousness of sins. But in those sacrifices there is a reminder of sins every year. For it is not possible that the blood of bulls and goats could take away sins. Therefore, when He came into the world, He said: "Sac-rifice and offering You did not desire, but a body You have prepared for Me. In burnt offerings and sacrifices for sin You had no pleasure. Then I said, 'Behold, I have come—In the volume of the book it is written of Me—To do Your will, O God.'" (Heb. 10:1-7)

By that will *we have been sanctified through the offering of the body of Jesus Christ once for all.* And every priest

---

[1] John R. Cross, *The Stranger on the Road to Emmaus*, 3rd ed. (Olds, Alberta: GoodSeed International, 2004), 233-34.

> stands ministering daily and offering repeatedly the same sacrifices, which can never take away sins. But this Man, after He had offered one sacrifice for sins forever, sat down at the right hand of God, from that time waiting till His enemies are made His footstool. *For by one offering He has perfected forever those who are being sanctified.* (Heb. 10:10-14)

The writer of the book of Hebrews logically explains, chapter by chapter, how Jesus Christ is "better" than the prophets (1:1-3), the angels (1:4–2:18), and Moses (3:1-6). He then clarifies how Jesus Christ provides a better rest (4:1-16), as a better high priest (5:1–8:5), with a better covenant (8:6–9:24), having offered a better sacrifice for sins (9:25–10:39).

Though the punishment for sin is *death* (Gen. 2:17; Rom. 6:23), and while the Old Testament sacrifices could picture the truth of substitutionary atonement, the blood of bulls and goats *could never take away sins* (10:4). Thus, according to this passage, the Old Testament priesthood and sacrifices were inferior to and stand clearly contrasted with the superior person and work of Jesus Christ (Heb. 10:10-12).

- many priests vs. Jesus Christ alone

- priests standing vs. Christ sat down

- repeated sacrifices vs. one sacrifice

- can never take away sins vs. for sins forever

Jesus Christ, in His eternal High Priesthood, offered His body as a sacrifice for all our sins—past, present, and future—without exception.

The reason He then "sat down" is because His once-for-all sacrifice for sins was totally complete. No more sacrifices for sin would ever be needed again. This is where religion repeatedly misses the mark. It fails to understand the finished work of Jesus Christ. All religious systems inevitably teach that salvation will ultimately be obtained by human merit and good works. They conclude if one believes in God (however the particular religion defines him/her/it) and sincerely tries to do his best (whatever religious works are prescribed), his chances of obtaining Heaven (nirvana, paradise, the after-life, etc.) are good but not guaranteed.

These merit approaches to eternal salvation run contrary to the Gospel of grace and say in effect that Christ's work on the cross *alone* is insufficient to save the sinner. Yet the Scriptures declare, "I do not frustrate the grace of God: for if righteousness come by the law, then Christ is dead in vain" (Gal. 2:21, KJV). With a merit approach to eternal salvation, any absolute assurance of a person's salvation is decimated, for how does a sinner know when he has done enough good works to finally qualify for Heaven?

Contrast this religious uncertainty with the assuring promises of God's Word.

> And this is the testimony: that God has given us eternal life, and this life is in His Son. He who has the Son has life; he who does not have the Son of God does not have life. These things I have written to you who believe in the name of the Son of God, *that you may know that you have eternal life*, and that you may continue to believe in the name of the Son of God. (1 John 5:11-13)

To truly grasp the significance and value of Christ's sacrifice on your behalf, you must come to grips with how God the Father viewed and responded to His Son's vicarious death.

> And *He Himself is the propitiation for our sins,* and not for ours only but also *for the whole world.* (1 John 2:2)

> In this the love of God was manifested toward us, that God has sent His only begotten Son into the world, that we might live through Him. In this is love, not that we loved God, but that He loved us and *sent His Son to be the propitiation for our sins.* (1 John 4:9-10)

The term "propitiation," which refers to a satisfactory payment, underscores God's perspective on the death of Christ. Christ's substitutionary sacrifice for you fully satisfied the holy demands of the righteous law-court of Heaven. The first proof that Jesus' propitiatory sacrifice for sins satisfied God's righteousness and justice is that Jesus Christ cried out on the cross, "It is finished" (John 19:30). The second proof of the Father having been propitiated by

Christ's cross-work was that God Himself ripped the Temple veil in two, which had separated the Holy Place from the Holiest of Holies. This was the divine death-blow for the Old Testament sacrificial system: "Then, behold, the veil of the temple was torn in two from top to bottom; and the earth quaked, and the rocks were split" (Matt. 27:51). Thus, the writer of Hebrews remarks, "Therefore, brethren, having boldness to enter the Holiest by the blood of Jesus, by a new and living way which He consecrated for us, through the veil, that is, His flesh" (Heb. 10:19-20). The third proof of propitiation was that God Himself raised Jesus Christ from the dead on the third day: "Who was delivered up because of our offenses, and was raised because of our justification" (Rom. 4:25). Our Lord's resurrection acts as the cancelled check that our sin debt to God was fully paid by the Savior and accepted at the bank of Heaven.

Since God has been fully propitiated, what did Christ's sacrifice accomplish for sinners who put their trust in Jesus Christ alone? First, *believers in Christ alone are permanently sanctified.* Hebrews 10 declares, "By that will we have been sanctified through the offering of the body of Jesus Christ once for all" (v. 10). All believers have been given a position in Christ in which they have been permanently set apart unto God (sanctified) by God Himself the very moment they placed their faith in Christ alone. As one classic Christian hymn declares, "To God be the glory, great things He hath done!"[2]

Second, *believers in Christ alone are perfected forever:* "For by one offering He has perfected forever those who are being sanctified" (v. 14). The Word of God declares that every believer has a perfect and permanent standing before God. We are "perfected forever." This speaks of a permanent reality.[3] This is true regardless of the believer's less-than-perfect state that God is seeking to progressively change through on-going spiritual growth ("them that are sanctified"—present tense). God does not accept us on the basis of *our* works or performance for Him, but because of Jesus Christ's sacrificial death *for* us ("for by one offering"). Dear friends, why would God declare believers in Christ to be permanently sanctified and perfected forever in their standing before Him if at some later time they could lose, forfeit, or give away their salvation? "*It is finished!*" That's eternal security!

---

[2] The Greek word translated "*sanctified*" (*hēgiasmenoi*) is a participle in the perfect tense and passive voice.

[3] The Greek word translated "*perfected*" (*teteleiōken*) is a perfect tense, indicative mood verb.

Regarding this, Leonard Radtke has insightfully written:

> To deny eternal security is to deny the finished work of
> Christ upon the Cross for the sins of the world and to
> reduce the sacrifice of Christ to the level of Old Testament
> sacrifices which could never take away sin (Heb. 10:4),
> thus putting a person in the hopeless position of always
> seeking to atone for his sin by his own religious works.
> One must see that the sin question has been forever
> taken care of once and for all (Heb. 10:10-14), and that
> God is no longer holding man's sins against him (2 Cor.
> 5:19), which is what God, in His love, did for man. One
> must see that it is no longer the Sin question, but the
> Son question. If sin, then, is no longer a condemning
> factor with the lost, how can sin be a condemning
> factor with the saved? The sinning believer loses God's
> blessing, not salvation. "He who believes in Him is not
> condemned; but he who does not believe is condemned
> already, because he has not believed in the name of the
> only begotten Son of God." (John 3:18)[4]

Dear reader, these wonderful truths of God's grace are foreign to
the natural thinking and pride of spiritually blind sinners who
repeatedly seek to earn and merit the blessings of God through
their good, religious works. Furthermore, those individuals who
think they can lose their salvation by committing a particular sin
(or pattern of sinning) fail to comprehend the reality of how God
has been fully propitiated through Christ's ransom payment for all
our sins. Is the Father fully satisfied regarding *your* sins through the
finished work of Christ or not? Must you do something *more* to gain
God's acceptance? Paul explains,

> For all have sinned and fall short of the glory of God;
> being justified freely by His grace through the redemp-
> tion that is in Christ Jesus, whom God set forth as a pro-
> pitiation by His blood, through faith, to demonstrate
> His righteousness, because in His forbearance God had
> passed over the sins that were previously committed.
> (Rom. 3:23-25a)

---

[4] Leonard A. Radtke, unpublished notes. Heritage Trail Bible Church, Gilbert, Minnesota.

What does all of this really mean? It means that true biblical Christianity is not a religion; it is a relationship with God through Jesus Christ alone. This eternal relationship is not accomplished by human achievement but by divine accomplishment. Good works or religious rituals do not obtain salvation; it is by God's grace through faith alone in Christ alone. So which do *you* have—a religion or a relationship with God? Are you trusting your imperfect works and holy life to obtain or maintain a right standing before God? Or have you rested by faith in the sufficiency of Christ's cross-work alone to save you forever? If God the Father is fully satisfied with what Jesus Christ has done for you on the cross, only one question remains: are *you* satisfied with what Jesus Christ has accomplished so as to now receive Him by faith as *your* personal Savior? "But as many as received Him, to them He gave the right to become children of God, to those who believe in His name" (John 1:12).

Well-known author Dr. Charles Ryrie challenges you to think deeply and personally about your salvation in a tract that he wrote years ago titled, "Think."

ABOUT GOD:

Do you realize, dear friend, that God is absolutely holy, and do you know what this means? It means that God cannot look upon sin, and that He, because of His holiness, can never take a sinner stained with sin to His spotless Heaven. Since "all have sinned, and come short of the glory of God" (Rom. 3:23), there is no possibility of our going to Heaven as we are. God is righteous and just and, since He is, He must demand death as the penalty for sin, "for the wages of sin is death" (Rom. 6:23). You cannot escape these truths about God. But, thank God, there is another side to the picture, so won't you think with me

ABOUT CHRIST:

The Lord Jesus Christ was sent to this earth by God's love, to die on the cross for your sins. God's love was so great that it could not rest until He had paid the full price for your sins even though it meant the death of His own Son. The death of an ordinary man could accomplish nothing for anyone's sin, but the death of the spotless Son of God accomplished everything by paying the price for the sins of the whole world (John 1:29). Now, because of what Christ has done on the cross, you have been made savable, for the holiness of God has been satisfied by the death of His Son, Jesus Christ. So now think

ABOUT YOURSELF:

God has made you savable, but are you saved? If you can't truthfully say yes, then listen to how you can be saved. "Believe on the Lord Jesus Christ, and thou shalt be saved" (Acts 16:31). That is all God asks you to do, and 200 times in the New Testament He offers salvation to you on the simple, single ground of believing that what Jesus Christ accomplished was done for you.

"But," you say, "surely there is something that I must do!" What could you do, my friend, that would build up enough merit to make you presentable to a holy, infinitely righteous God? If you worked all your life, still your sin—yes, even one sin—would be enough to keep you out of Heaven. The Bible says that "by grace are ye saved through faith . . . not of works" (Eph. 2:8-9).

God is satisfied with what Christ did on the cross in payment for your sin. The question is, are you satisfied? Think earnestly about this question, and if you are not absolutely sure you are saved, make it certain in your own heart right now by simply accepting the salvation which God has provided in the Person of the Lord Jesus Christ. Trust him now as your Savior. "Him that cometh to me I will in no wise cast out" (John 6:37).[5]

Dear reader, are you satisfied with what Christ has done for you? Is Christ's work at Calvary not merely necessary, but do you believe it is enough to save you forever? Why not settle this issue right now? Then you also will be satisfied.

---

[5] Charles C. Ryrie, *Think*. This tract was originally printed by Moody Press and is available by permission through the Duluth Bible Church.

Long ago I saw my Savior
Bearing shame upon a tree;
Then my heart was touched with sorrow,
For I saw He bled for me.

Lo, the sky was veiled in darkness;
Sudden trembling shook the ground
As the angry crowd was jeering,
Mocking Jesus all around.

Then my Savior called to heaven
As I saw His love anew,
O my Father; please forgive them,
For they know not what they do.

Free salvation now He offers;
Take His gift, O hear His plea;
On the bloody cross behold Him,
Join His shout of victory.

"It is finished," loud He cried;
Oh what love—for me He died.
In my stead He bled on Calvary;
Once for all Christ rescued me.[6]

---

[6] Ron Hamilton, *It Is Finished*.

CHAPTER 10

An Offer You Dare Not Refuse

The eternal security of the genuine believer in Christ is inherently connected with the Gospel of grace. For if a person could lose his salvation, he would have to *do* something to keep it. And if he has to *do* something to keep it (live a holy life, not sin, confess all known sin, etc.), he then is ultimately relying on his *own works* to get to Heaven—not on Jesus Christ and His finished work *alone*. In the previous chapter, we saw just how much Christ accomplished by his propitiatory sacrifice for our sins and how it makes our salvation eternal and secure. In this chapter, we will study Jesus Christ's salvation promises as recorded in the book of John. The purpose for John's written Gospel account underscores the great value of this examination: "And truly Jesus did many other signs in the presence of His disciples, which are not written in this book; *but these are written that you may believe that Jesus is the Christ, the Son of God, and that believing you may have life in His name*" (John 20:30-31).

Every believer in Christ is eternally secure because of the guaranteed PROMISES of Jesus Christ.

John 3:16

The first iron-clad promise we will observe is probably the most obvious and well-known of all. John 3:16 states, "For God so loved the world that He gave His only begotten Son, that whoever believes in Him should not perish but have everlasting life." These words fall directly on the heels of Jesus' explanation to religious-but-lost Nicodemus regarding the subject of being "born again":

There was a man of the Pharisees named Nicodemus, a
ruler of the Jews. This man came to Jesus by night and
said to Him, "Rabbi, we know that You are a teacher
come from God; for no one can do these signs that You
do unless God is with him." Jesus answered and said to
him, "Most assuredly, I say to you, unless one is born
again, he cannot see the kingdom of God." Nicodemus
said to Him, "How can a man be born when he is old?
Can he enter a second time into his mother's womb
and be born?" Jesus answered, "Most assuredly, I say
to you, unless one is born of water and the Spirit, he
cannot enter the kingdom of God. That which is born
of the flesh is flesh, and that which is born of the Spirit
is spirit. Do not marvel that I said to you, 'You must be
born again.' The wind blows where it wishes, and you
hear the sound of it, but cannot tell where it comes from
and where it goes. So is everyone who is born of the
Spirit." Nicodemus answered and said to Him, "How
can these things be?" Jesus answered and said to him,
"Are you the teacher of Israel, and do not know these
things? Most assuredly, I say to you, We speak what We
know and testify what We have seen, and you do not
receive Our witness. If I have told you earthly things
and you do not believe, how will you believe if I tell you
heavenly things? No one has ascended to heaven but He
who came down from heaven, that is, the Son of Man
who is in heaven. And as Moses lifted up the serpent in
the wilderness, even so must the Son of Man be lifted
up, that whoever believes in Him should not perish but
have eternal life. For God so loved the world that He
gave His only begotten Son, that whoever believes in
Him should not perish but have everlasting life." (John
3:1-16)

Our Lord clearly states the *necessity* of the spiritual birth (vv. 1-3),
along with the *nature* or *source* of a new birth which comes from
God the Holy Spirit (vv. 4-8). In light of Christ's confrontational and
urgent words, Nicodemus raises the question, "*How* can these things
be?" (v. 9). His inquiry opens the door for our Lord to clearly state
the *means* of the new birth, which is through *Christ* alone (vv. 9-13),
through His *cross* alone (v. 14), and thus through *faith in Christ alone*

(vv. 15-18).[1] To communicate and clarify the one human condition of the new birth, the word "believe" occurs seven times in this passage (vv. 12 [twice], 15, 16, 18 [three times]).

While scores of people know John 3:16, few seem to understand it. This confusion surfaces when they are asked, "Do you know John 3:16?" Many reply, "Oh my, yes." When next asked, "So do you know for sure that you have eternal life?" they answer with the agnostic, "How can anyone know that for sure?" Or if they are then asked, "What percentage of certainty do you have that you will go to heaven?" they almost always answer less than 100 percent. Dear friends, this is the point of John 3:16. God "loved" and "gave." We simply "believe" and "have." How this must have shocked lost Nicodemus who had a religion of "do" instead of "done," or "faith *plus* works" instead of "faith in Christ plus *nothing*." We see once again that the possession and assurance of eternal life are based solely on the person and the work of Christ coupled with the unfailing promises of God's Word. Notice closely the five parts of John 3:16:

- God's part ...."For God so loved the world"

- God's part ...."that He gave His only begotten Son"

- Your part ...."that whoever believes in Him"

- God's promise ...."should not perish"

- God's promise ...."but have everlasting life."

Can Jesus Christ lie? Does He keep His promises? Of course He does, for He is God![2] To emphasize further God's purpose in sending Jesus Christ to earth, verse 17 reads, "For God did not send His Son into the world to condemn the world, but that the world through Him might be saved." Salvation comes only through Jesus Christ who came not to condemn us, but to save us. This verse links being "born again" with salvation. In fact, the word "saved" is the

---

[1] For a more in-depth study of this passage and subject, see Dennis M. Rokser, *Bad News for Good People and Good News for Bad People* (Duluth, MN: Duluth Bible Church, 2007).

[2] The prologue of John's Gospel (1:1-18) answers the needed question, "Who is Jesus Christ?" He is God (v. 1) who became a man (v. 14). This provides the necessary doctrinal and historical context as to *the one whom* sinners must trust to receive eternal life.

identical grammatical construction as "born again" in verse three.[3] Salvation, like the new birth, is a work of God for man, not a work of man for God.[4] The cross-work of Christ paid the penalty of our sin 100 percent. "It is finished" (John 19:30) was the Savior's cry upon the cross. Salvation is not an 80 percent-God, 20 percent-man proposition. Christ's work accomplished it all. It is simply a matter of whether helpless, hopeless, hell-bound sinners will choose to rely on Jesus Christ and His finished work alone to save them. If they will, they are guaranteed to "have"[5] (right now) eternal life. However, a failure to trust in Christ alone means they remain condemned, as John 3:18 states, "He who believes in Him is not condemned; but he who does not believe is condemned already, because he has not believed in the name of the only begotten Son of God."

Dear readers, which half of verse 18 describes you? The whole issue of salvation revolves around whether you have trusted in Christ alone or not. If your faith has rested on Jesus Christ alone, verse 16 guarantees that you "have" (present tense) "everlasting life." And for how long does "eternal" or "everlasting" life last? Of course, *forever.* So how could you possibly lose "eternal" life? *Impossible!* If you could lose eternal life in five years because of a particular sin, or in ten years because of a pattern of sinning, or in fifteen years because of your unfaithfulness, was eternal life then "eternal"? And *if this were possible* (and it's not), think through the biblical ramifications:

- Your salvation would depend on your walk instead of solely on Christ's finished work, and on your works instead of God's grace. (Eph. 2:8-9)

- You would never have absolute assurance of going to heaven because you might lose eternal life somewhere along the way. (1 John 5:13)

- Your Christian life, instead of being built upon a firm assurance of salvation in Christ forever, would be a human experiment to see whether you will ultimately get to heaven or not. (2 Cor. 5:8)

---

[3] Both Greek verbs are in the aorist tense and passive voice.
[4] The passive voice makes this clear.
[5] The word "have" (*echō*) is in the present tense, indicating the present possession of eternal life.

- The condemning factor in your life would then be your "sins," though Christ paid for all of your sins on the cross and forgave them when you believed (Col. 2:13; Heb. 10:12; 1 Peter 3:18; 1 John 2:2).

Dear reader, if you are a believer, the Scriptures have great news for you. If "eternal life" lasts forever, and it does, *you can never lose your salvation!* That's eternal security!

To reinforce this truth, John 3:36 proclaims, "He who believes in the Son has everlasting life; and he who does not believe the Son shall not see life, but the wrath of God abides on him." Again, the sole human condition to possess eternal life is to simply believe or rely on Jesus Christ alone. The Greek verb translated "has" is in the present tense (right now, not sometime in the future) and indicative mood (a guaranteed fact). Eternal life is not something God gives you after you are dead *if* you have been good and faithful enough. Eternal life is a gift from God and is the *guaranteed present and forever possession* of every believer in Christ.

In striking contrast, John 3:18 declares, "He who believes in the Son has everlasting life; and he who does not believe the Son shall not see life, but the wrath of God abides on him."[6] The issue again is one of belief or unbelief in Jesus Christ alone. But please notice the middle of verse 36: "and he who does not believe the Son *shall not see life."* The Greek verb translated "shall . . . see" means "to see, perceive, or experience." Do you realize what this is saying? If you came to trust the Lord Jesus Christ for eternal life in 1975 but somehow you were able to lose, forfeit, or give it back in the year 2050, you would have "seen" or "experienced" eternal life for 75 years. However, God's perspective is stated in John 3:36, "He who

---

[6] In John 3:36, some English Bibles translate *ho apeithōn* as "he who does not obey" instead of "he who does not believe." This gives the unfortunate impression to some that the condition for eternal life is faith in Christ *plus* obedience to God. However, this passage is simply stating that unbelief in Christ is disobedience to God's command to believe in His Son (Acts 16:31). This is synonymous with not obeying the Gospel by not believing it (2 Thess. 1:8-10). For this reason Greek lexicologists Bauer, Arndt, Gingrich, and Danker state regarding *apeitheō*: "Since, in the view of the early Christians, the supreme disobedience was a refusal to believe their gospel, *apeitheō* may be restricted in some passages to the meaning *disbelieve, be an unbeliever.* This sense . . . seems most probable in John 3:36" (*A Greek-English Lexicon of the New Testament and Other Early Christian Literature,* 82). A thoughtful comparison to John 3:18 also supports this conclusion since it is a parallel passage to verse 36 where belief versus unbelief is contrasted along with the results of eternal life versus condemnation.

does not believe the Son *shall not see life*; but the wrath of God *abides*[7] *on him.*" Either you have eternal life (which cannot be lost) or *you never had it!* There is no such reality as possessing eternal life for 75 years and then losing it. So, dear friends, what does *eternal* life mean? That's right—it means an *eternal* relationship with God and Jesus Christ: "And this is eternal life, that they may know You, the only true God, and Jesus Christ whom You have sent" (John 17:3).

John 4:13-14

Jesus issued another great promise of eternal security to the immoral Samaritan woman (4:17-18) whom He encountered at a well in Sychar. John chapter 4 recounts the story:

> Now Jacob's well was there. Jesus therefore, being wearied from His journey, sat thus by the well. It was about the sixth hour. A woman of Samaria came to draw water. Jesus said to her, "Give Me a drink." For His disciples had gone away into the city to buy food. Then the woman of Samaria said to Him, "How is it that You, being a Jew, ask a drink from me, a Samaritan woman?" For Jews have no dealings with Samaritans. Jesus answered and said to her, "If you knew the gift of God, and who it is who says to you, 'Give Me a drink,' you would have asked Him, and He would have given you living water." The woman said to Him, "Sir, You have nothing to draw with, and the well is deep. Where then do You get that living water? Are You greater than our father Jacob, who gave us the well, and drank from it himself, as well as his sons and his livestock?" Jesus answered and said to her, "Whoever drinks of this water will thirst again, but whoever drinks of the water that I shall give him will never thirst. But the water that I shall give him will become in him a fountain of water springing up into everlasting life." (vv. 6-14)

Jesus Christ is telling the Samaritan woman about the only "water" that would quench the real need of her spiritually dry and empty soul. Our Lord's offer of eternal salvation to her reveals a striking

---

[7] The word "abides" (*menei*) is in the present tense. If a sinner does not possess eternal life, the wrath of God continues to abide on him.

contrast. He says, "Whoever drinks [present tense, demanding on-going action] of this water [in the well] will thirst again: But whoever drinks [aorist tense] of the water that I shall give him will never thirst. But the water that I shall give him will become in him a fountain of water springing up into everlasting life" (vv. 13-14).

Let me highlight these two striking contrasts. First of all, instead of eternal life requiring ongoing actions ("drinks"—present tense, v. 13), it requires only a simple act of faith in Christ ("drinks" – aorist tense, v. 14).[8] Secondly, instead of thirsting "again," the believer in Christ "shall *never* thirst" for eternal life.[9] These words emphasize that under *no* circumstances and under *no* conditions will the believer in Christ ever thirst again. Dear readers, do you realize what this means? If a believer could somehow lose his salvation, he would then "thirst again." But Jesus Christ guarantees in this promise that he "shall never thirst." That's eternal security!

In addition to this, the New King James Bible does not translate three Greek words in the text that underscore this wonderful truth of eternal security even more. Following the phrase "shall never thirst" are the Greek words *eis ton aiōna* which literally mean "into the age" or "forever."[10] Can you think of any stronger way to emphasize the guarantee of eternal life than by literally saying, "Whosoever drinks of the water I shall give him *shall never thirst again forever*"? What a wonderful guarantee of eternal salvation to a sinful woman who through faith alone in Christ alone could receive eternal life while deserving the very opposite. And according to John 4:26-42, she did receive it! What amazing grace!

John 5:24

The Lord Jesus gives yet another promise regarding the eternal security of salvation to angry Jews who sought to kill Him for breaking the Sabbath and declaring Himself equal with God. He said to them, "Most assuredly, I say to you, he who hears My word and believes in Him who sent Me has everlasting life, and shall not come into judgment, but has passed from death into life" (John 5:24). Eternal life is guaranteed to the individual who is willing to simply

---

[8] This striking contrast between the present tense and the aorist tense can also be found in Acts 16:30 "do" (present) and Acts 16:31 "believe" (aorist).

[9] The Greek particles *ou* and *mē* are here combined to emphasize a very strong negation.

[10] *Eis ton aiōna* will be explained, and its usage demonstrated, in the next chapter.

believe God's record of His Son. Again, the verb "has" (*echei*) is in the present tense and indicative mood, which sets forth the fact that eternal life is a *present* reality, not a future possibility. God gives a know-so, not hope-so salvation. Notice also the two-prong promise, followed by a definite statement from Jesus Christ Himself.

- **Promise #1**: "has everlasting life"

- **Promise #2**: "and shall not come into condemnation"

If you could lose or forfeit your salvation by committing a heinous sin, developing a pattern of sin, not confessing your sin, or turning your back on God, then you would relinquish eternal life and come under God's condemnation. Our Lord guarantees that *this is impossible*. Thus, as Lewis Sperry Chafer says, the promises of eternal life in the Gospel of John "should not be countermanded by an 'if.' The words of certainty must stand as they appear on the Sacred Page."[11] Jesus Christ's two-fold warranty declares for you the certain and forever salvation of every believer who permanently *"has passed*[12] *from death unto life."* Clearly, this is another wonderful promise from Jesus Christ regarding the believer's eternal salvation. That's eternal security!

Dear friend, have you ever drunk of the water of eternal life that Jesus Christ offers you? If God, by His grace, could save a religious Pharisee like Nicodemus or an immoral sinner like the Samaritan woman, He can save a wretch like you. By way of a personal paraphrase, John 3:16 is saying to you, "For God so loved *you*, that He gave His only Son to die on the cross for *you*, that if *you* would put your trust in Jesus Christ alone, *you* would not perish in Hell, but *you* would have right now eternal life." As a Mafia godfather would say, *"This is an offer you dare not refuse!"*

> Wonderful grace of Jesus,
> Greater than all my sin;
> How shall my tongue describe it,

---

[11] Lewis Sperry Chafer, *Systematic Theology* (Dallas: Dallas Seminary Press, 1948; reprint, Grand Rapids: Kregel, 1993), 3:267.

[12] The word "passed" (*metabebēken*) is in the perfect tense indicating that at a point in time in the past (new birth), the believer passed from death to life, with the results remaining to the present—the believer remains regenerated. At the moment of faith in Christ alone, the believer permanently passed out of separation from God (spiritual "death") and "into life" (union with God).

Where shall its praise begin?
Taking away my burden,
Setting my spirit free;
For the wonderful grace of Jesus reaches me.

Wonderful grace of Jesus,
Reaching to all the lost,
By it I have been pardoned,
Saved to the uttermost,
Chains have been torn asunder,
Giving me liberty;
For the wonderful grace of Jesus reaches me.

Wonderful grace of Jesus,
Reaching the most defiled,
By its transforming power,
Making him God's dear child,
Purchasing peace and heaven,
For all eternity;
And the wonderful grace of Jesus reaches me.

REFRAIN:
Wonderful the matchless grace of Jesus,
Deeper than the mighty rolling sea;
Higher than the mountain, sparkling like a fountain,
all sufficient for me, for even me.
Broader than the scope of my transgressions,
Greater far than all my sin and shame,
O magnify the precious Name of Jesus.
Praise His Name![13]

---

[13] Haldor Lillenas, *Wonderful Grace of Jesus*.

CHAPTER 11

A Double Negative Worth Knowing

In the English language, grammarians will be quick to point out that a double negative is a definite "no no." But in the language of the New Testament (Greek), the negatives *ou* and *mē* are occasionally combined (*ou mē*) to express how under *no* conditions and *no* circumstances could something *ever* happen. As we continue to observe select promises that Jesus Christ made regarding the eternal security of a believer's salvation as recorded in the Book of John, this double negative (*ou mē*) is worth noting.

John 6:35-40

In John chapter 6, Jesus Christ makes yet another promise that guarantees an eternal and secure salvation for those who trust in Him alone:

> And Jesus said to them, "I am the bread of life. He who comes to Me shall never hunger, and he who believes in Me shall never thirst. But I said to you that you have seen Me and yet do not believe. All that the Father gives Me will come to Me, and the one who comes to Me I will by no means cast out. For I have come down from heaven, not to do My own will, but the will of Him who sent Me. This is the will of the Father who sent Me, that of all He has given Me I should lose nothing, but should raise it up at the last day. And this is the will of Him who sent Me, that everyone who sees the Son and believes in Him may have everlasting life; and I will raise him up at the last day. (vv. 35-40)

In this great discourse on the bread of life, Jesus Christ compares Himself to the manna from heaven which provided life to the Exodus generation of Jews (vv. 31-33). And just as those Jews needed to personally accept God's gift of manna for it to benefit them personally, sinners need to come to Christ by faith (v. 35). The issue is not coming forward to the front of a church and praying the "sinner's prayer." Nor is it a matter of coming to a baptismal fount or baptistry to somehow wash away your sins. The issue is coming to Jesus Christ by faith. Verse 35 clearly states . . .

- The *Person* of the offer: "I am the bread of life."

- The *condition* of the offer: "he who comes to Me"

- The *promise* of the offer: "shall never [*ou mē*] hunger"

- The *condition clarified* of the offer: "he who believes in Me"

- The *promise restated*: "shall never [*ou mē*] thirst."

This verse is similar to the promise Christ made to the Samaritan woman (John 4:13-14). Once again, He emphatically teaches the absolute guarantee of eternal security through the use of the word "never." This combination of Greek negative particles (*ou mē*) stresses that under no circumstances or conditions shall the believer in Christ ever spiritually hunger or thirst again.

What issue does Christ now put his index finger on? What were Christ's hearers still missing? The simplicity of faith in Him alone. "But I said to you that you have seen Me *and yet do not believe*" (John 6:36). The word "believes" (v. 35) and "believe" (v. 36) indicate that faith involves a *choice* to trust in Christ.[1] Yet this was the decision Christ's audience was unwilling to make. To further support the eternal security of salvation, the Savior declares, "All that the Father gives Me will come to Me, and the one who comes to Me I will by no means [*ou mē*] cast out" (v. 37). This verse beautifully balances divine sovereignty in the first half of the verse with human responsibility in the second half. And please note that "all" means *all*. Christ's absolute pledge to *all* who come to Him by faith is that He "will by no means [*ou mē*—never] cast [them] out." If Jesus Christ will accept all believing sinners, why would He later kick someone out when He sees flaws and faults in that person's Christian walk? Being

---

[1] This is substantiated by the active voice.

omniscient, the Lord knew in advance whom He would accept and for whom He would die. Yet *He will never cast you out,* for He came "to seek and save that which was lost" (Luke 19:10). In fact, this litotes[2] in verse 37 indicates that Christ will do just the opposite—*he will keep you in.*

"For I have come down from heaven, not to do My own will, but the will of Him who sent Me. This is the will of the Father who sent Me, that of all He has given Me I should lose nothing, but should raise it up at the last day" (vv. 38-39). Did you realize that Christ's mission in fulfillment of the Father's will involved an eternal and secure salvation? Notice that He said, "I should lose *nothing,* but should raise it up at the last day." Interestingly, this same concept occurs earlier in this chapter in the feeding of the five thousand and His command to the disciples to "gather up the fragments that remain, *that nothing be lost*" (v. 12). No believer in Christ will ever be lost again! Is it guaranteed? "And this is the will of Him who sent Me, that everyone who sees the Son and believes in Him may have everlasting life; and I will raise him up at the last day" (v. 40).

Jesus Christ again guarantees that anyone may have "eternal life" if he puts his trust in Christ alone. What a powerful passage (John 6:35-40) and six-fold guarantee of eternal security!

- "shall never [*ou mē*] hunger" (v. 35)

- "shall never [*ou mē*] thirst" (v. 35)

- "I will by no means [*ou mē*] cast out " (v. 37)

- "I should lose nothing" (v. 39)

- "may have everlasting life" (v. 40)

- "I will raise him up at the last day" (v. 40)

Jesus Christ has promised that every sinner who chooses to trust Christ as Savior, via the convicting work of God (v. 44), will receive eternal life right now, as well as have a certain bodily resurrection in the future: "and I will raise him up at the last day." What a complete and guaranteed salvation! That's eternal security!

---

[2] Litotes is a literary device of understatement for effect, in which something is expressed by a negation of the contrary.

Dear readers, which verse describes you? Are you the sinner who, while recognizing your sin and worthiness of God's righteous condemnation, comes to Christ by faith for salvation? Or are you like those of whom Jesus said, "You have seen Me and yet *do not believe*"? Aren't these great and precious promises by Jesus Christ? So what is your decision? "Therefore I said to you that you will die in your sins; for if you do not believe that I am He, you will die in your sins" (John 8:24).

Every believer is eternally secure because of the divine PROTECTION of Jesus Christ.

The propitiatory sacrifice and the promises of Jesus Christ guarantee eternal salvation for those who place their trust in Him alone. The double negative *ou mē* adds emphasis to Christ's promises and also to His divine protection.

> Then Jesus said to them again, "Most assuredly, I say to you, I am the door of the sheep. All who ever came before Me are thieves and robbers, but the sheep did not hear them. I am the door. If anyone enters by Me, he will be saved, and will go in and out and find pasture. The thief does not come except to steal, and to kill, and to destroy. I have come that they may have life, and that they may have it more abundantly. I am the good shepherd. The good shepherd gives His life for the sheep. (John 10:7-11)

> I am the good shepherd; and I know My sheep, and am known by My own. As the Father knows Me, even so I know the Father; and I lay down My life for the sheep. And other sheep I have which are not of this fold; them also I must bring, and they will hear My voice; and there will be one flock and one shepherd. Therefore My Father loves Me, because I lay down My life that I may take it again. No one takes it from Me, but I lay it down of Myself. I have power to lay it down, and I have power to take it again. This command I have received from My Father. (John 10:14-18)

> Therefore there was a division again among the Jews because of these sayings. And many of them said, "He

has a demon and is mad. Why do you listen to Him?" Others said, "These are not the words of one who has a demon. Can a demon open the eyes of the blind?" Now it was the Feast of Dedication in Jerusalem, and it was winter. And Jesus walked in the temple, in Solomon's porch. Then the Jews surrounded Him and said to Him, "How long do You keep us in doubt? If You are the Christ, tell us plainly." Jesus answered them, "I told you, and you do not believe. The works that I do in My Father's name, they bear witness of Me. But you do not believe, because you are not of My sheep, as I said to you." (John 10:19-26)

John chapter 10 pictures the shepherd-sheep relationship of Jesus Christ with those who trust in Him. In verses 27-30, the end of the discourse, Jesus makes seven unconditional declarations which are true for *all* of Christ's sheep.

1) "My sheep hear My voice" (personal illumination)

2) "and I know them" (personal relationship)

3) "and they follow Me" (personal trust)

4) "And I give them eternal life" (present eternal life)

5) "and they shall never perish" (promised eternal security)

6) "neither shall anyone snatch them out of My hand." (promised double eternal security)

7) "My Father, who has given them to Me, is greater than all; and no one is able to snatch them out of My Father's hand." (divinely promised triple eternal security)

Please observe that there are no "ifs" in these statements, such as, "*If* My sheep hear My voice, and *if* I know them, and *if* they follow me, *then* I give them eternal life."[3] These declarations apply to everyone who has put his or her trust in Jesus Christ alone (v. 11). Every believer is one of Christ's "sheep."

[3] Robert G. Gromacki, *Salvation Is Forever* (Chicago: Moody Press, 1973; reprint, Schaumburg, IL: Regular Baptist Press, 1989), 76; and J. F. Strombeck, *Shall Never Perish: Eternal Security Examined* (Philadelphia: American Bible Conference Association, 1936; reprint, Grand Rapids: Kregel, 1992), 13-14.

If you recall chapter two of this book, the phrase "I know them" stands in stark contrast to those who trust in Jesus Christ *plus* their works for salvation (Matt. 7:22), regarding whom Christ declared, "*I never knew you*; depart from Me, you who practice lawlessness" (v. 23b).

To reinforce His words of assurance: "And I give unto them *eternal* life," Jesus Christ wonderfully adds, "and they shall *never perish*." The Greek *ou mē* construction, translated "never," underscores again that under no conditions and circumstances shall Christ's sheep ever perish. That's eternal security!

But for those who may be still skeptical of this wonderful truth, it would be helpful to note that virtually all English translations leave three Greek words in the text untranslated for stylistic reasons. In verse 28, Jesus Christ literally says that His sheep shall not perish "unto the ages" or "forever" (*eis ton aiōna*). Consider the other occurrences of this phrase in the book of John (of which some are translated and some are not).

> I am the living bread which came down from heaven. If anyone eats of this bread, he will live *forever* [*eis ton aiōna*]; and the bread that I shall give is My flesh, which I will give for the life of the world. (John 6:51)

> This is that bread which came down from heaven—not as your fathers ate the manna, and are dead. He who eats this bread will live *forever* [*eis ton aiōna*]. (John 6:58)

> And a slave does not abide in the house *forever* [*eis ton aiōna*], but a son abides *forever* [*eis ton aiōna*]. (John 8:35)

> And whoever lives and believes in Me shall never [*ou mē*] die [*eis ton aiōna*]. Do you believe this? (John 11:26)

> Peter said to Him, "You shall never [*ou mē*] wash my feet [*eis ton aiōna*]." Jesus answered him, "If I do not wash you, you have no part with me." (John 13:8)

> And I will pray the Father, and He will give you another Helper, that he may abide with you *forever* [*eis ton aiōna*]. (John 14:16)

How much stronger statement regarding the believer's eternal salvation and security could Christ make? "I give unto them *eternal life, and they shall never perish forever.*"

Are these promises absolutely guaranteed even if you fall, stumble, or live in carnality in the future? Yes, for Christ declares, "neither shall anyone snatch them out of My hand." The Greek verb translated "snatch" (*harpazō*) often carries the idea of seizing or snatching by force.[4] In fact, Jesus Christ uses it in John 10:12 of the wolf's violent snatching of sheep, and Paul uses it to refer to the Rapture of the Church in 1 Thessalonians 4:17 ("caught up").

The word picture in John 10:28 is that every believer is viewed as secure in the hand of Jesus Christ, so that no one even in the future "*shall . . . snatch them out of My hand.*"[5] Simply being Christ's sheep is the only condition attached to this, not the quality of your following, for the obtaining and maintaining of salvation is based on *Christ's work*, not your walk.[6] It does not rest on the believer's faithfulness or ability to cling, but on Christ's faithfulness and infinite power to keep His own in His hand. Remember, sheep have hoofs, they do not have hands. This is another promise of eternal security.

But there is more! "My Father, who has given them to Me, is greater than all; and no one is able to snatch them out of My Father's hand." Verse 29 then shifts from the emphasis being on Christ's hand, to His *Father's hand*, which "is greater than all." While verse 28 precludes anyone snatching the believer out of Christ's hand in the future, verse 29 guarantees that no one shall snatch the believer out of the Father's hand in the meantime.[7] Believer, you are in good

---

[4] Walter Bauer, William F. Arndt, and F. Wilbur Gingrich, *A Greek-English Lexicon of the New Testament and Other Early Christians Literature*, 3rd ed., rev. and ed. Frederick W. Danker (Chicago: University of Chicago Press, 2000), 134.

[5] The verb for "shall . . . snatch" (*harpasei*) in verse 28 is in the future tense.

[6] Christ's statement in verse 27 that believers are those who "follow Me" must be understood contextually. When Christ says, "My sheep hear My voice, and I know them, and they follow Me," the point of the passage is not the faithfulness of sheep in following the Shepherd (Thomas L. Constable, *Expository Notes on John* [Garland, TX: Sonic Light, 2008], 159). The statement that "they follow Me" does not imply salvation by faith plus works or obedience but simply that sheep trust the Shepherd. Christ is the object of their faith and not another. They trust the voice of their Shepherd and not a stranger or a thief (vv. 1-10). Furthermore, in the context it is the Shepherd who gives His life for the sheep and not vice versa (vv. 11, 15, 17-18). This section is rightly known as the "Good Shepherd Discourse" because the whole point is the goodness of Christ as Shepherd (vv. 11, 14), not the goodness of sheep as faithful followers. In fact, a well-known tendency of sheep is to go astray and need rescuing by the Shepherd. Christ is the good Shepherd because He knows us who have believed in Him and because He died for us, protects us, and keeps us eternally.

[7] The verb for "*snatch*" is the in the present tense in verse 29.

hands with Jesus Christ and God the Father as "I and my Father are one" (v. 30). This is another guarantee of eternal security! Could the passage be any plainer or stronger?

In spite of these tremendous promises, some still object, "But can't you jump out of the hands of Jesus Christ and God the Father?" Dear reader, if you could jump out, you would have to be stronger than God the Father, and remember, "My Father . . . is greater than all." Furthermore, if you could jump out of God's hands, you would then "perish." And that would contradict what Jesus declared when he promised, "and they shall *never perish*." If you possessed "eternal" life and lost it, in what sense was it "eternal"? Charles Stanley states this point well when he writes,

> If our salvation is not secure, how could Jesus say about those to whom He gives eternal life, "and they shall never perish" (John 10:28)? If even one man or woman receives eternal life and then forfeits it through sin or apostasy, will they not perish? And by doing so, do they not make Jesus' words a lie?[8]

Still others retort, "But doesn't eternal security violate free will?" Not at all. All believers are within God's hand, and yet we still have many choices to make as to the kind of Christian walk we will have and the quality of our decisions. Let me illustrate this truth with Noah's ark. Once Noah and his family made a decision to trust God's only provision for deliverance from the flood and went through the door of the ark, they were saved forever from God's judgment. Yet within the ark, they still had numerous decisions to make each day as to what to do, how to use their time, and how they would relate to one another. But from the day they walked through the one door to enter the ark, it was certain and clear that *they would never perish*. Likewise, when an unworthy sinner trusts Jesus Christ alone and receives God's gift of eternal life, he *shall never perish*. Within the ark of salvation, Jesus Christ, we still have numerous decisions to make each day as to what to do, how to use our time, whether we will walk by faith or walk by sight, and whether we will live for Jesus Christ or for ourselves. Yet one thing is settled forever: *we shall never perish*.

These promises from our Lord Jesus Christ do not violate your free will, but they do recognize what free will can and cannot do. For

---

[8] Charles Stanley, *Eternal Security: Can You Be Sure?* (Nashville: Thomas Nelson, 1990), 18.

example, you may want to jump off a building and go up; however, the law of gravity will make certain that you go down instead. Is your free volition violated? No! In such a case, your free volition is not violated, but it is certainly limited as to what it can and cannot accomplish. What Jesus Christ clearly and emphatically declares in John 10:27-30 is the guarantee of eternal life and the impossibility of ever losing your salvation. This wonderful Shepherd is all-powerful, and every sheep in Him has nothing to fear. Hallelujah! Praise the Lord! On one occasion when the late Dr. H. A. Ironside preached on the subject of the eternal security of the believer, a woman came up to him afterwards and said,

> "I don't agree with your doctrine."

> "What don't you agree with?" he asked her.

> "Well, this doctrine of once saved, always saved," she replied.

> "Let me read you a verse which supports this doctrine," he said.

> "Oh, I know what you are going to read. You're going to read John 10:28, aren't you?"

> "As a matter of fact, that is the verse I was going to read." So he read the words: "I give them eternal life, and they shall never perish; no one can snatch them out of my hand." Then he looked her in the eye and asked her, "Do you believe those words?"

> "Not as you interpret them," she replied.

> "But I didn't interpret them at all! I just read them to you."

> "Well," she replied, "I don't believe those words mean what you say they mean."

> "Then let me read the verse this way," he said. "Supposing Jesus said, 'I give them life for twenty

years, and they shall never perish for twenty years and no one can snatch them out of my hand for twenty years.' What would you think that means?"

"I think that means they would be safe for twenty years."

"Let us say we changed twenty years to forty years. Would they be safe for forty years?"

"Yes," she said, "I think they would be safe for forty years."

"But it doesn't say twenty years or forty years, it says forever: 'and they shall never perish.' The Greek text is very strong at that point. What it literally says is, 'They shall not ever perish forever.' Let's read it that way: 'I give unto them life forever and they shall never perish forever.' Do you believe that?"

"Not the way you interpret it," she replied.

At this point, Dr. Ironside could only throw up his hands.

But someone may object, "What about believers who fall into sin? Don't they lose their salvation?" Psalm 37:23-24 answers this by stating, "The steps of a good man are ordered by the LORD, and He delights in his way. Though he fall, he shall not be utterly cast down; for the LORD upholds him with His hand." When a believer falls, it is imperative to keep in mind that he falls *in* the hand of Christ, not *out* of the hand of Christ. Dear friends, I ask you: Did Jesus Christ not only die for every sin of all mankind but also forgive every sin of all believers when they trusted in Jesus Christ as Savior? "And you, being dead in your trespasses and the uncircumcision of your flesh, He has made alive together with Him, having forgiven you *all trespasses*" (Col. 2:13).

If you are willing to take God's Word at face value and not take the mental posture, "Don't confuse me with the facts," you will find these verses to be of great comfort and assurance. And since Jesus cannot lie, your eternal security does not depend on your feeble hold on Christ, but on His firm grip upon you. To think otherwise is a big "*no no*." Amen?

Born of the Spirit with life from above
Into God's family divine,
Justified fully thro' Calvary's love–
O what a standing is mine!
And the transaction so quickly was made
When as a sinner I came–
Took of the offer of grace
He did proffer. He saved me;
O praise His dear name!

Now I've a hope that will surely endure
After the passing of time.
I have a future in heaven for sure,
There in those mansions sublime.
And it's because of that wonderful day
When at the cross I believed;
Riches eternal and blessings supernal
From His precious hand I received.

Heaven came down and glory filled my soul,
When at the cross the Savior made me whole.
My sins were washed away,
And my night was turned to day.
Heaven came down and glory filled by soul![9]

---

[9] John W. Peterson, *Heaven Came Down.*

CHAPTER 12

God's Answers to Jesus Christ's Prayer

During Jesus Christ's earthly ministry, He remained deity—equal with the Father—though in becoming a man He voluntarily humbled Himself. His complete submission and dependence toward God the Father and His daily, repeated, believing prayers to God demonstrate His humility. Even on the night in which Judas betrayed Him and Peter denied Him three times, Jesus Christ entered again into the throne room of the Father in prayer:

> Now I am no longer in the world, but these are in the world, and I come to You. Holy Father, *keep through Your name those whom You have given Me, that they may be one as We are.* While I was with them in the world, I kept them in Your name. Those whom You gave Me I have kept; and *none of them is lost* except the son of perdition, that the Scripture might be fulfilled. . . . I do not pray for these alone, but also for those who will believe in Me through their word; that they all may be one, as You, Father, are in Me, and I in You; that they also may be one in Us, that the world may believe that You sent Me. And the glory which You gave Me I have given them, that they may be one just as We are one: I in them, and You in Me; that they may be made perfect in one, and that the world may know that You have sent Me, and have loved them as You have loved Me. Father, I desire that they also whom You gave Me *may be with Me where I am,* that they may behold My glory which You have given Me;

for You loved Me before the foundation of the world. O
righteous Father! The world has not known You, but I
have known You; and these have known that You sent
Me. And I have declared to them Your name, and will
declare it, that the love with which You loved Me may be
in them, and I in them." (John 17:11-12, 20-24)

Jesus Christ, because of His deep love for us which He expresses in
His prayer above, keeps us saved and eternally secure because of
His *propitiatory sacrifice* for us, His *promises* to us, and His *protection*
of us. But there is more.

Every believer is eternally secure because of the divine PRAYER of Jesus Christ. (John 17:1-26)

Knowing that He would be crucified the next day, Jesus Christ . . .

- prayed for Himself. (vv. 1-5)
- prayed for His disciples. (vv. 6-19)
- prayed for His future Church. (vv. 20-26)

In this historical context, it is important to note that Judas departed
earlier that night to betray Jesus (13:21-30). Christ's prayer is only
for His believing disciples (v. 8), whom He repeatedly describes as
those "whom You [the Father] have given Me [Jesus]" (vv. 2, 6, 7, 9,
11, 12, 24). This indicates that Jesus Christ views each believer as a
gift from the Father to the Son.

What, specifically, is Christ's first petition for His believing
disciples? "Now I am no longer in the world, but these are in the
world, and I come to You. Holy Father, *keep through Your name* those
whom You have given Me, that they may be one as We are" (v. 11).
Christ's first request to the Father is for Him to "keep," guard, or
preserve these believers "through Your name." This refers to the
Father keeping believers through His person and work.[1]

---

[1] The "name" of a person is a common Hebrew idiom representing the characteristics
or deeds of that person (Gen. 3:20; Josh. 9:9-10; Ruth 1:20-21; Ps. 20:1). See Hans Bieten-
hard, "*name*," in *The New International Dictionary of New Testament Theology*, ed. Colin
Brown (Grand Rapids: Zondervan, 1975), 2:650; idem, "*onoma*," in *Theological Dictionary
of the New Testament*, ed. Gerhard Friedrich and Gerhard Kittel, trans. and ed. Goeffrey
W. Bromiley, vol. 5 (Grand Rapids: Eerdmans, 1967), 272; and Thomas L. Stegall, *The
Gospel of the Christ* (Milwaukee: Grace Gospel Press, 2009), 129-52. In the writings of

And why does Jesus Christ ask for the keeping or preservation of these believing disciples? It is so "that they may be one as We are" (v. 11c). This positional, spiritual unity would be fulfilled on the day of Pentecost when Christ's Church began in answer to Christ's prayer. It was then that all believers in Christ (Jew or Gentile) became "one" in the Body of Christ (Acts 2; Eph. 2:11-18; 4:4). But why would this prayer of preservation be needed at that time? "While I was with them in the world, I kept them in Your name. Those whom You gave Me I have kept; and none of them is lost except the son of perdition, that the Scripture might be fulfilled" (v. 12) In anticipation of His crucifixion, resurrection, and ascension into Heaven, Jesus Christ asks for the Father's preservation of these genuine believers and that *"none of them is lost."*

Who is the exception to this truth? Who is lost? Verse 12 states, "except the son of perdition, that the Scripture might be fulfilled." Who is the "son of perdition"?[2] It was Judas Iscariot. While no genuine believer can ever lose salvation, there was one in the disciple band who was lost, namely Judas, for *he had never been saved!*

1. Judas never believed in Christ.

   "'But there are some of you who do not believe.' For Jesus knew from the beginning who they were who did not believe, and who would betray Him." (John 6:64)

2. Judas was never cleansed from his sins.

   "Jesus said to him, 'He who is bathed needs only to wash his feet, but is completely clean; and you are clean, but not all of you.' For He knew who would betray Him; therefore He said, 'You are not all clean.'" (John 13:10-11)

3. Judas was never chosen by Christ.

   "I do not speak concerning all of you. I know whom I have chosen; but that the Scripture may be fulfilled, 'He who eats bread with Me has lifted up his heel against Me.'" (John 13:18)

John, to believe in the name of Jesus Christ is to believe in His person and work (John 1:12; 3:18; 20:31; 1 John 2:12; 3:23; 5:13). Thus in John 17:11 Christ is requesting that believers be kept through the Father's own attributes and saving work.

[2] This is a Hebrew expression for a person characterized or identified with utter spiritual ruin; that is, destined to Hell.

4. Judas was never kept by Christ.

"Now I am no longer in the world, but these are in the world, and I come to You. Holy Father, keep through Your name those whom You have given Me, that they may be one as We are. While I was with them in the world, I kept them in Your name. Those whom You gave Me I have kept; and none of them is lost except the son of perdition, that the Scripture might be fulfilled." (John 17:11-12)

5. Judas was never given by the Father to the Son.

"Jesus answered, 'I have told you that I am He. Therefore, if you seek Me, let these [the eleven] go their way,' that the saying might be fulfilled which He spoke, 'Of those whom You gave Me I have lost none.'" (John 18:8-9)

Is Judas an example of a believer who lost his salvation? No, but he is a scriptural example of a religious hypocrite who engaged in various religious works and yet *never trusted in Christ alone* for his salvation.

Having prayed for divine preservation for His disciples, our Lord then prayed for their divine protection from the Devil. "I do not pray that You should take them out of the world, but that *You should keep them from the evil one*" (v. 15). If Satan cannot successfully prevent your justification before God, He certainly wants to prevent your practical sanctification and service for the Lord.

Jesus also prayed, "They are not of the world, just as I am not of the world. *Sanctify them by Your truth. Your word is truth.* As You sent Me into the world, I also have sent them into the world. And for their sakes I sanctify Myself, that they also may be *sanctified by the truth*" (vv. 16-19). The tool that the Holy Spirit utilizes for the progressive sanctification and spiritual growth of the believer is *the Word of God*. Dear believer, are you allowing the Bible to have a sanctifying effect in your daily walk with the Lord and . . .

- in your thought life? (With what are you mentally occupied?)

- with your tongue? (Does it express blessing or cursing?)

- in your motives? (Whether to please men or God?)

- in your objective dependence? (To depend on yourself or the Lord?)

Jesus' prayer confronts us again with the stark reality that the eternal security of the believer is designed to lead to personal and progressive sanctification; it is not designed to be a license to sin. God wants to impress upon you that He designed His gift of a *permanent salvation* to lead you to a *progressive sanctification* in your life resulting in *practical service* for Jesus Christ and others. Verses 18 and 19 make it clear that the purpose of God's preservation and progressive sanctification in your life is for service to others as unto the Lord: "As You sent Me into the world, *I also have sent them into the world.* And for their sakes I sanctify Myself, that they also may be sanctified by the truth."

Still someone may object, "But those verses only apply to the eleven believing disciples. They do not apply to us." This is a half-truth, for Jesus Christ goes on to pray, "I do not pray for these alone, *but also for those who will believe in Me through their word*" (v. 20). Christ's prayer stretches beyond His eleven believing disciples to "those who *will believe* in Me through their word." It would be through the "word" of these disciples in preaching the Gospel and writing the New Testament that sinners would hear the message of salvation and "believe" in Jesus Christ as Savior. Note again that the sole and singular condition to be saved and part of the true Church of Jesus Christ is only faith in Christ—not good works, church rituals, or law-keeping.

If you have trusted in Christ alone, what specifically did Jesus Christ pray for you that night?

> *That they all may be one*, as You, Father, are in Me, and I in You; that *they also may be one in Us*, that the world may believe that You sent Me. And the glory which You gave Me I have given them, that *they may be one just as We are one*: I in them, and You in Me; that they may be made perfect in one, and that the world may know that You have sent Me, and have loved them as You have loved Me. (John 17:21-23)

Jesus Christ first prayed for an actual, spiritual, positional unity of all genuine believers in Christ produced by the Holy Spirit and based on the Gospel of grace amidst ethnic and gender diversity (Eph. 2:11-19). The practical purposes of this true unity among believers were to promote the believer's fellowship with God (v. 21b) and evangelism toward the lost (v. 21c).

Christ's second request for you pertains to the *heavenly glorification* of His future Church: "Father, I desire that they also whom You gave Me *may be with Me where I am,* that they may behold My glory which You have given Me; for You loved Me before the foundation of the world" (v. 24). The Savior's prayer for you as a Church-age believer is that you would "be with Me [Christ] where I am." Where is Jesus Christ today? He is in Heaven!

> Let not your heart be troubled; you believe in God, believe also in Me. *In My Father's house are many mansions;* if it were not so, I would have told you. *I go to prepare a place for you.* And if I go and prepare a place for you, I will come again and receive you to Myself; *that where I am, there you may be also.* (John 14:1-3)

> Now when He had spoken these things, while they watched, He was taken up, and a cloud received Him out of their sight. And while they looked steadfastly toward heaven as He went up, behold, two men stood by them in white apparel, who also said, "Men of Galilee, why do you stand gazing up *into heaven*? This same Jesus, who was taken up from you *into heaven,* will so come in like manner as you saw Him go *into heaven.*" (Acts 1:9-11)

So what are believers presently doing in Heaven? What did our Lord pray? He prayed, "that they may behold My glory" (v. 24). In order for you to behold the glory of Jesus Christ in Heaven, what must be guaranteed? *That you are going to Heaven!*

Thus, we have observed in this high priestly prayer of Jesus Christ that He prayed for the preservation, positional unity, and heavenly glorification of not only His eleven believing disciples but also His future Church. This begs the question, "Did God the Father hear and answer His requests?" Just before the raising of Lazarus, Jesus prayed to the Father.

> Then they took away the stone from the place where the dead man was lying. And Jesus lifted up His eyes and said, "Father, I thank You that You have heard Me. *And I know that You always hear Me,* but because of the people who are standing by I said this, that they may believe that You sent Me." (John 11:41-42)

God the Father always heard and favorably answered every prayer Jesus Christ uttered. And if this is true, the believer's permanent salvation and heavenly glorification is eternally secure because of the *prayer of Jesus Christ.*

So, was Jesus' prayer in John 17:20, *"for those who will believe in Me,"* for you? Let me ask you: as Jesus Christ looked down the corridors of time in anticipation of His future Church and at those who would put their trust in Him alone, did He see you? Was Jesus Christ praying for you that night? Have you ever put your trust in Him alone as presented in the Gospel to give you eternal life? You may have been part of many local churches, but have you ever become a member in the true Church of Jesus Christ by receiving Him through faith?

If you have never transferred your faith from a church, ritual, sacrament, or work (including your good, religious works) to the Son of God who loved you and gave Himself for you, why don't you make that decision right now? Do not put it off. God wants to forgive all your sins and make you His child. But He is a perfect gentleman, and He will not force you to put your trust in Christ alone. In His mercy, love, and grace, God is tapping His toe waiting to bless you and give you eternal life.

You may ask, "But what about my sins?" They have all been fully paid for by Jesus Christ and will be totally forgiven the moment you receive Him as your Savior. "To Him all the prophets witness that, through His name, *whoever believes in Him will receive remission of sins"* (Acts 10:43). You may say, "But I don't deserve this." You are right. It's all because of God's grace that He will save you from a Hell you deserve to a Heaven you do not. *"For by grace you have been saved through faith,* and that not of yourselves; it is the gift of God, not of works, lest anyone should boast" (Eph. 2:8-9).

You may ask, "But don't I need to change my life first?" No. Your life is secondary. Your eternal destiny is primary. And through faith in Jesus Christ, you will become a new creation in Christ. *"But to him who does not work but believes on Him* who justifies the ungodly, his faith is accounted for righteousness" (Rom. 4:5). And you might also ask, "But haven't my good works gained *some* favor with God?" No, they have not, for Isaiah 64:6 tells us that "we are all like an unclean thing, and all our righteousnesses are like filthy rags; we all fade as a leaf, and our iniquities, like the wind, have taken us away."

Dear friends, remember: if you could go to heaven by your good works, Jesus Christ would not have needed to come to earth and die on the cross for your sins. It would have been for nothing. "I do not set aside the grace of God; for *if righteousness comes through the law, then Christ died in vain"* (Gal. 2:21).

So let me ask you again. Was Jesus praying for you that very night before He would go to the cross of Calvary where His body and soul would be made an offering for your sins, my sins, and the sins of the whole world? On the night He was crucified, was Jesus Christ praying for you, knowing that in the 1960s, 70s, 80s, 90s, or in the twenty-first century you would hear the Gospel, come under the conviction of the Holy Spirit, and, as a result, believe in Jesus Christ and His work alone to be saved?

If you have trusted in Jesus Christ alone to save you, your salvation is eternal and secure—not based on your performance but because of the *prayer of Jesus Christ.* Dear believer, would it not be fitting for you to now pause and offer a prayer of thanksgiving to God for His matchless grace? Would it not be appropriate to praise Jesus Christ not only for His sacrificial death for your sins and bodily resurrection from the grave to give you eternal life, but also for His personal prayer for you that assures you that your salvation is eternal and secure, both now and forever? Amen! That's eternal security!

The songwriter, Philip P. Bliss, captures the wonderful truth of eternal security:

Children of God, O glorious calling,
Surely His grace will keep us from falling;
Passing from death to life at His call,
Blessed salvation, once for all.

Once for all, O sinner receive it;
Once for all, O brother believe it;
Cling to the cross, the burden will fall,
Christ hath redeemed us once for all.[3]

---

[3] Philip P. Bliss, *Once For All.*

CHAPTER 13

Does Eternal Salvation Depend on Your Faithfulness or Christ's?

Many who profess to be Christians live under an erroneous assumption that results in a stressful daily grind. They believe that while Christ died on the cross, whether they make it to heaven or not ultimately depends on their ongoing faith, faithfulness, holy life, avoidance of major sins, perseverance, good works, and so forth. Charles Stanley addresses this problem when he asks, "If salvation hinges on the consistency of our faith, by what standard are we to judge our consistency? Can we have any doubts at all? How long can we doubt? To what degree can we doubt? Is there a divine quota we dare not exceed?" In addition to that, we should ask, "How faithful must I be to maintain or prove my salvation? In what areas and how often? What if I am faithful but fail right before I die? Will I still go to Heaven? What if I sin and fail to confess it five minutes before I die? Will I miss Heaven due to one sin and five minutes?" All these questions boil down into one crucial question: *does eternal salvation depend on your faithfulness or Christ's?*

> You therefore, my son, be strong in the grace that is in Christ Jesus. And the things that you have heard from me among many witnesses, commit these to faithful men who will be able to teach others also. You therefore must endure hardship as a good soldier of Jesus Christ. No one engaged in warfare entangles himself with the affairs of this life, that he may please him who enlisted him as a soldier. And also if anyone competes in athletics, he is

not crowned unless he competes according to the rules.
The hard-working farmer must be first to partake of the
crops. Consider what I say, and may the Lord give you
understanding in all things. Remember that Jesus Christ,
of the seed of David, was raised from the dead according
to my gospel, for which I suffer trouble as an evildoer,
even to the point of chains; but the word of God is not
chained. Therefore I endure all things for the sake of the
elect, that they also may obtain the salvation which is in
Christ Jesus with eternal glory. This is a faithful saying:
For if we died with Him, we shall also live with Him.
If we endure, we shall also reign with Him. If we deny
Him, He also will deny us. If we are faithless, He remains
faithful; He cannot deny Himself. (2 Tim. 2:1-13)

In addition to His *propitiatory sacrifice*, His *guaranteed promises*, His
divine protection, and His *intercessory prayer*,

**Every believer in Christ is eternally secure because of the PRE-
VAILING FAITHFULNESS of Jesus Christ.**

The context of these verses involves the apostle Paul writing to his
son in the faith, Timothy, regarding faithful service to the Savior
amidst days of apostasy (vv. 1-8). Paul reminds Timothy of God's
sufficient grace (v. 1), the importance of passing on the baton of truth
to other faithful men (v. 2), the need to endure hardship (v. 3), and
the imperative of singular focus (v. 4), resulting in the expectation of
future reward (vv. 5-6). Timothy was to seriously ponder these truths
(v. 7) and remember the Savior he preached (v. 8), even as Paul was
suffering imprisonment for Christ's sake (v. 9a). Though Paul was
chained, the Word of God was not (v. 9), and his persecution was
worth enduring in light of the salvation of others (v. 10).

Beginning in verse 11, Paul introduces a series of four "if" clauses,
each of which assumes a reality. " This is a faithful saying, for:

- If we died with Him we shall also live with Him.

- If we endure, we shall also reign with Him.

- If we deny Him, He also will deny us.

- If we are faithless, He remains faithful; He cannot deny Himself."

The plural pronoun "we" occurs six times in these verses, referring to no less than Paul and Timothy as well as all believers in Christ. Therefore, this passage refers to genuine possessors of salvation, not mere professors of Christ.

The declarations of verses 11 and 13 act as divine bookends or supernatural pillars underscoring God's faithfulness in guaranteeing the eternal security of every sinner who has trusted Christ, while verse 12 highlights two possibilities regarding the believer's walk and service for the Lord.

Eternal Security

OPTIONS

v. 12

If we endure, we shall also reign with Him. If we deny Him, He also will deny us.

Eternal Security

v. 11

This is a faithful saying: For if we died with Him, we shall also live with Him.

v. 13

If we are faithless, He remains faithful; He cannot deny Himself.

At the point of faith in Christ, every believer has died and been crucified with Christ (Rom. 6:1-10; Gal. 2:20; Col. 2:20). Assuming this reality to be true, God's guarantee[1] is that we shall also live with Jesus Christ in the future.[2] This underscores the certainty and security of eternal salvation from beginning to end.

Now that the believer's identity and future destination are securely settled, what are his options in the meantime? Verse 12 sets forth two possibilities. If believers are willing to endure under pressure, tribulation, and persecution in faithfully serving the Savior in this lifetime, they will receive the reward of specific privileges in ruling and reigning with Christ in the future.[3] Regarding this, it is

---

[1] The verb for "died with" (*sunapethanomen*) is in the indicative mood, setting forth a fact of reality.

[2] The verb for "live with" (*suzēsomen*) is in the future tense.

[3] The word for "endure" (*hupomenomen*) is in the present tense; whereas the verb for "reign with" (*sumbasileusomen*) is in the future tense, indicating Christ's future Millennial Kingdom is in view.

important to distinguish eternal salvation (which is a gift of God's grace) and believers' rewards (which they earn through faithful service).[4] This verse is teaching that the perseverance of the saints does not result in eternal salvation but in future reward at the Judgment Seat of Christ (1 Cor. 3:11-15; 4:4-5; 2 Cor. 5:9-10).

In contrast to this preferred possibility in the first half of verse 12, Paul then presents a second possible option for the believer's life and service under pressure and persecution, namely, "If we deny Him, He also will deny us." The plural, first person pronouns of "we" and "us" draw attention to these possibilities in the lives of Paul and Timothy—who were clearly genuine believers in Christ. In addition to this, the word "deny" is the same word that is used to describe the apostle Peter's three denials of Jesus Christ.[5] Can a genuine believer deny the Lord? Yes, and Peter did. But did Peter lose his salvation when he denied His Savior and Lord? Never! But his faith faltered and his fellowship with Christ was temporarily broken and needed to be restored.[6]

Thomas Stegall emphasizes this when he writes,

> 2 Timothy 2:12b is not addressing either the loss of salvation by denying Christ (Arminianism) or the disproving of our salvation (Calvinism). Instead it is teaching the flip-side of v. 12a, that if we deny Christ He also will deny us one day in the future at His Judgment Seat by not giving us a reward (1 Cor. 3:10-15; 2 Cor. 5:9-10). By so teaching in v. 12b, Paul has returned to the theme of rewards discussed in the immediately preceding context of 2 Timothy 2:4-6 and elsewhere throughout this epistle (1:18; 4:1, 7-8, 14).[7]

---

[4] Lewis Sperry Chafer, *Systematic Theology* (Dallas: Dallas Seminary Press, 1948; reprint, Grand Rapids: Kregel, 1993), 3:307-9.

[5] The NIV translates this "disown" which is contextually and linguistically inappropriate in this passage; whereas the KJV, NKJV, and NASB accurately translate this "deny." The Greek word for "deny" is *arneomai*, which is elsewhere normally translated by all of these English Bibles and versions simply as "deny" rather than "disown" (Matt. 26:70, 72; Mark 14:68, 70; Luke 22:57; John 13:38; 18:25, 27).

[6] And the Lord said, "Simon, Simon! Indeed, Satan has asked for you, that he may sift you as wheat. But I have prayed for you, that your faith should not fail; and when you have returned to Me, strengthen your brethren." But he said to Him, "Lord, I am ready to go with You, both to prison and to death." Then He said, "I tell you, Peter, the rooster shall not crow this day before you will deny three times that you know Me." (Luke 22:31-34)

[7] Thomas L. Stegall, "Must Faith Endure for Salvation to Be Sure? Part 8," *Grace Family Journal* 6 (Summer 2003): 23.

Can a believer in Christ lose his potential reward due to unfaithfulness yet still be saved forever by God's grace and power? The same writer, Paul, makes this possibility crystal clear:

> For no other foundation can anyone lay than that which is laid, which is Jesus Christ. Now if anyone builds on this foundation with gold, silver, precious stones, wood, hay, straw, each one's work will become clear; for the Day will declare it, because it will be revealed by fire; and the fire will test each one's work, of what sort it is. *If anyone's work which he has built on it endures, he will receive a reward. If anyone's work is burned, he will suffer loss;* but he himself will be saved, yet so as through fire. (1 Cor. 3:11-15)

All believers have Jesus Christ as their sure foundation (v. 11). They must then determine how and with what materials they will build upon this foundation in their Christian lives and ministries. "Wood, hay, straw" set forth the believer's post-justification works comprised of human wisdom and produced by the flesh. These works will perish when the fire of God's judgment tests their quality at the Judgment Seat of Christ. In contrast, "gold, silver, and precious stones" symbolize the Christian's works involving divine wisdom and produced by the Holy Spirit. These works are permanent and will withstand the fire test of Jesus Christ, resulting in the receiving of "a reward." But what happens to the child of God who built his life and ministry with the perishable materials of "wood, hay, and straw"? The Bible is undeniably clear: "If anyone's work is burned, he will suffer loss; *but he himself will be saved,* yet so as through fire" (v. 15b). The believer who lived according to the flesh will have his work burned and will suffer the loss of a reward he could have received. But while a genuine Christian can lose a future reward, God guarantees that "he himself will be saved" by God in the future.[8] Why is this? It is because while his works may burn up, his Foundation still remains—Jesus Christ.

No wonder 2 Timothy 2:13 goes on to confirm that, "If we are faithless, He remains faithful; He cannot deny Himself." Based on

---

[8] The Greek word for "saved" (*sōthēsetai*) is in the indicative mood, which sets forth a fact of reality; and it is in the passive voice, which indicates that God does the act of saving rather than a person saving himself; and it is in the future tense, referring to salvation from sin's presence in Heaven.

the first-class condition "if" in the Greek text, Paul assumes that
some believers will be faithless, yet Jesus Christ remains faithful to
His person and His promises. Isn't it encouraging to be assured that
the believer's faithlessness never diminishes Christ's faithfulness?
The word translated "faithless" can mean unfaithful, unbelieving,
or even to stop believing. Yet in spite of the Christian's failures and
faithlessness, our Savior remains faithful to keep every sinner who
has trusted in Him saved and eternally secure as "He cannot deny
Himself." We can conclude from this that the perseverance of the
saints will be worthy of a tremendous reward from Jesus Christ in
the future, though the preservation of the Savior grants the believer
an absolute assurance of his salvation now and forever.

DOES THE BIBLE TEACH THAT ALL BELIEVERS
WILL PERSEVERE IN THE FAITH TO THE END?

Does the Bible teach that all genuine believers *will* persevere in the
faith? Consistent Calvinist theology answers "Yes" as it teaches that
if a person is truly elect, he will persevere in the faith until the end of
his life. Arminian theology answers "No" as it teaches that a believer
can lose his faith and in doing so can lose his salvation. Both of these
views rob the believer of the absolute assurance of salvation. But
what does the Bible say? The Bible actually teaches that it is possible
for one who is eternally saved by God's grace to . . .

1) commit idolatry and apostasy (1 Kings 11:1-10)
2) believe only for a while (Luke 8:13)
3) not continue in the Word of Christ (John 8:31)
4) not abide in Christ (John 15:1-8)
5) become disqualified in the race of the Christian life
    (1 Cor. 9:24-27)
6) resist God's chastening and correction to the point of physical
    death (1 Cor. 11:30-32)
7) stray from the faith (1 Tim. 1:5-6)
8) shipwreck faith (1 Tim. 1:18-20)
9) fall away from the faith (1 Tim. 4:1-3)
10) deny the faith (1 Tim. 5:8)
11) cast off initial faith and follow Satan (1 Tim. 5:12-15)
12) stray from the faith by loving money (1 Tim. 6:9-10)
13) stray from the faith by professing false doctrine (1 Tim. 6:20-21)
14) deny Christ and be faithless (2 Tim. 2:11-13)

15) have faith overthrown (2 Tim. 2:14-18)[9]

When answering this critical question about the perseverance of the saints, one should keep in mind both Old and New Testament believers such as . . .

- Lot, who lived in ongoing carnality (Gen. 11-19; 2 Peter 2:7-8)

- Solomon, who died worshiping false deities (1 Kings 11)

- King Saul, who committed suicide after visiting a witch (1 Sam. 28-31)

- Soil #2 believer, who believed for a while, but when persecution came, fell away (Luke 8:13)

- Justified, regenerated Corinthian believers whom God divinely disciplined through physical death (1 Cor. 11:30-31)

- Demas, a fellowlaborer for the gospel (Col. 4:14; Philem. 24), who forsook Paul, having loved this present world (2 Tim. 4:10)

- Alexander and Hymenaeus, whose faith was made shipwreck (1 Tim. 1:18-20)

- Believers at Ephesus, who would not endure sound doctrine but would be turned to fables (2 Tim. 4:3-4)

- The warning passages in Hebrews about apostasy, directed toward believers in Christ (Heb. 3, 6, 10)

Does God desire all believers to persevere in a life of faith and good works? Absolutely yes! Does God reward those believers who persevere in the faith? Yes (2 Tim. 4:6-8)! But does God guarantee that all believers will persevere in the faith? No! This is desired, but not guaranteed, resulting in either reward or loss of reward, but never the loss of eternal salvation (2 Tim. 2:11-13).

Does eternal salvation depend on your faithfulness or Christ's? The Word of God is clear: "If we remain faithless, He remains faithful; He cannot deny Himself" (v. 13). That's eternal security! Praise the Lord!

---

[9] Thomas L. Stegall, "Must Faith Endure for Salvation to Be Sure? Parts 1-9" *Grace Family Journal* 5-6 (March/April 2002 – Winter 2003).

Standing on the promises of Christ my King,
Through eternal ages let His praises ring,
Glory in the highest, I will shout and sing,
Standing on the promises of God.

Standing on the promises that cannot fail,
When the howling storms of doubt and fear assail,
By the living Word of God I shall prevail,
Standing on the promises of God.

Standing on the promises of Christ the Lord,
Bound to Him eternally by love's strong cord,
Overcoming daily with the Spirit's sword,
Standing on the promises of God.[10]

---

[10] R. Kelso Carter, *Standing on the Promises*.

CHAPTER 14

A Seal That Cannot Be Broken

It is wonderful to know from the Scriptures that God the Father and God the Son both guarantee the eternal salvation of every believer in Jesus Christ. As the Godhead is a trinity, the Holy Spirit guarantees our eternal security as well.

1. **Every believer in Christ is eternally secure because of the PERPETUAL PRESENCE of the Holy Spirit.**

    And I will pray the Father, and He will give you another Helper, *that He may abide with you forever.* (John 14:16)

The Lord Jesus Christ spoke these words on the eve of His crucifixion in what is commonly referred to as "The Upper Room Discourse" (John 13-17). Having washed the disciples' feet and instituted the Lord's Supper, Jesus Christ announces that one of His disciples would betray Him (13:21-27), another disciple would deny Him (13:36-38), and that He would depart to His Father's house (14:1-6). In light of this, our Lord seeks to comfort the troubled hearts of the disciples (14:1), as well as instruct them about His future grace provisions for their needs after His departure (14:13ff). This would include "another Helper" (14:16) who is the Holy Spirit (15:26).

How long does the Holy Spirit abide with every child of God during this present age? Our Lord Jesus said: "that He may abide with you *forever*" (14:16). The Greek words translated "forever" are once again *eis ton aiōna*. This Helper or Comforter (*parakletos*) would come alongside to comfort, help, and enable these believers as God the Father's answer to Jesus Christ's request. And unlike previous dispensations when the Holy Spirit would come and go,[1] He would abide with them *forever.*

Jesus Christ did not declare, "The Holy Spirit will abide with you until you sin, keep sinning, fall away, or turn your back on Me." No, dear friends, the Holy Spirit will abide with you *forever.* And what stands true for every believer in Christ today? "But you are not in the flesh but in the Spirit, if indeed the Spirit of God dwells in you. *Now if anyone does not have the Spirit of Christ, he is not His"* (Rom. 8:9). This verse indicates that every genuine, born-again child of God in this age has the Holy Spirit. In fact, if one does not possess the Holy Spirit today, "he is none of His" (i.e., he does not belong to Jesus Christ). If the Holy Spirit will abide with believers *forever,* and if the mark of being a genuine Christian in this present age is possessing the Holy Spirit, it stands to reason that it would be *impossible* to lose your salvation. That's eternal security!

2. **Every believer in Christ is eternally secure because of the PERMANENT INDWELLING of the Holy Spirit.**

On the night before His death, Jesus Christ also announced to His disciples the promise of the indwelling of the Holy Spirit, saying, "The Spirit of truth, whom the world cannot receive, because it neither sees Him nor knows Him; but you know Him, for He dwells with you *and will be in you"* (John 14:17). Notice the shift in the Holy Spirit's ministry at that time ("for He dwells *with* you") versus the Comforter's ministry *now* ("and will be *in* you").

This "will be in you" promise was later fulfilled for every believer on the day of Pentecost (Acts 2). Our Lord had previously predicted the Holy Spirit's indwelling during the Feast of Tabernacles:

> On the last day, that great day of the feast, Jesus stood and cried out, saying, "If anyone thirsts, let him come to Me and drink. He who believes in Me, as the Scripture has said, out of his heart will flow rivers of living water." But this He spoke concerning the Spirit, *whom those believing in Him would receive;* for the Holy Spirit was not yet given, because Jesus was not yet glorified. (John 7:37-39)

---

[1] This was true in the Old Testament. See Judges 14:6, 19; 15:4; 1 Samuel 10:10; 11:16; 16:13-14; Psalm 51:12.

How does a lost sinner receive the Holy Spirit today? Ephesians 1:13 plainly explains, *"In Him you also trusted,* after you heard the word of truth, the gospel of your salvation; in whom also, *having believed, you were sealed with the Holy Spirit* of promise" (Eph. 1:13).

Notice the sequence of events this verse explains:

a.   They heard the Word of Truth—the Gospel of salvation.

b.   They trusted in Jesus Christ alone.

c.   They were then sealed with the Holy Spirit.

The phrase "having believed" indicates a completed action in the past (aorist tense) which they chose (active voice). This could be understood as "when you believed."[2] These individuals put their trust in Christ through hearing the Gospel which resulted in their being "sealed with the Holy Spirit." Regarding the sealing ministry of the Holy Spirit, the Scofield Study Bible explains, "The Holy Spirit is Himself the seal. In the symbolism of Scripture a seal signifies: (1) a *finished transaction* (Jer. 32:9-10; John 17:4; 19:30). (2) *ownership* (Jer. 32:11-12; 2 Tim. 2:19); and (3) *security* (Esth. 8:8; Dan. 6:17; Eph. 4:30)."[3]

The sealing of the Holy Spirit reveals that your salvation is a finished transaction (you are not on probation), that you belong to the Lord as His child (ownership), and that your salvation is secure (security). This is a completed reality[4] that God did for you the moment you trusted in Jesus Christ to save you based on His finished work on the cross. But that's not all! Ephesians 1:14 goes on to add, "Who [referring back to the Holy Spirit] *is the guarantee of our inheritance* until the redemption of the purchased possession, to the praise of his glory" (Eph. 1:14). The sealing of the Holy Spirit further acts as "the guarantee" (the first installment of a guaranteed final purchase) that you will one day receive a new, glorified, redeemed body (Rom. 8:23; 2 Cor. 1:22).

But what is the duration of the Holy Spirit's sealing ministry to each believer? The book of Ephesians later specifies, "And do not grieve the Holy Spirit of God, by whom *you were sealed for the day*

---

[2] This is an aorist participle.

[3] *The Scofield Study Bible, New King James Version,* ed. C. I. Scofield, et al. (Oxford: Oxford University Press, 2002), 1620 (emphasis added).

[4] The verb for "sealed" (*esphragisthēte*) is in the aorist tense (completed action), indicative mood (mood of reality), and passive voice.

of redemption" (4:30). While believers grieve the Holy Spirit through sin and unwillingness to walk by faith, He is never grieved away. This verse does *not* warn us, "And do not grieve the Holy Spirit of God by whom you are sealed until you sin, backslide, apostatize, or blaspheme." In fact, if the Holy Spirit seals you permanently, and if you could somehow lose your salvation, the Holy Spirit would then have to go to Hell forever with you. God forbid! Furthermore, Charles Stanley raises a legitimate question when he asks, "What is the significance of a seal that can be continually removed and reapplied? What does it really seal?"[5] The sealing of the Holy Spirit underscores once again the tremendous truth of eternal security.

3.   Every believer in Christ is eternally secure because of the POSITIONAL BAPTIZING of the Holy Spirit.

> For as the body is one, and hath many members, and all the members of that one body, being many, are one body: so also is Christ. *For by one Spirit are we all baptized into one body,* whether we be Jews or Gentiles, whether we be bond or free; and have been all made to drink into one Spirit. (1 Cor. 12:12-13)

The baptizing work of the Holy Spirit places every believer into union with Christ and His spiritual Body, which is the Church (Rom. 6:3-5; 1 Cor. 12:27; Gal. 3:26-29). This amazing identification with Christ is true of all believers ("we all"); therefore, it must happen at the moment you trust in Christ.[6] This is a spiritual reality that God does for you and is a scriptural fact[7] though it is intangible and invisible. How can you know this? Simply because God's Word says so! This is why the New Testament epistles repeatedly emphasize the prepositional phrase "in Christ."

How does the baptizing work of the Holy Spirit guarantee a believer's eternal salvation? If Christ is the Head and you are a member of His body, are not the two inseparable? And if Christ is presently seated at the throne of God in Heaven, and you are already seated there with Christ, where is your eternal destiny and the place that God now sees you? Ephesians 2:4-6 provides the answer:

---

[5] Charles Stanley, *Eternal Security: Can You Be Sure?* (Nashville: Thomas Nelson, 1990), 59.

[6] The aorist tense combined with the indicative mood emphasizes the reality that the "baptizing" which was completed in the past.

[7] This is highlighted by the passive voice and indicative mood.

> But God, who is rich in mercy, because of His great love
> with which He loved us, even when we were dead in
> trespasses, *made us alive together with Christ (by grace you
> have been saved), and raised us up together, and made us sit
> together in the heavenly places in Christ Jesus.*

Furthermore, if Christ is the beloved Son in whom the Father is well
pleased, and you are "in Him," what does that mean about you? "To
the praise of the glory of his grace, wherein *he hath made us accepted
in the beloved*" (Eph. 1:6).

Thus, the baptizing ministry of the Holy Spirit unites and
identifies all believers with the Lord Jesus Christ so that God the
Father now views them "in Christ" and blesses them with "all
spiritual blessings in the heavenly places in Christ" (Eph. 1:3). If
this is true of you, here is a sampling of the spiritual blessings that
became yours the moment you put your trust in Christ alone:

1. You are part of God's eternal plan. (Rom. 8:28-30)

2. You are redeemed from the slave market of sin. (1 Peter 1:18-19)

3. You are reconciled to God. (Rom. 5:10)

4. You are saved from sin's penalty. (Eph. 2:8)

5. You have eternal life. (John 3:16)

6. You are no longer condemned. (Rom. 8:1)

7. You are a child of God. (Gal. 3:26)

8. You are accepted in Christ. (Eph. 1:6)

9. You are forgiven all sin. (Col. 1:14)

10. You are dead to sin. (Rom. 6:6, 11a)

11. You are alive unto God. (Rom. 6:4, 11b)

12. You are free from the law as a way of life. (Rom. 6:14; 8:2)

13. You are justified in God's sight. (Rom. 3:24-30)

14. You are sanctified in Christ. (1 Cor. 1:2)

15. You are brought near to God. (Eph. 2:13)

16. You are rescued from Satan's power. (Col. 1:13a)

17. You are translated into Christ's kingdom. (Col. 1:13)

18. You are given by God to Christ. (John 10:29)

19. You will never be separated from God's love. (Rom. 8:35-39)

20. You are a king-priest. (1 Peter 2:5)

21. You are a chosen and protected person. (1 Peter 2:9)

22. You are a citizen of Heaven. (Phil. 3:20)

23. You are a new creation in Christ. (2 Cor. 5:17)

24. You are born again. (1 Cor. 4:15)

25. You are light in the Lord. (Eph. 5:8)

26. You are complete in Christ. (Col. 2:10)

27. You have a standing in grace. (Rom. 5:2)

28. You are glorified in Christ. (Rom. 8:30)

29. You are joint-heir with Christ. (Rom. 8:17)

30. You are regenerated, baptized, indwelt, and sealed by the Holy Spirit. (John 3:3-5, 16; 1 Cor. 12:13; Eph. 1:13-14)

31. You are crucified to the world. (Gal. 6:14)

32. You are secure in Christ. (1 Peter 1:4-5)

33. You have peace with God. (Rom. 5:1)

34. You own every spiritual blessing in Christ. (Eph. 1:3)[8]

Why would God bless you in all these ways if He knew you would lose your salvation and be lost forever anyway? Such a conclusion makes no logical sense. So, believer, rejoice, for you are eternally secure because of the ministries of the Holy Spirit. That's eternal security!

> There is a Redeemer—
> Jesus, God's own Son,
> Precious Lamb of God, Messiah,
> Holy One.
>
> Jesus, My Redeemer,
> Name above all names,

---

[8] Lewis Sperry Chafer, *Salvation: A Clear Doctrinal Analysis* (reprint, Grand Rapids: Zondervan, 1977), 44-50.

Precious Lamb of God, Messiah,
O for sinners slain.

When I stand in Glory,
I will see His face;
There I'll serve my King forever
In that holy place.

Thank You, O my Father,
For giving us Your Son,
And leaving Your Spirit 'til
The work on earth is done.[9]

---

[9] Melody Green, *There Is a Redeemer.*

CHAPTER 15

A Few More Verses to Catch Your Eye

I read of a man who was dining in a fancy restaurant, and there was a gorgeous redhead at the next table. He had been checking her out since he sat down, but he lacked the nerve to talk to her. Suddenly, she sneezed, and her glass eye flew out of its socket right towards him. He reflexively reached out, grabbed it out of the air, and handed it back. "Oh my, I am sooo sorry," the woman said as she popped her eye back in place. "Let me buy your dinner to make it up to you," she said. They enjoyed a wonderful dinner together and afterwards the woman invited him to the theater. So they proceeded to enjoy a movie together. The evening ended with the redhead inviting him over for dinner the next day, to which he agreed. The next day, she cooked a tremendous gourmet meal with all the trimmings. The guy was amazed! Everything was incredible! "You know," he said, "you are the perfect woman. Are you this nice to every guy you meet?" "No," she replied, "but you caught my eye."

As we further consider the wonderful truth of eternal security, it is amazing how many verses in the New Testament "catch your eye" regarding the keeping power and grace of God in the believer's life. We have previously considered numerous passages that teach how God the Father, God the Son, and the Holy Spirit keep us saved and secure. In this chapter we want to analyze several other verses that clearly teach the eternal security of the believer in Christ.

1. **Every believer in Christ is eternally secure because SALVATION IS AN IRREVOCABLE GIFT FROM GOD.**

   For the wages of sin is death, but *the gift of God is eternal life* in Christ Jesus our Lord. (Rom. 6:23)

Though "death" (separation from God) is what all sinners have earned ("wages") because of Adam's sin and their own, God has provided by His grace the gift of eternal life for you and me. *God alone is the giver of this gift* (2 Cor. 9:15). *Jesus Christ alone shed His blood and died for your sins* to pay for the gift of salvation (Rom. 5:6-10). God now offers the gift of eternal life to you because of His unconditional love (John 3:16) and amazing grace (Eph. 2:8-9). Yet, like any gift, it is of no personal value to you until you receive it. Faith alone in Christ alone is the hand that receives God's gift of His forgiveness (Acts 10:43; 13:38-39; 16:31). But can a believer ever lose or forfeit eternal life because of his sin(s), unfaithfulness, or backsliding? Must God ever be required to take back the gift of salvation that He has faithfully promised, offered, and given? Again, the Bible gives us God's answer: *"For the gifts and the calling of God are irrevocable"* (Rom. 11:29). The word "irrevocable" means "incapable of being recalled, undone, altered, or revoked; that cannot be reversed repealed, or annulled."[1] God does *not* change His mind or break His promises. In the context of Romans 11, God is addressing Israel's past election and His faithfulness in keeping His covenantal promises in spite of the Jews' past failures. The same biblical principle is true regarding the "gift" and "calling" involved in salvation.

> *For you see your calling, brethren,* that not many wise according to the flesh, not many mighty, not many noble, are called. But God has chosen the foolish things of the world to put to shame the wise, and God has chosen the weak things of the world to put to shame the things which are mighty; and the base things of the world and the things which are despised God has chosen, and the things which are not, to bring to nothing the things that are, *that no flesh should glory in His presence. But of Him you are in Christ Jesus, who became for us wisdom from God—and righteousness and sanctification and redemption.* (1 Cor. 1:26-30)

> But we are bound to give thanks to God always for you, brethren beloved by the Lord, because God from the beginning chose you for salvation through sanctification

---

[1] *Webster's New Universal Unabridged Dictionary*, 2nd ed. (New York: Simon & Schuster, 1979), 971.

by the Spirit and belief in the truth, to which *He called you by our gospel, for the obtaining of the glory of our Lord Jesus Christ*. (2 Thess. 2:13-14)

Who has saved us and called us with a holy calling, not according to our works, but according to His own purpose and grace which was given to us in Christ Jesus before time began. (2 Tim. 1:9)

If salvation is a free gift of God's grace to undeserving sinners who trust in Christ and His finished work alone, and His "gifts and calling are irrevocable," how could you ever lose your salvation or forfeit your calling? You can't, and that's eternal security! No wonder Paul ends Romans 11 with great adoration and exaltation to the God of all grace:

O the depth of the riches both of the wisdom and knowledge of God! How unsearchable are His judgments, and His ways past finding out! For who has known the mind of the Lord? Or who has become His counselor? Or who has first given to Him and it shall be repaid to him? For of Him and through Him and to Him are all things, to whom be glory forever. Amen. (Rom. 11:33-36)

2. The believer in Christ is eternally secure because SALVATION IS A PERMANENT REALITY WHICH IS *NOT* OBTAINED OR MAINTAINED BY A HOLY LIFE OR GOOD WORKS.

For by grace are ye saved through faith; and that not of yourselves: it is the gift of God: Not of works, lest any man should boast. (Eph. 2:8-9, KJV)

The phrase "have been saved" is especially pregnant with meaning in the Greek text. It contains the present tense verb *este* (translated "are ye") and the perfect participle *sesōsmenoi* (translated "saved"). The combination of this present tense verb and perfect participle is technically called a "perfect periphrastic construction." The King James translators gave a more superior rendering than many modern translations when they translated this "for by grace are ye saved." On the basis of God's grace ("for by grace"), these Ephesian believers had been saved (perfect tense) from Hell by God (passive voice) when they trusted Christ in the past, with the result being that they remained saved in the present (perfect tense). The addition of the present tense verb translated "are" doubly reinforces the permanency and present possession of their salvation. Again, we see the inspired original text of the New Testament emphatically and dogmatically teaching the *eternal security of salvation.*

Furthermore, your salvation is "not of works lest any man should boast" (v. 9). Those who deny eternal security inevitably require believers to maintain their salvation by good works, a holy life, personal faithfulness, and avoiding alleged "significant" sins. This amounts to salvation by faith *plus* some form of works, not faith in Christ *period*, and results in merely a "hope-so" salvation versus a "know-so" salvation. Thus, if you were required to obtain or maintain your salvation by your perseverance and godly living, you would have a basis to boast or brag about what *you have done* instead of what *Christ has done for you!* God's grace obliterates human pride so "that, as it is written, 'He who glories, *let him glory in the Lord*'" (1 Cor. 1:31).

3. **You, as a believer in Christ, are eternally secure because "YOU DIED, AND YOUR LIFE IS HIDDEN WITH CHRIST IN GOD." (Col. 3:3-4)**

In the wonderful epistle of Colossians, which exalts the supremacy and sufficiency of Jesus Christ's person and work, the apostle Paul reminds these believers of their eternal and unchanging identity with Christ. Prior to salvation, they were positioned in Adam, and "For as in Adam all die, even so in Christ all shall be made alive" (1 Cor. 15:22).

Before coming to faith in Christ, they also were spiritually "dead in trespasses and sins" (Eph. 2:1) and lived under the reigning power of Satan and their sin natures. But through the new birth they became new creations in Christ (2 Cor. 5:17) and were co-crucified, co-buried, and co-raised in union with Christ and freed from the power of the indwelling sin nature. "Knowing this, that our old man was crucified with Him, that the body of sin might be done away with, that we should no longer be slaves of sin. For he who has died has been freed from sin" (Rom. 6:6-7). God wants every believer to "know" (Rom. 6:3, 6, 9) and to daily faith-rest ("reckon") in these tremendous truths. "Likewise you also, reckon yourselves to be dead indeed to sin, but alive to God in Christ Jesus our Lord" (Rom. 6:11).

Furthermore, every believer is "complete" in Christ with all spiritual blessings.

> And you *are complete in Him*, who is the head of all principality and power. (Col. 2:10)

> Blessed be the God and Father of our Lord Jesus Christ, *who has blessed us with every spiritual blessing in the heavenly places in Christ*. (Eph. 1:3)

> As His divine power *has given to us all things that pertain to life and godliness*, through the knowledge of Him who called us by glory and virtue, by which have been given to us exceedingly great and precious promises, that through these you may be partakers of the divine nature, having escaped the corruption that is in the world through lust. (2 Peter 1:3-4)

Miles Stanford writes,

> Our position, the source of our Christian life, is perfect. It is eternally established in the Father's presence. When we received the Lord Jesus as our personal Savior, the Holy Spirit caused us to be born into Him. He created us in the position that was established through His work at Calvary. "Therefore if any man be in Christ, He is a new creature [creation]" (2 Cor. 5: 17). This is the eternal position in which every believer has been placed, whether he is aware of it or not. The Christian who comes to see his position in the Lord Jesus begins to experience the benefit of all that he is in Him. His daily state is developed from the source of his eternal standing.

> Our condition is what we are in our Christian walk, in which we develop from infancy to maturity. Although our position remains immutable, our condition is variable. Through the exercise of faith, our eternal position (source) affects our daily condition, but in no way does our condition affect that heavenly position.[2]

---

[2] Miles J. Stanford, *The Complete Green Letters* (Grand Rapids: Zondervan, 1975), 71.

This position in or identity with Jesus Christ forms the basis for each believer's walk with Christ. *"If then you were raised with Christ, seek those things which are above,* where Christ is, sitting at the right hand of God. *Set your mind on things above,* not on things on the earth" (Col. 3:1-2). Verses 3 and 4 appropriately follow to provide the reasons and motivations for true spirituality. Regarding *their past,* God says, "for you died" as every believer has died with Christ positionally. Their history "in Adam" ended at the cross. This is God's perspective of the believer in Christ.

This truth reminds me of two girls who loved the party scene. But as a result of putting their trust in Christ as Savior, they responded to a party invitation with the written reply, "We regret that we cannot attend, for we recently died."

The second reason or motivation to live a life that honors the Lord pertains to these believers' *present identity*: "and your life is hidden with Christ in God" (Col. 3:3b). Underscoring the eternal and secure position of these Colossian Christians, God emphatically declares as an established fact that He has permanently "hidden" their "life" since the day of their salvation. Where are their lives now, and why are they so secure? "Your life is hid *with Christ in God.*" This is double eternal security. It is like putting something valuable in a security box ("with Christ") inside of a safe ("in God"). This passage does not instruct believers to seek the things above and to pursue a heavenly mindset (3:1-2) in order to be saved, stay saved, or prove they are saved, but *because they have been saved and remain secure in Christ forever.*

And relating to *their future,* Paul gives a third motivation or reason to fulfill the two commands of verses 1 and 2. In Colossians 3:4, he states, "When Christ who is our life appears, then you also will appear with Him in glory." Jesus Christ is not only the believer's Savior and Lord, but He is also his/her *life*! Why?

> He who has the Son has life; he who does not have the Son of God does not have life. These things I have written to you who believe in the name of the Son of God, that you may know that you have eternal life, and that you may continue to believe in the name of the Son of God. (1 John 5:12-13)

In typical emphatic, New Testament fashion, without any hint of uncertainty, Paul spells out the believer's guarantee of glory in the most assuring of terms: "When Christ who is our life appears, *then you also will appear with Him in glory*" (Col. 3:4).

I can almost hear someone saying, "But what if these Christians backslide, sin, fall, or fail the Lord? What of their future then?" Notice that there are no qualifying statements attached to these tremendous divine guarantees. "When Christ, who is our life, shall appear," God promises that "you" (plural—all these believers, no exceptions) "will also appear[3] with Him in glory." That is God's ironclad promise, and that is eternal security!

4. The believer in Christ is eternally secure because GOD AL-READY SEES THE BELIEVER AS A CITIZEN OF HEAVEN.

> *For our citizenship is in heaven*, from which we also eagerly wait for the Savior, the Lord Jesus Christ, who will transform our lowly body that it may be conformed to His glorious body, according to the working by which He is able even to subdue all things to Himself. (Phil. 3:20-21)

The word "citizenship" had great significance in Philippi as these residents were actually citizens of Rome as a Roman colony, though they lived in Macedonia. In the same way, believers in Christ are already citizens of Heaven though they live on planet Earth. Because of this certain citizenship in Heaven, Paul can state without reservation, "from which we also eagerly wait for the Savior, the Lord Jesus Christ, *who will transform our lowly body that it may be conformed to His glorious body*, according to the working by which He is able even to subdue all things to Himself" (Phil. 3:20-21). Does this citizenship in Heaven and future bodily transformation sound conditional, iffy, or uncertain? Not at all! It rings with absolute assurance and certainty. This passage sets forth yet another example of the *eternal security* of the believer by God's grace and power!

5. As a believer in Christ, you are eternally secure because CHRIST WILL NEVER LEAVE YOU, NOR FORSAKE YOU.

> Let your conduct be without covetousness; be content with such things as you have. For He Himself has said, *I will never leave you, nor forsake you.* (Heb 13:5)

---

[3] The verb for "will . . . appear" (*phanerōthēsesthe*) is in the future tense and indicative mood.

Chapter 11 explained the Greek *ou mē* double negative construction. The writer of Hebrews is even more dogmatic using *five negatives* in this verse to strengthen one another. In the Greek text it looks this way:

> *ou mē se anō*
> not not you shall I desert
>
> *oud' ou mē se egkatalipō*
> not not not you shall I forsake

Dear believer, Christ was already forsaken by God on the cross when He died for your sins (Matt. 27:46), so that you as a believer will *never ever* be forsaken or deserted by God. What good news! However, if your salvation could be lost, forfeited, or given back, Christ would have to leave you and forsake you as He cannot go to Hell with you. Since this is impossible, according to this precious divine promise, it also stands to reason that your salvation is eternal and secure. Again, this is eternal security! No wonder the writer of Hebrews can confidently add, "So that we may boldly say, The Lord is my helper, and I will not fear what man shall do unto me" (Heb. 13:6).

6. **If you've trusted in Christ alone, your salvation is eternal and secure because you are a CHILD OF GOD forever.**

> He came to His own, and His own did not receive Him. But as many as received Him, to them He gave the right to become children of God, to those who believe in His name: who were born, not of blood, nor of the will of the flesh, nor of the will of man, but of God. (John 1:11-13)

In contrast to those who rejected Christ in His first coming, some received Him. How does one receive Jesus Christ? The answer is "even to those who believe in His name" as His name represents *who* He is and *what* He has done.[4] When people receive Christ by faith in Him, they are "born of God" (1:13) and have the right to call themselves "children of God" (1:12). Jesus Christ uses this same analogy when He announces to Nicodemus, "Except a man is born again, he cannot see the kingdom of heaven" (3:3).

---

[4] Walter Bauer, William F. Arndt, and F. Wilbur Gingrich, *A Greek-English Lexicon of the New Testament and Other Early Christians Literature*, 3rd ed., rev. and ed. Frederick W. Danker (Chicago: University of Chicago Press, 2000), 134.

Every person who receives Jesus Christ as Savior by faith alone in His person and finished work ("His name") is instantaneously born again and becomes a child of God. Just like physical birth occurs only once at a point in time and is never to be reversed or repeated, so spiritual birth occurs only once at a point in time, never to be reversed or repeated. As God's child, you also have God's DNA in you. First Peter 1:23 reminds us that we "have been born again, not of corruptible seed, but of incorruptible through the Word of God which lives and abides forever." This divine, procreative act can never be undone. The issue after the new birth is not, "Will you remain a child of God?" but "Will you be a growing and obedient child of God?"

To encourage growth and to prevent or correct sin in the life of His children, what does God do to them as a loving heavenly Father? Hebrews 12:5-8 tells us,

> And you have forgotten the exhortation which speaks to you as to *sons*: "My *son*, do not despise the chastening of the LORD, nor be discouraged when you are rebuked by Him; for whom the LORD loves He chastens, and scourges every *son* whom He receives." If you endure chastening, God deals with you as with *sons*; for what *son* is there whom a father does not chasten? But if you are without chastening, of which all have become partakers, then you are illegitimate and not *sons*.

If you could lose your salvation through sin or unfaithfulness, you would either become unborn or need to be born again and again and again. Either option is absurdly unbiblical. God disciplines His born-again children out of love, but He never condemns them like He does with the lost (1 Cor. 11:30-32). And though sin in the life of the believer breaks *fellowship* with God, requiring confession of sin as needed (1 John 1:3-10), you can never lose your eternal salvation and sonship because you are a child of God forever.[5] That is eternal security!

Years I spent in vanity and pride,
Caring not my Lord was crucified,

---

[5] The critical distinction between being a child of God in the family of God versus abiding in fellowship with God as a child of God is covered in greater detail in chapter 19.

Knowing not it was for me He died
On Calvary.

By God's Word at last my sin I learned;
Then I trembled at the law I'd spurned,
Till my guilty soul imploring turned
To Calvary.

O the love that drew salvation's plan!
O the grace that bro't it down to man!
O the mighty gulf that God did span
At Calvary![6]

---

[6] William R. Newell, *At Calvary*.

Part III

The Absolute Assurance of Eternal Security

CHAPTER 16

Can You Know for Sure?

A Christian friend of mine told me about a time he had to fly to another U.S. city for business. In doing so, he needed to rent a car. But when he went to drive the car out of the rental lot, he wondered, "Does my car insurance cover this rental?" He honestly did not know. This lack of assurance caused him to drive anxiously, fearful that any accident would leave him in great debt. It was not until the next day that he heard news from his insurance agent that his policy covered the rental car. What relief this news brought to his heart.

Unfortunately, many people live their lives like my friend drove his rental car—anxiously and fearful of God's judgment in Hell. They are convinced that no one can have absolute assurance of eternal salvation before death. Can you know for sure *before* you die that you are absolutely saved by God's grace and certain of going to Heaven? And have you ever known someone who professed to trust in Jesus Christ as personal Savior (perhaps as a child or teenager) but later in life struggled with doubts about his salvation? He may mentally and emotionally torture himself with questions such as:

- "Am I really saved?"

- "Have I truly believed in Jesus Christ?"

- "Is all this Bible stuff actually true?"

Maybe you have known someone with these vexing queries. Or perhaps that person is *you*. Are there any scriptural solutions for these perplexing problems? Praise God there are clear-cut answers for you and me in the timeless pages of the written Word of God.

We have so far studied verse after verse after verse teaching that God's grace and power keep the genuine believer in Christ saved and secure forever. But perhaps you are thinking, "The Bible repeatedly declares that believers in Christ cannot lose the possession and security of their salvation; however, can a person lose the *assurance* of salvation? And if so, how?"

THE IMPORTANCE OF THE BELIEVER'S ASSURANCE

Does it matter to God whether or not you know with absolute certainty[1] that you are saved forever? The Lord answers this question by openly testifying in His Word, "These things I have written to you who believe in the name of the Son of God, that *you may know that you have eternal life*" (1 John 5:13). What is this verse saying? First, God put His guarantee of our assurance in writing ("these things I have written"). Second, this promise is for *all* believers: "to you who believe in the name of the Son of God," not just the spiritual, mature, or elite. Third, God designed this written pledge to cause all believers to have not merely a hope-so salvation but a know-so salvation ("that you may know"). The word "that" (*hina*) sets forth a purpose clause expressing God's intent that all believers "know" of their possession of eternal life. It is one thing for believers to "have" eternal life and another to "know" they possess it. Fourth, John's use of the present tense for "have" (*echete*) shows that believers possess eternal life from the moment of initial faith in the Savior alone up to the present. This is consistent with the fact that "eternal life"—by its very definition— lasts forever. First John 5:13 is a key passage of Scripture promising absolute assurance of eternal salvation to all believers whether newly saved or mature in the Lord or at any point in between.

Contrary to the postmodern culture that denies absolute truth and views certainty of anything as arrogance (all under the guise of

---

[1] It is not wrong or unbiblical to use the adjective "absolute" to modify the words "certainty" or "assurance," as though "absolute assurance" or "absolute certainty" imply that the words "certainty" and "assurance" by themselves indicate some degree of doubt that one is truly saved. "Assurance" and "certainty" are sufficient by themselves to indicate 100-percent confidence or persuasion that one is going to heaven. But the expression "absolute assurance" can be helpful since many professing Christians who trust in their works claim to have some degree of "assurance" when they really mean that they will "probably" or "most likely" go to heaven. Adding the adjective "absolute" is similar to adding the adjective "free" to "grace" (e.g., "Free Grace theology") to clarify the nonmeritorious nature of God's grace. Many professing Christians claim to believe that salvation is by God's "grace" while simultaneously believing that good works are required to be saved.

pseudo-humility), God has given His eternal, unchangeable Word so that believers may know His truths with clarity and certainty. The Scriptures are replete with verses indicating that God wants believers to *know* His principles and promises.[2] Thus, God expects people to *know* His truths, as Jesus said to Nicodemus, "Are you the teacher of Israel, and do not *know* these things?" (John 3:10). The fact that God *expects* us to know these things means they *can be* known, as Jesus also said to the Samaritan woman at the well, "You worship what you do not *know*; we *know* what we worship, for salvation is of the Jews" (John 4:22).

In light of all these divine declarations indicating that God wants people to *know* His Word and that His promises *can be* known, it is astonishing that many professing believers in Christ do not know they are saved for sure and forever. In fact, some even think that a lack of assurance of salvation is a good option.[3] Nowhere does the Bible give the slightest intimation that God's children are to be anything but completely sure of their eternal relationship to God their Father. "I write to you, little children, because your sins are forgiven you for His name's sake" (1 John 2:12). The phrase "little children" is a term of endearment applied to *all* believers. Thus, God Himself assures all believers that their sins are forgiven and that He is their Father. Hannah Whitall Smith captured this idea well when she wrote:

> Even the little children in Bible times were supposed to know that their sins were forgiven, and that God was their Father. In fact, common-sense would tell us that the knowledge of one's position and standing in any relation of life is always the essential foundation of all

---

[2] See for example, John 4:42; 6:69; 7:17; 8:30-32; 1 Cor. 2:12; 6:19; 2 Cor. 5:12; 8:9; Phil. 3:7-9; 1 John 3:5, 16; and 5:19-20.

[3] Noted Reformed theologian and author R.C. Sproul writes, "A while back I had one of those moments of acute self-awareness, and suddenly the question hit me: R.C., what if you are not one of the redeemed? What if your destiny is not Heaven after all, but Hell? Let me tell you that I was flooded in my body with a chill that went from my head to the bottom of my spine. I was terrified. I tried to grab hold of myself. I thought, 'Well, it's a good sign that I am worried about this. Only true Christians really care about salvation.' But then I began to take stock of my life, and I looked at my performance. My sins came pouring into my mind, and the more I looked at myself, the worse I felt. I thought, 'Maybe it's true. Maybe I'm not saved after all.' I went to my room and began to read my Bible. On my knees I said, 'Well, here I am. I can't point to my obedience. There's nothing I can offer.' I know some people only flee to the Cross to escape Hell. Then I remembered John 6:68. Peter was also uncomfortable, but he realized that being uncomfortable with Jesus was better than any other option" (*Table Talk* [November 1989]: 20).

action in that relation; and how Christians ever came to tolerate (if they do not even sometimes inculcate) such a mist of doubt and uncertainty in regard to the soul's relations with God, is incomprehensible to me. No service could be rightly performed by any Israelite who was doubtful as to his nationality or his family record.

In the first chapter of Numbers we are told that only those Israelites who could "declare their pedigree" might be numbered among the men of war; and in the second chapter of Ezra no one who could not "find his register" and "reckon his genealogy" was allowed to exercise the office of priest. Any doubts and uncertainties on these points made them "as polluted," and consequently unfit to serve (see Num. 1:2, 17, 18; 2:2; Ezra 2:62- 63). I believe the same thing is also true of Christians now. We can neither be numbered among the Lord's soldiers, nor enter into priestly relations with Him, until we also can "declare our pedigree" as children of God, and "reckon our genealogy" as being born of Him.[4]

If you will look at the opening verses of each Epistle, you will see that they are all addressed to people of whom it was taken for granted that they *knew*, without a shadow of doubt, their standing as reconciled and forgiven children of God. . . . (Rom. 1:7; 1 Cor. 1:1-3).[5]

Can you know with absolute certainty that you are the "beloved" of God, that you are "children of God," and that one day you will "be like Him" (glorified)? Yes!

Behold what manner of love the Father has bestowed on us, that we should be called *children of God*! Therefore the world does not know us, because it did not know Him. *Beloved, now we are children of God*; and it has not yet been revealed what we shall be, but *we know* that when He is revealed, *we shall be like Him, for we shall see Him as He is*. And everyone who has this hope in Him purifies himself, just as He is pure. (1 John 3:1-3).

---

[4] Hannah Whitall Smith, *Every-Day Religion: The Common Sense Teaching of the Bible* (New York: Revell, 1893), 5.

[5] Ibid., 8.

The question you need to resolve is simply, "Will you believe the testimony of God or make Him out to be a liar by your unbelief?" For,

> If we receive the witness of men, the witness of God is greater; for this is the witness of God which He has testified of His Son. *He who believes in the Son of God has the witness in himself; he who does not believe God has made Him a liar, because he has not believed the testimony that God has given of His Son.* And this is the testimony: that God has given us eternal life, and this life is in His Son. He who has the Son has life; he who does not have the Son of God does not have life. *These things I have written to you who believe in the name of the Son of God, that you may know that you have eternal life."* (1 John 5:9-13)

Yet various theological systems and traditions of Christendom obscure this marvelous biblical truth and rob believers in Christ of absolute assurance until the day they die. For instance, Roman Catholicism, with its emphasis on works-salvation, claims that possessing assurance of one's salvation is a sin of presumption.[6] This religious system denies even its most illustrious devotees this blessing from God (which is understandable in this merit system of salvation). Thus one newspaper reporter summarizes the Catholic Church's teaching on assurance and quotes the late Cardinal John O'Connor of New York:

> On the subject of heaven and hell, the Cardinal stated emphatically that no one can know the fate of a particular person's soul. "Church teaching is that I don't know, at any given moment, what my eternal future will be," the Cardinal wrote. "I can hope, pray, do my very best—but I still don't know. Pope John Paul II doesn't know absolutely that he will go to heaven, nor does Mother Teresa of Calcutta, unless either has had a special divine revelation."[7]

---

[6] Henry Denzinger, *The Sources of Catholic Dogma*, trans. Roy J. Deferrari, 13th ed. (London: Herder, 1955), 255.

[7] Sam Howe Verhovek, "Cardinal Defends a Jailed Bishop Who Warned Cuomo on Abortion," *New York Times*, February 1, 1990.

Protestantism, unfortunately, is no better. Classic Arminianism teaches that you will lose your salvation if you do not persevere to the end of your life with a fruitful, working faith. Conversely, but similarly, consistent Calvinism maintains that though salvation cannot be lost, if you do not persevere in faith and godliness to the end of your life, this proves that you were never one of God's elect, and you will not attain final salvation. No wonder many Puritan divines cried out to God for His mercy while on their deathbeds without absolute certainty of their salvation. They did not know that they were saved and children of God. Even popular Calvinist and Lordship Salvation teacher, John Piper, acknowledges his own lack of absolute assurance of going to Heaven when he confesses, "I probably pray the prayer, 'Keep me and preserve me' as often as I pray any prayer. I mean, 'Keep me saved,' because I think God uses means to cause us to persevere."[8] Only when one believes the Gospel of grace in its simplicity and takes God at His Word by faith can he *know for sure* that he is *saved forever*.

At this point, it may be helpful for you to consider the differences between the objective truth of eternal security (salvation is eternal and secure by God's grace and power) and the subjective assurance of salvation ("I know I'm saved forever by God's grace and power"). In distinguishing these related siblings of doctrine, we will first need to answer the question:

WHAT IS THE BASIS FOR A BELIEVER'S ASSURANCE OF ETERNAL SECURITY?

1. The absolute assurance of eternal salvation is based on the FINISHED WORK OF JESUS CHRIST.

Some seven hundred years before the birth of Jesus Christ, the Holy Spirit inspired the writing of the prophet Isaiah to accurately predict the substitutionary death of Jesus Christ on the cross.

> He is despised and rejected by men, a man of sorrows, and acquainted with grief. And we hid, as it were, our faces from Him; He was despised, and we did not esteem Him. Surely He has borne our griefs and carried our sorrows; yet we esteemed Him stricken,

---

[8] John Piper and Justin Taylor, *Stand: A Call for the Endurance of the Saints* (Wheaton, IL: Crossway, 2008), 142.

smitten by God, and afflicted. *But He was wounded for our transgressions, He was bruised for our iniquities: the chastisement of our peace was upon Him; and by His stripes we are healed. All we like sheep have gone astray; we have turned, every one, to his own way; and the LORD has laid on Him the iniquity of us all.* He was oppressed and He was afflicted, yet He opened not his mouth; He was led as a lamb to the slaughter, and as a sheep before her shearers is silent, so He opened not his mouth. He was taken from prison and from judgment, and who will declare his generation? For He was cut off from the land of the living; *for the transgression of My people he was stricken.* And they made His grave with the wicked—but with the rich at His death, because He had done no violence, nor was any deceit in His mouth. (Isa. 53:3-9)

Why was our Lord "wounded"? It was "for our transgressions" (v. 5a). Why was Jesus Christ "bruised"? It was "for our iniquities" (v. 5b). Was all this really necessary? Yes, for "all we like sheep have gone astray; we have turned, every one, to his own way" (v. 6a). Dear reader, is this not a vivid description of you and me as helpless, hopeless, hell-bound sinners? But, instead of dropping the gavel of justice upon us, God in His wonderful love sacrificed His Son in our place as "the LORD has laid on Him the iniquity of us all" (v. 6b).

Do you realize what all of this means? It indicates that . . .

- God's holy punishment for our sins has been fully paid for by our Substitute, the Lord Jesus Christ.

    Yet it pleased the LORD to bruise Him; He has put Him to grief. When you make His soul an offering for sin, He shall see His seed, He shall prolong His days, and the pleasure of the LORD shall prosper in His hand. (Isa.53:10)

- God's righteous and just demands against our transgression have been satisfied so that He has been propitiated.

    He shall see of the labor of His soul, and be satisfied. By His knowledge My righteous servant shall justify many, for He shall bear their iniquities. (Isa. 53:11)

- Though all sinners are worthy of God's judgment, God offers salvation from Hell to all people.

  Ho! Everyone who thirsts, Come to the waters; and you who have no money, come, buy and eat. Yes, come, buy wine and milk without money and without price. Why do you spend money for what is not bread, and your wages for what does not satisfy? Listen carefully to Me, and eat what is good, and let your soul delight itself in abundance. *Incline your ear, and come to Me. Hear, and your soul shall live.* (Isa. 55:1-3)

- Satan's bondage of fear has been broken.

  But we see Jesus, who was made a little lower than the angels, for the suffering of death crowned with glory and honor, that *He by the grace of God might taste death for every man.* (Heb. 2:9)

  Inasmuch then as the children have partaken of flesh and blood, He Himself likewise shared in the same, *that through death He might destroy him who had the power of death, that is, the devil, and release those who through fear of death were all their lifetime subject to bondage.* (Heb. 2:14-15)

- Religion's deception and futile efforts to atone for man's sin and act as a mediator to God have been exposed.

  Who desires all men to be saved and to come to the knowledge of the truth. *For there is one God* and *one Mediator between God and men, the man Christ Jesus, who gave Himself a ransom for all,* to be testified in due time. (1 Tim. 2:4-6)

The prophet Isaiah exploded the religious myth of salvation by good works or religious rituals a few chapters later when he wrote,

  But we are all like an unclean thing, and *all our righteousnesses are like filthy rags;* we all fade as a leaf; and our iniquities, like the wind, have taken us away. (Isa. 64:6)

Dear reader, if you seek the assurance of salvation based on your good works or religious rituals, you will never have assurance of eternal life, for how good is good enough? And how do you know when you have attained it? We may think we're doing quite well and that we even have a "high degree of probability" we will be saved.[9] However, the standard of righteousness by which God judges us is His very own perfect righteousness, not the relative standard of comparing us to other sinful human beings. God does not grade on a curve. Since He is perfectly righteous, and He judges by that standard, everyone—even the best of us—falls desperately short (Rom. 3:23). "If You, LORD, should mark iniquities, O Lord, who could stand?" (Ps. 130:3). We must realize that the bar of God's justice is so high that even *near* moral perfection in doing the will of God results in guaranteed condemnation (Gal. 3:10; James 2:10).

The only solution, therefore, is to look outside ourselves—to the Christ of Calvary whose finished work for human redemption stands perfect and complete (John 19:30). All human religions are characterized by their requirement for just one more ritual to perform, one more sacrifice to be made, one more sin to atone for, one more act of devotion to fulfill, one more charitable deed to accomplish, and all the while assurance of one's salvation dangles like the unattainable carrot before the horse. It is for this reason that the author of Hebrews grounds our assurance (Heb. 10:18-22) on the sufficiency and finality of Christ's sacrifice for us (Heb. 10:1-14).[10] It is never grounded by God in the Bible on the believer's subjective level of perceived practical sanctification since this is ever changing from week to week and year to year, sometimes for the better and sometimes for the worse.[11] Instead, the Bible instructs believers to rest their assurance on Jesus Christ and His finished work because

---

[9] Ludwig Ott, *Fundamentals of Catholic Dogma*, trans. Patrick Lynch (Rockford, IL: Tan, 1974), 244.

[10] Michael D. Halsey, *Truthspeak: The True Meaning of Five Key Christian Words Distorted through Religious Newspeak* (Milwaukee: Grace Gospel Press, 2010), 31-43.

[11] An example of this subjectivity can be seen by the statement, "Christ did not die to forgive sinners who go on treasuring anything above seeing and savoring God. And people who would be happy in heaven if Christ were not there, will not be there. The gospel is not a way to get people to heaven; it is a way to get people to God. It's a way of overcoming every obstacle to everlasting joy in God. If we don't want God above all things, we have not been converted by the gospel" (John Piper, *God Is the Gospel: Meditations on God's Love as the Gift of Himself* [Wheaton, IL: Crossway, 2005], 47). Can any and all believers in Christ know with certainty that they want God above all things?

He never changes (Heb. 13:8), and therefore certainty of salvation can be guaranteed.[12]

2. The absolute assurance of eternal salvation is based on the unfailing and sure PROMISES OF GOD.

The apostle Paul illustrates the truth that justification before God is by faith alone from the lives of Abraham (Rom. 4:1-3) and David (Rom. 4:6-8). Sandwiched in between these two examples, he emphatically states, "Now to him who *works*, the *wages* are not counted as *grace* but as *debt*. But to him who *does not work* but *believes on Him* who justifies the ungodly, *his faith* is accounted for *righteousness*" (Rom. 4:4-5). The great apostle to the Gentiles then explains that to be declared righteous before God (justification) is wholly apart from any good works, (Rom. 4:2-5), religious ritual (Rom. 4:9-12) and law-keeping (Rom. 4:13-15). What then is the conclusion of the matter? "Therefore it is of *faith* that it might be according to *grace*, so that the *promise* might be *sure* to all the seed, not only to those who are of the law, but also to those who are of the *faith* of Abraham, who is the father of us all" (Rom. 4:16).

It is important to underscore four key words in verse 16: "faith," "grace," "promise" and "sure." If justification before God is received

---

[12] Ironically, in recent years some Free Grace proponents have gone so far as to say that assurance of salvation is actually undermined when lost people *are required* to believe in Christ's substitutionary, sufficient sacrifice for their eternal salvation. They say a person must merely believe the "message of life" — that Jesus Christ guarantees eternal life to all who believe Him for it. See Zane C. Hodges, "The Hydra's Other Head: Theological Legalism," *Grace in Focus* 23 (September/October 2008): 2-3; and Bob Wilkin, "Four Free Grace Views Related to Two Issues: Assurance and the Five Essentials," *Grace in Focus* 24 (July/August 2009): 1-2. This is a radical departure from Scripture and the classical Free Grace view. Advocates of this new view reason that if we must believe in Christ's death and resurrection to be saved, then what else must we believe? Requiring belief in Christ's person and work is too subjective, they say, to provide certainty and assurance. They compare required belief in the cross-work of Christ to the way Lordship Salvation requires good works and a surrendered, obedient life of faith to be saved. Just as they ask, "How can we ever know if we have obeyed, surrendered, or worked enough?" they similarly reason, "How will we ever know if we have believed enough doctrine to be saved?" But this is not a valid comparison. The critical difference is that God *has revealed* the content of saving faith in His Word and this message has not changed in two thousand years. The Gospel of Christ is objective, unchanging, and knowable precisely because it has been revealed by God in Scripture; whereas a certain required amount of obedience, good works, and surrender has never been revealed in Scripture and is too subjective to provide any real assurance. For further explanation see Dennis Rokser, "A Critique of Zane Hodges's Article: 'The Hydra's Other Head: Theological Legalism,'" *Grace Family Journal* 11 (2008): 2-11.

through *faith* alone in Jesus Christ alone on the basis of God's *grace* (and not religious works, ritual, and law-keeping), then, because of God's *promise*, we can be absolutely *sure* of our salvation as it does not depend on what we have done for God but on what Christ has done for us.

This passage demonstrates with unmistakable clarity that justification from God comes to the one "who does not work but believes" (v. 5) and is by faith "apart from works" (v. 6). If God Himself assures us of our justification on the basis of imputed not imparted righteousness, what right do some Christians have to alter the basis of personal assurance so that it becomes a matter of faith *plus* works or faith *with* works? The common Reformed and Lordship Salvation view is that faith alone justifies, but the faith that justifies before God is never alone—it is always accompanied by a fruitful, persevering faith that works. Consequently, they say assurance of salvation is only the right of one who has a working faith! Yet to insist that God offers assurance only on the basis of a faith accompanied by works directly contradicts the basis on which God Himself promises justification in His Word, namely, by faith "apart from works"! This explains why God emphatically guarantees His forgiveness and eternal life to believers in Christ and why believers can be sure of their salvation.

> Most assuredly, I say to you, he who believes in Me *has everlasting life.* (John 6:47)

> I write to you, little children, because *your sins are forgiven you* for His name's sake. (1 John 2:12)

> And this is the *promise* that he has *promised* us—*eternal life.* (1 John 2:25)

> Behold what manner of love the Father has bestowed on us, that we should be called children of God! Therefore the world does not know us, because it did not know Him. Beloved, *now we are children of God; and it has not yet been revealed what we shall be, but we know that when He is revealed, we shall be like Him,* for we shall see Him as He is. (1 John 3:1-2)

Is it presumptuous to *know* that you have been saved? Is it arrogant to *know* that you possess eternal life? Is it rash to *know* that you are a child of God and will be going to heaven when you die? Not according to these wonderful promises, unless you are trusting in your own holiness or good works to get you there. Assurance is the believer's birthright! It is not a matter of your performance or perseverance, but of Christ's perfect sacrifice and God's unfailing promises. "These things I have written to you who believe in the name of the Son of God, that you may *know* that you have eternal life" (1 John 5:11-13).

This is the absolute assurance that the "chief of sinners" possessed (1 Tim. 1:12-16); and God wants you to have the same! Notice the personal assurance of salvation that the apostle Paul expresses in 2 Timothy 1:12: "I am not ashamed, for I *know* whom [Jesus Christ] I have believed [not surrendered to, worked for, or sacrificed for] and am persuaded [perfect tense—in the past with the results abiding in the present] that He is able to keep what I have committed [i.e., "entrusted" NASB, NIV] to Him until that Day." Paul also expresses his personal assurance in Romans 8:38-39: "For I am *persuaded* [perfect tense] that neither death nor life, nor angels nor principalities nor powers, nor things present nor things to come, nor height nor depth, nor any other created thing, shall be able to separate us from the love of God which is in Christ Jesus our Lord." Are you persuaded of your eternal salvation because of the finished work of Christ and the unfailing promises of God? If the apostle Paul had such assurance, you can have the same if you are a believer in the Lord Jesus Christ.

Any theology that denies a person the absolute assurance of eternal life from the moment of faith in Christ alone is clearly unscriptural. Yet some theological systems do exactly that, such as classical Reformed theology in the Westminster tradition. According to Reformed theology, full assurance is not possible when a person initially believes in Christ for salvation. Assurance is only a future possibility. "This infallible assurance doth not so belong to the essence of faith, but that a true believer may wait long, and conflict with many difficulties before he be partaker of it."[13] According to this view, assurance of salvation is not "of the essence of saving faith." However, since biblical faith is the very antithesis of doubt,

[13] Westminster Confession, chapter XVIII, article III, "Of the Assurance of Grace and Salvation," in *The Creeds of Christendom: With a History and Critical Notes*, ed. Philip Schaff, rev. David S. Schaff, 6th ed. (New York: Harper and Row, 1931; reprint, Grand Rapids: Baker, 1993), 3:637.

whenever people become sure of the person, work, and promise of Christ contained in the Gospel, they have believed the Gospel and thereby trusted in Christ (Luke 16:30-31; Acts 17:1-5 [cf. 2 Thess. 1:8-10]; 19:8; 28:23-24). They not only possess eternal salvation from that moment onward but they are certain they possess it, at least at that moment. This is why Robert P. Lightner says, "We can go so far as to say that at the moment of faith they also have assurance or they simply haven't exercised faith."[14]

Assurance is inherent to initial faith in Christ for eternal salvation, and it does not wait until we produce good works in our Christian lives. Unfortunately, assurance of salvation is often stripped from believers who are falsely taught that they must have a special "kind" of faith if they are truly saved—a working, fruitful, productive, obedient, committed, enduring faith.[15] However, assurance never comes from looking at the nature of our faith but at the object of our faith—the all-sufficient Savior. Lightner concludes:

> Sometimes people speak of "saving faith." By this they imply faith for salvation is different from faith exercised for other things. But God does not require some special kind of faith for salvation different from ordinary faith. . . . It is not, however, the person's faith which saves. The New Testament teaches that Christ and Christ alone saves. No one can be saved without faith in the Lord Jesus Christ and His death in the sinner's place. But it is not the kind nor the amount of faith that brings life to the one dead in trespasses and sin.[16]

Therefore the only sure basis on which to rest one's faith and find genuine assurance of salvation is the finished work of Christ and the unfailing promises of God. On this solid foundation God wants believers to know with certainty that they have been, and will be, saved forever.

---

[14] Robert P. Lightner, *Sin, the Savior, and Salvation: The Theology of Everlasting Life* (Nashville: Thomas Nelson, 1991), 240.

[15] MacArthur states, "If a person fails to love and obey the Lord through the trials of life, then there is no evidence that he possesses saving faith. How many people do you know who came to church for a while, had a little trouble in their lives, and left? Although they may have made a profession of faith in Christ, they cannot be identified as those who love Him because their lives are not characterized by an enduring obedience" (John F. MacArthur, Jr., *Saved without a Doubt* [Colorado Springs, CO: Chariot-Victor, 1992], 177).

[16] Ibid., 241-42.

Dear reader, do you *know* that you have eternal life? Have you trusted in Christ alone to save you based on His death and resurrection? Or are you trusting to some degree on the filthy rags of your good works as well?

> Not saved are we by trying;
>   From self can come no aid;
> 'Tis on the blood relying,
>   Once for our ransom paid.
> 'Tis looking unto Jesus,
>   The Holy One and Just;
> 'Tis His great work that saves us—
>   It is not "try" but "trust"!
> No deeds of ours are needed
>   To make Christ's merit more:
> No frames of mind or feelings
>   Can add to His great store;
> 'Tis simply to receive Him,
>   The Holy One and Just;
> 'Tis only to believe Him—
>   It is not "try" but "trust"!

Because of Christ's finished work on the cross and God's unfailing promises, we can join with grateful hearts in the chorus of old,

> Enough for me that Jesus saves,
> This ends my fear and doubt;
> A sinful soul I come to Him,
> He'll never cast me out.
>
> My heart is leaning on the Word,
> The written Word of God;
> Salvation by my Savior's name,
> Salvation through His blood.
>
> I need no other argument,
> I need no other plea!
> It is enough that Jesus died!
> And that He died for me.[17]

---

[17] Lidie H. Edmunds, *My Faith Has Found a Resting Place*.

CHAPTER 17

Evidences and Examples of Assurance

W hile the assurance of salvation rests sufficiently on the finished work of Christ and the unfailing promises of God, what role, if any, does our Christian life play in assuring us of our salvation? Are there not normally some evidences of new birth?

EVIDENCES OF A BELIEVER'S REGENERATION

While "justification" is God's divine courtroom announcement that believers in Christ have been declared righteous before Him because He has imputed his own righteousness to them, "regeneration" is the gracious act of God in imparting divine life to believing sinners (Titus 3:5). This new birth (John 3:3, 7) results in the impartation of a new nature (2 Peter 1:4), a new resident—the Holy Spirit (1 Cor. 6:19), and a new Life—Jesus Christ (Col. 1:27, 3:4), which is fitting for a new creation in Christ (2 Cor. 5:17) with a new destiny (1 Peter 1:3-5). All of this occurs when ungodly sinners believe the Gospel of God's grace (Rom. 1:16-17; 1 Cor. 4:15; Eph. 1:3). God divinely designed this so that believers "should walk in newness of life" (Rom. 6:4) and "should serve in newness of Spirit" (Rom. 7:6). While a birth certificate gives objective assurance of the reality of a physical birth, there are also subjective indicators that provide empirical evidence of physical life. For example, babies get hungry, they cry, they grow, and so forth. While the title deed of salvation is the unfailing promises of God because of the finished work of Christ, there are subjective evidences of spiritual life, such as believers' desire for the Word of God (1 Peter 2:2), their cry of "Abba Father" (Gal. 4:6), and normally their growth in grace (1 John 2:12-14).

The late Dr. Lewis Sperry Chafer comments regarding the believer's assurance of salvation:

> There is a normal Christian experience. There are new and blessed emotions and desires. Old things do pass away, and behold all things do become new; but *all such experiences are but secondary evidences*, as to the fact of salvation, in that they grow out of that positive repose of faith which is the primary evidence.[1]

In this matter of assurance, we do well to distinguish between the primary basis of assurance and the secondary evidences. This distinction occurs even in the physical realm as newborn children who are genuinely, physically alive may have been born with birth defects or later manifest certain disorders that cause stunted growth or bodily malfunction. Likewise, in the spiritual realm, carnal Christians (1 Cor. 3:1) experience stunted spiritual growth (v. 2) which manifests itself by a walk like that of the unsaved (v. 3), thus blurring at times any empirical evidence of their relationship to Jesus Christ (2 Peter 1:8-9).

In understanding and underscoring the distinction between the primary basis of assurance in contrast to its secondary evidences, Dr. Chafer again writes,

> Such a precious experience as is described by these passages may become clouded by sin or lost in the depression of some physical weakness, and were we depending upon the experience as primary evidence that we are saved, all grounds of assurance would be swept away. The primary evidence is clearly stated in the same Epistle as the final word of testing here given and the final grounds of confidence: "If we receive the witness of men, the witness of God is greater: for this is the witness of God which he hath testified of his Son. He that believeth on the Son of God hath the witness in himself: he that believeth not God hath made him a liar; because he believeth not the record that God gave of his Son. And this is the record, that God hath given to us eternal life, and this life is in his Son. He that hath the Son

---

[1] Lewis Sperry Chafer, *Salvation: A Clear Doctrinal Analysis* (reprint, Grand Rapids: Zondervan, 1977), 60 (emphasis added).

hath the life; and he that hath not the Son of God hath not life. These things [about having the life] have I written unto you that believe on the name of the Son of God; that ye may know that ye have eternal life, and that ye may believe on the name of the Son of God" (1 John 5:9-13).

The possession of the indwelling Son of God is the abiding fact of the newly created life in Him and should never be confused with some imperfect and changeable experience in the daily life."[2]

The writer of Hebrews sets forth another secondary evidence of a person's salvation:

And you have forgotten the exhortation which speaks to you as to sons: "My son, do not despise the chastening of the LORD, nor be discouraged when you are rebuked by Him; for whom the LORD loves He chastens, and scourges every son whom He receives." If you endure chastening, God deals with you as with sons; for what son is there whom a father does not chasten? But if you are without chastening, of which all have become partakers, then you are illegitimate and not sons. (Heb. 12:5-8)

Verse 7 makes it clear that genuine believers in Christ experience the loving chastisement of God in their lives, while unbelievers and religious professors do not. God's child-training (or the lack thereof) distinguishes a person as either "illegitimate" or a "son."

These passages demonstrate that there can be some secondary, corroborating evidences of salvation in the believer's life, but these are neither decisive nor necessary for our assurance. Instead, they function like circumstantial evidence in a court of law in that these secondary evidences have confirmatory value. They are not to be deemed as incontrovertible evidence that can stand alone to either prove or disprove the reality of our salvation. They have value only when combined with incontrovertible evidence (i.e., Christ's finished work and the promises of God); otherwise, they are immaterial and indecisive. One writer explains this point further:

Good works and the evidences of God's grace do not provide assurance. They provide warrant to assurance,

---
[2] Ibid., 61.

but not assurance itself. Perhaps a good analogy is how a Christian knows the love of God. He experiences the love of God every day in a myriad of ways. However, all those countless blessings merely affirm what the Christian already knows—God loves him. Even during those times when the good favor of God seems to be circumstantially absent and that Christian's confidence is tested, he still knows that God loves him the same way he has always known this—by the promises of God. So it is with the assurance of salvation. Good works play the mere supporting role of confirmation.[3]

Despite the confirmatory value of these secondary evidences of salvation, believers must be aware that the inclusion of such evidences as support for one's assurance does present potential problems that need further clarification.

1. These secondary evidences are subjective and experiential.

If desire for the Word of God is a secondary evidence of salvation, then how much desire for the Word of God must you have before you can know for sure that you have been saved? What if you are not growing? What about when you do not love the brethren? What if you don't forgive someone? What about when your love for Christ wanes? What about the carnal Christian? What about the "sin unto death"?[4] Must you wait for a period of time after trusting in Christ for salvation to discern whether there is sufficient fruit to assure yourself that you are genuinely saved? A time delay is not necessary to be sure of salvation. After all, a baby does not have to walk in order to prove it has physical life or that it has been born. Rather, it should learn to walk because it has life. The means of salvation must not be confused with the intended results of salvation.[5]

---

[3] Kenneth Keathley, *Salvation and Sovereignty: A Molinist Approach* (Nashville: Broadman & Holman, 2010), 188-89.

[4] The "sin leading to death" mentioned in 1 John 5:16 is illustrated in 1 Corinthians 11:28-32 by many obstinate, unrepentant Corinthian believers who were progressively disciplined by God. "For this reason many *are* weak and sick among you, and many sleep" (v. 30). "Sleep" was a common, first-century metaphor indicating physical death. The "sleep" spoken of here was nothing short of maximum divine discipline whereby God prematurely took these believers home to heaven. They missed any opportunity for further growth and service, thus affecting their eternal reward. Ananias and Sapphira (Acts 5:1-11) are a similar example.

[5] One five-point Calvinist teacher goes so far as to write, "Readers, if there is a re-

There is another potential problem with grounding assurance on good works. With respect to religious, unsaved people who are trusting in their works, they may also display an interest in the Bible, a willingness to pray, and demonstrate some degree of change in their lives. Externally they may appear to be Christians when in reality they are unregenerate. Therefore, perceived change and supposed sanctification in peoples' lives does not prove the genuineness of salvation. Perhaps the greatest problem with this approach to assurance is that it may actually lead to a false assurance among religious, unsaved people. When people who are already trusting in their own holiness or good works for salvation are told to look at their lives for positive evidence of being a genuine Christian, this may foster in them further self-deception and a false assurance. They may display interest in the Bible, willingness to pray, and even some change in their lives, but they are still unregenerate. As they continue to look away from Christ and to themselves, they will further establish and confirm their own self-reliance. Remember what our Lord taught,

> Many will say to Me in that day, *"Lord, Lord, have we not prophesied* in Your name, *cast out demons* in Your name, and *done many wonders in Your name?"* And then I will declare to them, *"I never knew you;* depart from Me, you who practice lawlessness!" (Matt. 7:22-23)

2. These secondary evidences revolve around the Christian's walk instead of Christ's work.

There is a great danger in seeking to find assurance based on observing what God is doing *in* you (practical sanctification), instead of believing what God has done *for* you (justification). This is, in fact, what many popular evangelical leaders are teaching today, such as John MacArthur who says, "Genuine assurance comes from seeing the Holy Spirit's transforming work in one's life."[6] However, since

serve in your obedience, you are on the way to hell" (A. W. Pink, *Practical Christianity* [Grand Rapids: Guardian, 1974], 16).

[6] John F. MacArthur, Jr., *The Gospel According to Jesus: What Does Jesus Mean When He Says, "Follow Me"?* (Grand Rapids: Zondervan, 1988), 23. This is the classical Reformed position, as also stated by Theodore Beza, "Therefore, that I am elect, is first perceived from sanctification begun in me, that is, by my hating of sin and my loving of righteousness" (*A Little Book of Christian Questions and Responses* [Allison Park, PA: Pickwick, 1986], 96-97 as quoted in Keathley, *Salvation and Sovereignty*, 173).

the believer's condition or practice is prone to change, you should not base the assurance of your salvation on your *fluctuating walk* but on Christ's *finished work*. Based on the former approach, no one would have absolute assurance of salvation at the moment he places his faith in Christ alone. Dear readers, let's not confuse the means of salvation with the intended results of salvation.

D. L. Moody, the gifted and down-to-earth evangelist of the nineteenth century, had an uncanny ability of personalizing a scripture verse for a needy heart. J. Wilbur Chapman tells the following story of how Moody used John 5:24 to help him gain assurance of salvation.

> I was studying for the ministry, and I heard that D. L. Moody was to preach in Chicago. I went down to hear him. Finally I got into his after meeting. I shall never forget the thrill that went through me when he came and sat down beside me as an inquirer. He asked me if I was a Christian. I said, "Mr. Moody, I am not sure whether I am a Christian or not."

> He very kindly took his Bible and opened it at the fifth chapter of John, and the twenty-fourth verse, which reads as follows: "Verily, verily, I say unto you, he that heareth My word, and believeth on Him that sent Me, hath everlasting life, and shall not come into condemnation; but is passed from death unto life."

> "Suppose you had read it through for the first time, wouldn't you think it was wonderful?" I read it through, and he said, "Do you believe it?"

> I said, "Yes."

> "Do you accept it?" I said, "Yes."

> "Well, are you a Christian?"

> "Mr. Moody, I sometimes think I am, and sometimes I am afraid I am not."

> He very kindly said, "Read it again."

So I read it again: "Verily, verily, I say unto you, he that heareth My word, and believeth on Him that sent me, hath everlasting life, and shall not come into condemnation; but is passed from death unto life."

Then he said, "Do you believe it?" I said, "Yes."

"Do you receive Him?" I said, "Yes."

"Well," he said, "are you a Christian?"

I just started to say over again that sometimes I was afraid I was not, when the only time in all the years I knew him and loved him, he was sharp with me. He turned on me with his eyes flashing and said, "See here, whom are you doubting?"

Then I saw it for the first time, that when I was afraid I was not a Christian I was doubting God's Word. I read it again with my eyes over-flowing with tears.

Since that day I have had many sorrows and many joys, but never have I doubted for a moment that I was a Christian, because God said it.[7]

Basing our assurance of salvation on our walk can lead not only to doubt and discouragement but also to spiritual pride as we convince ourselves that we are so faithfully serving Christ and growing in holiness that we must be one of God's elect. But honest introspection should lead us to the opposite conclusion as we weigh our sin in light of the true standard of righteousness—God Himself. We should agree with the apostle Paul who wrote, "For I know that in me (that is, in my flesh) nothing good dwells" (Rom. 7:17). Even for believers who have been justified and regenerated, it is still true prior to glorification that "the heart is deceitful above all things and desperately wicked; who can know it?" (Jer. 17:9). Moreover, the Lord Jesus said there was a sense in which His saved disciples were presently still "evil" (Luke 11:13). This introspection then hardly provides a sufficient basis for certainty of salvation. No wonder James H. Brookes

---

[7] "A Conversation between J. Wilbur Chapman and D. L. Moody," *Sword of the Lord* (October 28, 1988) as cited in Dennis Rokser, "Can You Know for Sure that You Are Eternally Saved and Secure? Part 2," *Grace Family Journal* 4 (May/June 2001): 27.

says concerning assurance based on introspection, "If you expect to get assurance in this way, you might as well expect to get health by looking at disease, to get light by looking at darkness, to get life by looking at a corpse."[8]

Are you looking to yourself, your walk, and your works for the assurance of salvation? This is a subjective roller-coaster approach that many encourage you to enter into.[9] Jesus Christ is immutable; His work is finished; and His promises never change. He is the one we must look to in faith. "Most assuredly, I say to you, he who hears My word and believes on Him who sent Me *has everlasting life, and shall not come into judgment, but has passed from death into life*" (John 5:24).

JUSTIFICATION BEFORE GOD VERSUS JUSTIFICATION BEFORE OTHER PEOPLE
(James 2:14-26)

Another clarification is essential to properly understand the basis for the believer's absolute assurance of eternal salvation. Scripture distinguishes between justification in God's sight versus justification in the sight of other people. Before God, we do not need works of righteousness to be declared righteous by Him. He sees the heart, "For the Lord does not see as man sees; for man looks at the outward appearance, but the LORD looks at the heart" (1 Sam. 16:7). Since God sees the heart, He knows whether or not we have believed in Christ without having to see good works as the proof of initial "saving" faith. In several places in Scripture, the apostle Paul speaks of being declared righteous in God's sight solely by means of faith, not works.

> "Therefore by the deeds of the law no flesh will be *justified in His sight,* for by the law is the knowledge of sin" (Rom. 3:20).

---

[8] James H. Brookes, *The Way Made Plain* (Philadelphia: American Sunday School Union, 1871; reprint, Grand Rapids: Baker, 1967), 295.

[9] "The crucial test of true faith is endurance to the end, abiding in Christ, and continuance in the Word. . . . He cannot abandon himself to sin; he cannot come under the dominion of sin; he cannot be guilty of certain kinds of unfaithfulness. . . . Let us appreciate the doctrine of the perseverance of the saints and recognize that we may entertain the faith of our security in Christ only as we persevere in faith and holiness to the end" (John Murray, *Redemption Accomplished and Applied* [Grand Rapids: Eerdmans, 1965], 152, 154-55).

"For if Abraham was justified by works, he has
something to boast about, but *not before God*" (Rom. 4:2).

"But that no one is justified by the law *in the sight of God*
is evident, for 'the just shall live by faith'" (Gal. 3:11).

This is in stark contrast to James 2:14-26 where the subject is a
believer's walk of faith (1:2-12) after having been born again (1:18),
resulting in practical sanctification (1:19-21) and good works (1:22-
27). James 2 is not written to cause believers to evaluate the reality
and assurance of their salvation by taking their eyes of faith off the
finished work of Christ and the promises of God and instead look to
their walk and works for assurance. This is easily disproven by the
many times James refers to his readers as Christian "brethren" (1:2,
16, 19; 2:1, 5, 14; 3:1, 10, 12; 4:11; 5:7, 9, 10, 12, 19) who have faith in
Christ (2:1, 5, 20). Thus James 2 is not written to prove that we are
born again by the manifestation of good works later in our Christian
lives. Good works later in life are not the required proof of initial,
"saving" faith. As the Christian walks by faith under the enablement
of the Holy Spirit, he will experience practical sanctification. This
normally results in good works that become visible to others (but
not always, Matt. 6:1-6) as the demonstration to others of a genuine
walk of ongoing faith. Thus James 2:18 says, "Show me your faith
without your works, and I will show you my faith by my works." We
can avoid great confusion by recognizing that James 2 is not dealing
with justification *before God* by *faith alone* but rather justification
before other people (vv. 21-25) on the basis of *faith resulting in profitable
works* (vv. 15-17). God will declare sinners righteous on the basis
of faith alone (Rom. 4:1-5), but other men will declare believers as
righteous only as they see their faith manifested by good works (vv.
21-25). James 2 should not be used, therefore, as a passage requiring
faith and good works to either be born again or to prove that we
were originally born again. The passage is not intended to gauge the
genuineness of a believer's eternal salvation but the genuineness of
his or her practical walk of faith and sanctification.[10]

---

[10] This conclusion is supported by the fact that none of the five uses of *sōzō* ("save")
in the Epistle of James (1:21; 2:14; 4:12; 5:15, 20) deal with first-tense salvation, which
is deliverance in the past from sin's penalty, namely, eternal condemnation. The epistle is addressed to people who were considered to be already born again (1:21) and
had faith in Christ (2:1). The reference to "save" in 2:14 is therefore not to justification
before God or first-tense salvation; rather it deals with second-tense deliverance or
practical sanctification by means of a walk of genuine faith issuing in good works.

SOME BIBLICAL EXAMPLES OF PERSONAL ASSURANCE

Can you as a believer know that you have trusted in Christ, and can you know that you have eternal life *before* you die? Some religions teach that you can only reach a "high degree of probability" that you will be saved but not the certainty of salvation since this can be obtained "by special Revelation only."[11] The fact is God has already given us special revelation in the Bible testifying that believers can know they are saved in this lifetime. At least a dozen scriptural examples take the witness stand to prove this.

1. **Job.** *"For I know that my Redeemer lives,* and He shall stand at last on the earth; and after my skin is destroyed, this I know, that in my flesh *I shall see God"* (Job 19:25-26).

2. **David.** "Surely goodness and mercy shall follow me all the days of my life; *and I will dwell in the house of the LORD forever"* (Ps. 23:6).

3. **The Apostles.** "Nevertheless do not rejoice in this, that the spirits are subject to you, but rather rejoice because *your names are written in heaven"* (Luke 10:20). "Then Jesus said to the twelve, 'Do you want to go away?' But Simon Peter answered Him, 'Lord, to whom shall we go? You have the words of eternal life. *Also we have come to believe and know that You are the Christ, the Son of the living God'"* (John 6:67-69).

4. **Martha.** "Jesus said to her, 'I am the resurrection and the life. He who *believes in Me,* though he may die, *he shall live.* And whoever lives and believes in Me *shall never die.* Do you believe this?' She said to Him, *'Yes, Lord, I believe* that You are the Christ, the Son of God, who is to come into the world'" (John 11:25-27).

5. **The apostle Paul.** "We are confident, yes, well pleased rather to *be absent from the body and to be present with the Lord"* (2 Cor. 5:8). "But if I live on in the flesh, this will mean fruit from my labor; yet what I shall choose I cannot tell. For I am hard pressed between the two, *having a desire to depart and be with Christ,* which is far better. Nevertheless to remain in the flesh is more needful for you" (Phil. 1:22-24).

---

[11] Ludwig Ott, *Fundamentals of Catholic Dogma,* trans. Patrick Lynch (Rockford, IL: Tan, 1974), 244.

6. **The Corinthian believers.** "To the church of God which is at Corinth, to those *who are sanctified in Christ Jesus, called to be saints,* with all who in every place call on the name of Jesus Christ our Lord, both theirs and ours" (1 Cor. 1:2). "*Or do you not know that your body is the temple of the Holy Spirit* who is in you, whom you have from God, and you are not your own? For you were bought at a price; therefore glorify God in your body and in your spirit, which are God's" (1 Cor. 6:19-20). "Behold, I tell you a mystery: *We shall not all sleep, but we shall all be changed*—in a moment, in the twinkling of an eye, at the last trumpet. For the trumpet will sound, and the dead will be raised incorruptible, and *we shall be changed*" (1 Cor. 15:51-52).

7. **The Thessalonian believers.** "But I do not want you to be ignorant, brethren, concerning those who have fallen asleep, lest you sorrow as others who have no hope. *For if we believe that Jesus died and rose again,* even so God will bring with Him those who sleep in Jesus. For this we say to you by the word of the Lord, that we who are alive and remain until the coming of the Lord will by no means precede those who are asleep. For the Lord Himself will descend from heaven with a shout, with the voice of an archangel, and with the trumpet of God. And the dead in Christ will rise first. *Then we who are alive and remain shall be caught up together with them* in the clouds to meet the Lord in the air. And thus we shall always be with the Lord. Therefore comfort one another with these words" (1 Thess. 4:13-18).

8. **The Ephesian believers.** "*For by grace you have been saved through faith,* and that not of yourselves; it is the gift of God, not of works, lest anyone should boast. *For we are His workmanship,* created in Christ Jesus for good works, which God prepared beforehand that we should walk in them" (Eph. 2:8-10).

9. **The Philippian believers.** "*For our citizenship is in heaven,* from which we also eagerly wait for the Savior, the Lord Jesus Christ, *who will transform our lowly body that it may be conformed to His glorious body,* according to the working by which He is able even to subdue all things to Himself" (Phil. 3:20-21). "And I urge you also, true companion, help these women who labored with me in the gospel, with Clement also, and the rest of my fellow workers, *whose name are in the Book of Life*" (Phil. 4:3).

10. **The Colossian believers.** *"For you died, and your life is hidden with Christ in God. When Christ who is our life appears, then you also will appear with Him in glory"* (Col. 3:3–4).

11. **Jewish believers in Christ.** "Blessed be the God and Father of our Lord Jesus Christ, who according to His abundant mercy *has begotten us again to a living hope* through the resurrection of Jesus Christ from the dead, to *an inheritance incorruptible and undefiled and that does not fade away, reserved in heaven for you, who are kept by the power of God* through faith for salvation ready to be revealed in the last time" (1 Peter 1:3-5).

12. **The apostle John's readers.** "Behold what manner of love the Father has bestowed on us, that *we should be called children of God!* Therefore the world does not know us, because it did not know Him. Beloved, now *we are children of God*; and it has not yet been revealed what we shall be, *but we know that when He is revealed, we shall be like Him*, for we shall see Him as He is" (1 John 3:1-2).

Dear friend, if you have trusted in Jesus Christ and His finished work upon the cross, you can *know* with absolute certainty that you have been saved and are secure in Christ forever. Thus, you can be *assured* that whether you die today or five years from now, that "absent from the body" will mean that you will be "present with the Lord" for you "have everlasting life." Praise the Lord!

How can I say thanks
For the things You have done for me
Things so undeserved,
Yet you give to prove Your love for me?
The voices of a million angels
could not express my gratitude.
All that I am and ever hope to be,
I owe it all to Thee.

To God be the glory.
To God be the glory.
To God be the glory
For the things He has done.

With His blood He has saved me;
With His power He has raised me.
To God be the glory
For the things He has done.

Just let me live my life;
Let it be pleasing, Lord, to Thee.
And should I gain any praise,
Let it go to Calvary.

With His blood He has saved me;
With His power He has raised me.
To God be the glory
For the things He has done.[12]

---

[12] Andrae Crouch, *My Tribute*.

CHAPTER 18

Why Do People Lack the Absolute Assurance of Eternal Salvation?

While the assurance of salvation is the birthright of every believer in Christ (1 John 5:10), why don't more people who claim to be Christians or born again have the absolute assurance of salvation as promised in the Word of God (1 John 5:11-13)? I recommend for your Berean examination (Acts 17:10-11) the following seven reasons as analytical answers to this personal and pertinent question.

#1: Because they are NOT TRULY SAVED.

I believe this is the number one reason people do not have assurance of Heaven. Many are like the religious Jews of Jesus' day to whom He said, "You search the Scriptures, for in them you think you have eternal life; and these are they which testify of Me. *But you are not willing to come to Me that you may have life*" (John 5:39-40). Commenting on the meaning of the Greek word translated "think" (v. 39), Greek linguists Louw and Nida write that it means "to regard something as presumably true, but without particular certainty; to suppose; to presume; to assume; to imagine; to think but not to be sure."[1] These religious Jews believed that a messiah would come based on their knowledge of the Word of God, but they rejected *Jesus* as the Christ because they trusted in their own good works and religious rituals to declare them righteous before God. The Lord Jesus warned them of this, saying, "Do not think that I shall accuse you to the

---

[1] Johannes P. Louw and Eugene A. Nida et al. *Greek-English Lexicon of the New Testament Based on Semantic Domains* (New York: United Bible Societies, 1988), 1:369.

Father; there is one who accuses you—*Moses, in whom you trust*" (v. 45). They trusted in their own ability to keep the Law of Moses and sought to establish their own righteousness before God (Rom. 9:30–10:4) instead of receiving it as a gift of God's grace by faith in Jesus Christ. This is why they did not *know* that they had eternal life; they could only *presume* it. In like manner, scores of religious but unregenerate seek to earn heaven by trusting some false messiah or Jesus Christ plus their own good works. In doing so, they are rejecting God's gift of salvation by His grace. When sinners seek to earn God's forgiveness by their works or church rituals, they can never have real certainty of salvation, for they never know when they have done enough! While many religious people have some measure of confidence that they will be saved or go to heaven based on their works or law-keeping (Matt. 7:21-23; Luke 18:9-14; Acts 15:1 cf. Gal. 2:4), this is a false assurance that falls short of the *absolute* assurance that comes from trusting in Jesus Christ alone whose work is sufficient and complete.[2]

#2: Because they GO BY THEIR FEELINGS instead of faith in God's promises.

> And this is the testimony: that God has given us eternal life, and this life is in His Son. He who has the Son has life; he who does not have the Son of God does not have life. *These things I have written to you* who believe in the name of the Son of God, that you may know that you have eternal life, and that you may continue to believe in the name of the Son of God. (1 John 5:11-13)

Verse 13 declares that the title deed of the believer in Christ is to *"know* that you have eternal life." It does not say "feel," "hope," or "wish." Some days you may not feel like a member of the family into which you were born, yet your birth certificate reassures you that you do belong. In the same way, the Word of God certifies that you are a child of God if you have believed in Jesus Christ alone for eternal life. Assurance is not a divine zap from heaven or a feeling in your soul that grants you the assurance of salvation. Assurance comes when you accept by faith the unfailing promises of God.[3]

---

[2] Dennis Rokser, *Seven Reasons NOT to Ask Jesus into Your Heart: Clarifying the Condition of Salvation* (Duluth, MN: Duluth Bible Church, n.d.).

[3] Robert P. Lightner, *Sin, the Savior, and Salvation* (Nashville: Thomas Nelson, 1991), 247-48.

Can you imagine a married man who wakes up morning after morning, turns to his wife, and asks, "Am I married? I don't feel married today." At first, the wife can't believe her husband's stupidity, but she patiently responds, "Yes."

"But how do I know I'm married?"

"Because we live together," she replies.

"But, honey, many people live together who aren't married."

"True, but don't you remember that you took me at my word on our wedding day."

"Yes, I remember. But I don't *feel* married."

In a fit of frustration, his wife thrusts their marriage certificate before his eyes and declares, "See, honey, no matter how you feel today, we are married, *for it is written* right here!" Is this not what God declares to the believer in Christ in 1 John 5:13?

Feelings come and feelings go,
And feelings are deceiving;
My warrant is the Word of God—
Nothing else is worth believing.

Though all my heart should feel condemned
For want of some sweet token,
There is One greater than my heart
Whose Word cannot be broken.

I'll trust in God's unchanging Word
Till soul and body sever,
For, though all things shall pass away,
His Word shall stand forever!

Dear friends, it is false humility to think that you are too humble to claim that you are certain that you have been saved forever. In fact, it is actually calling God a liar when you don't believe His testimony (1 John 5:10-13)! Now if your claim of eternal salvation is based on your own good works, holiness, perseverance, faithfulness, and so forth, it would then be very arrogant to claim that you know that you are going to Heaven. That's why Ephesians 2:9 ends with, "lest anyone should boast." But if you were rescued from drowning by another, is it arrogant to claim, "*I have been saved*"? This is not a claim of self-righteousness or arrogance but of absolute assurance and sincere gratitude for the rescuing work of another. Such is also the humble recognition and joyful assurance of every sinner saved by Another, the Lord Jesus Christ, all because of the wonderful grace of God!

#3: Because they SEEK ASSURANCE BY THEIR WALK AND WORKS instead of by Christ's completed work.

All churches and religions that reject salvation by grace alone and eternal security must eventually view the believer's assurance from this standpoint. It logically follows that if people seek assurance based on their walk or works, then they cannot have absolute assurance from the moment they trust in Christ as Savior since a time lapse is needed to check for good works and fruitfulness in their lives. At the Judgment Seat of Christ, where He will evaluate and possibly reward believers' post-conversion faithfulness and works,[4] some believers' works may be burned up, but they themselves will be saved. But what do the Scriptures say?

> *For no other foundation can anyone lay than that which is laid, which is Jesus Christ.* Now if anyone builds on this foundation with gold, silver, precious stones, wood, hay, straw, each one's work will become clear; for the Day will declare it, because it will be revealed by fire; and the fire will test each one's work, of what sort it is. If anyone's work which he has built on it endures, he will receive a reward. *If anyone's work is burned, he will suffer loss; but he himself will be saved, yet so as through fire.* (1 Cor. 3:11-15)

The problem with this walk/works approach to assurance is that it focuses the believer on himself and his own subjective walk instead

---

[4] For the critical distinction between the free gift of eternal salvation and rewards which are earned by good works, see chapter 19. See also, Thomas L. Stegall, "Rewards and the Judgment Seat of Christ" in *Freely by His Grace: Classical Free Grace Theology*, ed. J.B. Hixson, Rick Whitmire, and Roy B. Zuck (Duluth, MN: Grace Gospel Press, 2012), 434-46.

of the objective promises of God's Word and finished work of Christ.[5] This is the deadly problem of believing in the perseverance of the saints instead of the preservation of the saints by the Savior! Ironically, Calvinist/Lordship Salvation teacher, John MacArthur, acknowledges this problem, apparently without perceiving the cause and effect relationship that his teaching induces or promotes. He writes,

> Rather than leading their people to examine themselves and make sure their assurance is valid, many preachers feel it's their duty to make everyone feel good. However, those who preach as they should will find some in their congregation plagued with doubt. Recently I received the following letter: "Dear John, I've been attending Grace Church for several years. As a result of a growing conviction in my heart, your preaching, and my seeming powerlessness against the temptations which arise in my heart and which I constantly succumb to, my growing doubts have led me to believe that I'm not saved.
>
> How sad it is, John, for me not to be able to enter in because of the sin which clings to me and from which I long to be free. How bizarre for one who has advanced biblical training and who teaches in Sunday School with heartfelt conviction! So many times I have determined in my heart to repent, to shake loose my desire to sin, to forsake all for Jesus only to find myself doing the sin I don't want to do and not doing the good I want to do.
>
> After my fiancée and I broke up I memorized Ephesians as part of an all-out effort against sin, only to find myself weaker and more painfully aware of my sinfulness, more prone to sin than ever before, and grabbing cheap thrills to push back the pain of lost love. This occurs mostly in the heart, John, but that's where

---

[5] Occasionally people cite 2 Corinthians 13:5, "examine yourselves whether you are in the faith," as a proof text to support the notion of looking to self versus Christ for assurance of salvation. The context of the passage, however, clearly deals with the validation of Paul's apostleship amidst the accusation of false teachers (2 Cor. 10-12) by examining their own salvation. For if they were "in the faith" (and they were), then how did they get there? If it was through Pau's ministry (1 Cor. 4:15; 15:1-11), then he was a legitimate apostle. See J. Hampton Keathley III, *ABCs for Christian Growth: Laying the Foundation* (n.p.: Biblical Studies Press, 2002), 28-29; and Perry C. Brown, "What Is the Meaning of Examine Yourselves in 2 Corinthians 13:5?" *Bibliotheca Sacra* 154 (April-June 1997): 175-88.

it counts and that's where we live. I sin because I'm a sinner. I'm like a soldier without armor running across a battlefield getting shot up by fiery darts from the enemy.

I couldn't leave the church if I wanted to. I love the people and I'm enthralled by the gospel of the beautiful Messiah. But I'm a pile of manure on the white marble floor of Christ, a mongrel dog that sneaked in the back door of the King's banquet to lick the crumbs off the floor, and, by being close to Christians who are rich in the blessings of Christ, I get some of the overflow and ask you to pray for me as you think best."

Is the author of that poignant letter a Christian? One thing that jumps out at me is his desire to do right, which sounds more like Paul in Romans 7 than an unbeliever. The pulpit is the creator of anxious hearts, but it is also to give comfort and assurance to those who love Christ.[6]

But in this case was the pulpit the solution or did it contribute to the problem? This poor soul is thoroughly confused because he is seeking assurance by looking at Christ's work *in* him (by way of sanctification) in his walk and works instead of looking by faith at Christ's work *for* him (in justification) accomplished at Calvary.

#4: Because they SUCCUMB TO THE WILES OF THE DEVIL.

Finally, my brethren, be strong in the Lord and in the power of His might. Put on the whole armor of God, that you may be able to stand against the wiles of the devil. . . . And take the helmet of salvation, and the sword of the Spirit, which is the word of God. (Eph. 6:10-11, 17)

Satan designed his first wile toward Eve in the Garden of Eden to cause her to doubt the Word of God (Gen. 3:1). The "sword of the Spirit" is the "word [*rhēma*, i.e., specific sayings] of God." Believing the specific promises of God thwarts this particular fiery dart of the Wicked One.

A new Christian was confiding with a mature believer about a period of darkness and doubt he was going

---

[6] John MacArthur, *A Believer's Assurance: A Practical Guide to Victory over Doubt* (Panorama City, CA: Grace to You, 2011), 3-4.

through. "In the meeting yesterday I was filled with the joy of salvation, and I thought I would never be in the dark again. But now it's all gone, and I'm in the depths. What's the matter with me?" "Did you ever pass through a tunnel?" asked his friend. "Certainly I have," said the convert. "But I don't see what that has to do with my present situation." "When you were in the tunnel, did you think the sun had been blotted out of the sky?" "No, I knew the sun was in the sky the same as ever, although I couldn't see it just then. But what does that have to do with my experience" he inquired. "Were you distressed when you were in the dark tunnel?" asked the other. "No, I knew I'd soon be out in the light again." "And did you get out?" "Of course! I'm out now!" replied the new Christian. Then he paused as the truth dawned on his heart. "I see what you mean. Divine facts remain the same no matter how I feel. I should rejoice in God's Word not in my feelings! I see! I see!"[7]

#5: Because they live in PROLONGED CARNALITY and FAIL TO GROW SPIRITUALLY.

For if these things are yours and abound, you will be neither barren nor unfruitful in the knowledge of our Lord Jesus Christ. *For he who lacks these things is shortsighted, even to blindness, and has forgotten that he was cleansed from his old sins.* Therefore, brethren, be even more diligent to make your call and election sure, for if you do these things you will never stumble. (2 Peter 1:8-10)

Is it possible for a genuine believer ("brethren") to be barren, unfruitful, shortsighted, and even forget that he was cleansed from his old sins? God's Word says yes! While Christians who live in prolonged carnality cannot lose the eternal security of their salvation, they may lose the personal assurance of it by losing spiritual perspective. According to Jesus' parable in Luke 15, this is exactly what happened to the prodigal son living in the pigpen of the world. When he returned home to the Father he said, "Father, I have

[7] *Our Daily Bread*, February 27, 2001.

sinned against heaven and before you, and *I am no longer worthy to be called your son*. Make me like one of your hired servants" (vv. 18-19). The fact is that he was never worthy of being a son in the first place! Believers who live in extended carnality often lose sight of God's grace and the basis for their acceptance and assurance.

#6: Because they think that they have to know the EXACT DATE AND TIME of their salvation.

This dilemma can especially be true of children raised in Christian homes. No believer has "always been saved" since we all were born "lost." Yet the issue is not a matter of knowing the exact moment of personal faith in Christ (though some believers do).[8] Some people, especially from third-world countries, do not even know their own birthday, and yet they are certain they have been born! The apostle Paul clarified this when he wrote, "For I know *whom* I have believed and am persuaded that He is able to keep what I have committed to Him until that Day" (2 Tim. 1:12). The bottom-line issue is not knowing exactly "when" but "whom" (Jesus Christ) you have trusted to save you from a Hell you deserve to a Heaven you don't.

#7: Because they have fallen prey to FALSE TEACHING.

> Preach the word! Be ready in season and out of season. Convince, rebuke, exhort, with all longsuffering and teaching. For the time will come when they will not endure sound doctrine, but according to their own desires, because they have itching ears, they will heap up for themselves teachers; *and they will turn their ears away from the truth, and be turned aside to fables.* (2 Tim. 4:2-4)

False teaching of this sort often takes believers' eyes off of Christ and puts the focus themselves (Gal. 3:1). Only God actually knows how many individuals have heard the Gospel, put their trust in Christ alone, and known they were saved by God's grace, only to later hear false doctrine that undermined their absolute assurance of Heaven. The Son of God has spoken and He has not stuttered: "All that the Father gives Me will come to Me, and the one who comes to Me I will by no means cast out" (John 6:37).

---

[8] Charles C. Ryrie, *Basic Theology* (Wheaton, IL: Victor, 1986), 329.

#8: Because they REJECT the biblical doctrine of ETERNAL SECURITY.

Though assurance of salvation and eternal security are distinct, they are definitely related. What people believe about eternal security will affect their daily assurance of salvation. Thus, Charles Ryrie concludes, "If one does not believe in the security of the believer, then he will undoubtedly lack assurance more than once in his lifetime."[9] If people who claim to be believers in Christ think they can lose, forfeit, or give back God's gift of salvation, they cannot honestly know with absolute certainty *that they will go to heaven at any point in the future.* Why? Because they could possibly lose their salvation at any point along the way because of sin, unbelief, a pattern of carnality, and so forth. Instead, the best they could possess is some relative assurance of Heaven for today because they are remaining faithful to the Lord (at least from their own subjective perception). But since they may fail between now and tomorrow (like the apostle Peter who denied the Lord three times in a short period of time), they cannot honestly know with certainly that they have eternal life and will go to Heaven tomorrow should they die. But again we must ask, how long does "eternal life" last?

Others who reject the eternal security of the believer (God's preservation of the saints) and embrace the Calvinist doctrine of the "perseverance of the saints" lack absolute assurance of salvation because their enduring faith and good works act as the test-case to see if they are *truly* saved. And should their faith falter or fail at some later date, this supposedly would prove that they were never elect. R. C. Sproul, for example, states:

> Believers can have a radical fall, but such falls are temporary and impermanent. We have all known people who have made professions of faith and exhibited zeal for Christ, only to repudiate their confessions and turn away from Christ. What should we make of this? We consider two possibilities. The first possibility is that their profession was not genuine in the first place. . . . The second possible explanation . . . is that they are true believers who have fallen into serious and radical apostasy, but who will repent of their sin and be restored before they die. If they persist in apostasy until death, then theirs is a

---

[9] Ibid.

full and final fall from grace, which is evidence that they were not genuine believers in the first place.[10]

Logically, then, those who reject eternal security for the doctrine of perseverance lack the absolute certainty of salvation, for they must wait to see if their faith endures to the end of their life. But what do the Scriptures say? "And he [the Philippian jailor] brought them out and said, 'Sirs, what must I do to be saved?' So they said, '*Believe* [*pisteuson* – aorist tense] *on the Lord Jesus Christ, and you will be saved* [*sōthēsē* – future tense, passive voice, indicative mood]'" (Acts 16:30-31). The sole condition for salvation in this verse is simply to "believe," without requiring a special kind of faith that works and perseveres to the end. Ryrie explains:

> Some years ago a book by Robert Shank, entitled *Life in the Son*, argued against eternal security on the basis that believing in the New Testament was always in the present tense. Therefore, if a believer did not continue to believe he could and would lose his salvation. Today proponents of lordship/discipleship/mastery salvation . . . conclude that if someone does not continue to believe, then he or she was never a believer in the first place. However, notice that when Abraham's faith is described in the New Testament, an aorist, not a present, tense is used consistently (Romans 4:3; Galatians 3:6; James 2:23). Many Samaritans believed (aorist) the harlot's testimony and were saved (John 4:39, 41). Others believed (aorist) (John 10:42; 11:45; Acts 14:1; 1 Corinthians 15:11). And in response to the Philippian jailer's question, Paul said, "Believe" (aorist, Acts 16:31).[11]

Let me end this chapter with this fitting story.

> How did the first-born sons of the thousands of Israel know for certain that they were safe the night of the Passover and Egypt's judgment?

---

[10] R. C. Sproul, *Grace Unknown: The Heart of Reformed Theology* (Grand Rapids: Baker, 1997), 208-9.

[11] Charles C. Ryrie, *So Great Salvation: What It Means to Believe in Jesus Christ* (Wheaton, IL: Victor, 1989), 142-43.

Let us take a visit to two of their houses and hear what they have to say.

We find in the first house we enter that they are all shivering with fear and suspense.

What is the secret of all this paleness and trembling? We inquire; and the first-born son informs us that the angel of death is coming round the land, and that he is not quite certain how matters will stand with him at that solemn moment.

"When the destroying angel has passed our house," says he, "and the night of judgment is over, I shall, then know that I am safe, but I can't see how I can be quite sure of it until then. They say they are sure of salvation next door; but we think it very presumptuous. All I can do is to spend the long dreary night hoping for the best."

"Well," we inquire, "but has the God of Israel not provided a way of safety for His people?"

"True," he replies, "and we have availed ourselves of that way of escape. The blood of the spotless and unblemished first-year lamb has been duly sprinkled with the bunch of hyssop on the lintel and two side-posts, but still we are not fully assured of shelter." Let us now leave these doubting, troubled ones, and enter next door.

What a striking contrast meets our eye at once! Joy beams on every countenance. There they stand with girded loins and staff in hand, enjoying the roasted lamb.

What can be the meaning of all this joy on such a solemn night as this? "Ah," say they all, "we are only waiting for Jehovah's marching orders and then we shall bid a last farewell to the task-master's cruel lash and all the drudgery of Egypt."

"But hold. Do you forget that this is the night of Egypt's judgment?"

"Right well we know it; but our first-born son is safe. The blood has been sprinkled according to the wish of our God."

"But so it has been the next door," we reply, "but they are all unhappy because all uncertain of safety."

"Ah," responds the first-born firmly, "but we have MORE THAN THE SPRINKLED BLOOD, WE HAVE

THE UNERRING WORD OF GOD ABOUT IT. God has said, 'WHEN I SEE THE BLOOD I will pass over you.' God rests satisfied with the blood outside, and we rest satisfied with His word inside."

The sprinkled blood makes us SAFE.

The spoken word makes us SURE. Could anything make us more safe than the sprinkled blood, or more sure than His spoken word? Nothing, nothing.

Now, reader, let me ask you a question, "Which of those two houses think you was the safer?"

Do you say No. 2, where all were so happy? Nay, then you are wrong. Both are safe alike.

Their safety depends upon what God thinks about the blood outside and not upon the state of their feelings inside.

If you would be sure of your own blessing then, dear reader, listen not to the unstable testimony of inward emotions, but to the infallible witness of the Word of God.

"Verily, verily, I say unto you, He that believeth on Me HATH everlasting life."[12]

Oh, what a Savior that He died for me!
From condemnation He hath made me free;
"He that believeth on the Son" saith He,
"Hath everlasting life."

All my iniquities on Him were laid,
All my indebtedness by Him was paid;
All who believe on Him, the Lord hath said,
"Hath everlasting life."

Though poor and needy, I can trust my Lord;
Though weak and sinful, I believe His word;
Oh, glad message; every child of God
"Hath everlasting life."

---

[12] George Cutting, *Safety, Certainty & Enjoyment* (Addison, IL: Bible Truth Publishers), 9-12.

Though all unworthy, yet I will not doubt;
For him that cometh He will not cast out:
"He that believeth" — oh, the good news shout!
"Hath everlasting life."

"Verily, verily, I say unto you;"
"Verily, verily," message every new!
"He that believeth on the Son" — 'tis true! —
"Hath everlasting life."[13]

---

[13] James McGranahan, *Verily, Verily.*

CHAPTER 19

Why Do People Object to Eternal Security?

If you recall, this book began with an examination of Jesus Christ's indictment of the Sadducees who were challenging Him. He said to them, "You are mistaken, not knowing the Scriptures nor the power of God" (Matt. 22:29). The very same ignorance or confusion lies at the core of why people err regarding the wonderful truth of eternal security and, consequently, the lack of assurance about going to Heaven when they die. The reasons people give for not personally believing or embracing this biblical doctrine reflect the condition of "not knowing the Scriptures nor the power of God." Why are there objections to eternal security?

#1: Because of a failure to ACCEPT THE WORD OF GOD OVER PERSONAL EXPERIENCE, HUMAN OPINION, or RELIGIOUS TRADITION.

The teaching of God's grace is foreign and contrary to our natural thinking because we normally think, "There is no free lunch." Yet God has said, "'For my thoughts are not your thoughts, nor are your ways My ways' says the LORD. 'For as the heavens are higher than the earth, so are My ways higher than your ways, and My thoughts than your thoughts'" (Isa. 55:8-9). Often, those who reject eternal security rely on their emotions and experiences to determine right from wrong in these important matters, instead of God's unfailing and inerrant Word, the Bible. "So then faith comes by hearing, and hearing by the word of God" (Rom 10:17).

In his classic book, *The Green Letters* (*Principles of Spiritual Growth*), Miles Stanford writes,

Since true faith is anchored on scriptural facts, we are certainly not to be influenced by *impressions*. George Mueller said, "Impressions have neither one thing nor the other to do with faith. Faith has to do with the Word of God. It is not impressions, strong or weak, which will make the difference. We have to do with the Written Word and not ourselves or our impressions." Then, too, *probabilities* are the big temptation when it comes to exercising faith. Too often the attitude is: "It doesn't seem probable that he will ever be saved." "The way things are going, I wonder if the Lord really loves me." But Mueller wrote: "Many people are willing to believe regarding those things that seem probable to them. Faith has nothing to do with probabilities. The province of faith begins where probabilities cease and sight and sense fail. Appearances are not to be taken into account. The question is—whether God has spoken it in His Word."[1]

In this book you have seen many verses from the Scriptures that individually and corporately make a strong case for the teaching of eternal security. So will you take God at His Word by faith, or will you elevate your experience or opinion over this myriad of biblical verses?

#2: Because of a failure to BE CORRECTLY TAUGHT THE WORD OF GOD.

Satan is the master deceiver, and as some sage has quipped, "When you look for the devil, make sure to look in the pulpit." Sometimes, even sincere and well-intended teachers and pastors erroneously teach a garbled gospel with a non-eternal security twist. However, it has been my observation that when one examines various passages on this subject, using proper exegesis that carefully considers context, content, and comparisons of Scripture with Scripture, the result is a correct understanding of the Gospel that embraces eternal security and the absolute assurance of salvation. I have sought to carefully examine and exegete the various passages we have studied in this book. I have given meticulous attention to the

---

[1] Miles J. Stanford, *The Green Letters: Principles of Spiritual Growth* (Grand Rapids: Zondervan, 1975), 10.

context and *content* of each passage, along with *comparing Scripture with Scripture*, in order to arrive at correct and exact interpretations of each passage.

Unfortunately, many unsuspecting individuals have heard verses twisted out of their contexts and displayed as proof texts that supposedly deny the teaching of eternal security. We'll examine some of these passages starting in chapter twenty-two. However, the net result of this Scripture-twisting is that there are those who are "tossed to and fro and carried about with every wind of doctrine, by the trickery of men" (Eph. 4:14).

#3: Because of a failure to truly UNDERSTAND THE COMPLETENESS OF CHRIST'S WORK on the Cross.

Why do I say this? It is because those who reject eternal security almost always make our "sins" the issue for either obtaining or maintaining eternal life. Dear reader, I ask you, "*What* did Jesus Christ die for and completely pay for on the cross?" Our *sins!* How many sins did Christ die for when He died? All of them—past, present, and future! So how can sin ultimately condemn a sinner when Christ paid for it in full? It can't!

When you trusted Jesus Christ alone as your Savior, how many of your sins did He immediately and eternally forgive? All of them—past, present, and future!

> To Him all the prophets witness that, through His name, whoever believes in Him will receive remission of sins. (Acts 10:43)

> And you, being dead in your trespasses and the uncircumcision of your flesh, He has made alive together with Him, having forgiven you all trespasses. (Col. 2:13)

> He has not dealt with us according to our sins, nor punished us according to our iniquities. For as the heavens are high above the earth, so great is His mercy toward those who fear Him; as far as the east is from the west, so far has He removed our transgressions from us. (Ps. 103:10-12)

It is imperative to note that when those in pulpit or pew deny eternal security, they still make *sin* the issue instead of fully grasping the completeness Jesus Christ's work on the cross. For while those who deny eternal security may give lip service to the sacrifice of Christ for our sins, they fail the grace of God by still making *sin* the issue instead of the *Son*. But what do the Scriptures say? "He who believes in him is not condemned; but he who does not believe is condemned already, *because he has not believed in the name of the only begotten Son of God*" (John 3:18). This verse makes it clear that it is unbelief that condemns a person, not sin.

#4:   Because of a failure to DISCERN THE NATURE OF SALVATION BY GRACE ALONE.

Though many opponents of eternal security claim to believe a sinner is saved by God's grace, they still condition ultimate entrance into Heaven on good works such as living a holy life, not sinning certain sins, confessing your sins, submitting daily to Christ's lordship, and persevering in godliness. This is inconsistent with God's grace which is free, underserved, unmerited favor and blessing from God apart from human efforts or works.

> Being justified freely by His grace through the redemption that is in Christ Jesus, whom God set forth as a propitiation by His blood. (Rom. 3:24-25a)

> And if by grace, then it is no longer of works; otherwise grace is no longer grace. But if it is of works, it is no longer grace; otherwise work is no longer work. (Rom. 11:6)

> For by grace you have been saved through faith, and that not of yourselves; it is the gift of God, not of works, lest anyone should boast. (Eph. 2:8-9)

> Who has saved us and called us with a holy calling, not according to our works, but according to His own purpose and grace which was given to us in Christ Jesus before time began, but has now been revealed by the appearing of our Savior Jesus Christ, who has abolished death and brought life and immortality to light through the gospel. (2 Tim. 1:9-10)

Your salvation does not ultimately depend on your walk or works, nor your conduct or confession of sins, but on Jesus Christ's finished cross-work alone. While some erroneously frontload the Gospel by requiring religious works to be saved initially, others backload the Gospel by claiming that a genuine "saving faith" necessarily results in submission to Christ's mastery over one's life and personal commitment to obey Christ evidenced by persevering faithfulness or fruitfulness to the end of one's life (Lordship Salvation). This false teaching shifts the basis of one's absolute assurance of salvation from simple faith in Christ's work *for* you in justification (Christ's finished work) and God's promises to you (as a believer in Christ), to Christ's work *in* you in sanctification (which is incomplete and even erratic at times). False teaching on the Gospel has often taken three prevalent forms:

- Faith in Jesus Christ + good works = maybe Heaven (Romanism & much of Protestantism)

- Faith in Jesus Christ = maybe Heaven *if* you maintain a holy life, confess your sins, remain faithful, etc. (Arminianism)

- Faith in Jesus Christ = salvation + good works to ultimately arrive at Heaven (Calvinism). No works = no real salvation and no Heaven.

In each of these options, the bottom-line ends up being the same: lack of good works means no real salvation and no ultimate entrance to heaven. For example, one dedicated Reformed author states,

> Thus, good works may be said to be a condition for obtaining salvation in that they inevitably accompany genuine faith. . . . The question is not whether good works are necessary to salvation, but in what way are they necessary. As the inevitable outworking of saving faith, they are necessary for salvation.[2]

---

[2] John H. Gerstner, *Wrongly Dividing the Word of Truth: A Critique of Dispensationalism* (Brentwood, TN: Wolgemuth & Hyatt, 1991), 210.

This is *not* salvation by grace. Though good works are an integral part of God's will for every Christian's life, and God designed them that we *should* walk in them after we receive His gift of salvation, it is not certain that we *will* walk in them. Good works are neither the grounds of our acceptance before God, nor the *means* of obtaining or maintaining salvation. If God required good works to enter Heaven, even as a post-conversion requirement, how would people ever know they have done enough?

> For by grace you have been saved through faith, and that not of yourselves; it is the gift of God, not of works, lest anyone should boast. For we are His workmanship, created in Christ Jesus for good works, which God prepared beforehand that we should walk in them. (Eph. 2:8-10)

> Not by works of righteousness which we have done, but according to His mercy He saved us, through the washing of regeneration and renewing of the Holy Spirit. (Titus 3:5)

> This is a faithful saying, and these things I want you to affirm constantly, that those who have believed in God should be careful to maintain good works. These things are good and profitable to men. (Titus 3:8)

> And let our people also learn to maintain good works, to meet urgent needs, that they may not be unfruitful. (Titus 3:14)

#5: Because of a failure to DISTINGUISH BETWEEN JUSTIFI-CATION BEFORE GOD AND PRACTICAL SANCTIFICA-TION IN TIME.

When these two biblical concepts (justification before God and practical sanctification) are homogenized and not distinguished, confusion regarding the eternal security of the believer will result. The following chart clarifies this important distinction.

Justification Before God	Practical Sanctification
1. God *declares righteous* the believing sinner (Rom. 4:1-3).	1. God *makes righteous* the yielded, dependent believer who responds to God's Word (John 17:17; Gal. 5:16).
2. God *imputes* righteousness to the believer in his standing before God (Rom. 4:4-8).	2. God *imparts* righteousness to the believer, affecting his state practically (Heb. 13:21).
3. Occurs *outside* the believing sinner (1 Cor. 6:11).	3. Occurs *inside* the responsive believer (Eph. 3:16).
4. Is a one-time event at a *point in time* when a sinner believes in Christ (Gal. 2:16).	4. Is to be an *ongoing* process as the believer walks by faith under the Spirit's control (2 Cor. 3:18).
5. Involves salvation from sin's *penalty* (Rom. 5:9).	5. Involves salvation from sin's *power* practically (Rom. 6:11-13).
6. Changes a believer's *eternal destiny* (Titus 3:7).	6. Changes a believer's *present life* (Eph. 5:15-16).
7. Results in having *peace with* God (Rom. 5:1).	7. Results in having the *peace of* God (Phil. 4:9).
8. Is *absolute* and not a matter of degrees (1 Cor. 1:30).	8. Can *increase* as believers grow in grace (1 Thess. 4:1-3).
9. Is solely by God's *grace* through faith (Rom. 3:24).	9. Is solely by God's *grace* through faith resulting in good works (Rom. 6:14).

How does a failure to recognize these clear biblical distinctions lead to a denial of eternal security and doubt about one's eternal destiny? God promises in Scripture that all who are justified will also be glorified (Rom. 5:9; 8:30, 33-39). What is not guaranteed is the believer's practical sanctification. This is evident from the examples of "just" or "righteous" Lot (2 Peter 2:7) and many justified yet carnal Corinthians whom the Lord chastened to the point of physical death (1 Cor. 3:1-4; 6:11; 11:28-32). But consistent Calvinism's doctrine of the perseverance of the saints denies this and insists that all who possess true saving faith will become practically sanctified with a life of faith and good works that endures to the end. According to this system of doctrine, God gives the gift of faith to the elect and in His sovereign grace assures that they will also be faithful until death. They argue that without a life of practical sanctification, a person cannot be glorified; and without a life of sanctification, it is also certain that a person was never truly justified. This ultimately makes assurance of justification and glorification conditioned on a life of sanctification. But who is responsible for the believer's sanctification? Is it God's responsibility, the believer's, or both?

Roman Catholicism openly teaches that salvation is conditioned on a life of faith plus works with God giving the believer enabling grace to do those works. Salvation becomes a collaborative effort between God and the believer. It teaches that "We cannot 'earn' our salvation through good works, but our faith in Christ puts us in a special grace-filled relationship with God so that our obedience and love, combined with our faith, will be rewarded with eternal life."[3] It is only consistent, therefore, that Catholicism openly declares that sanctification is part of justification. "The Holy Spirit is the master of the interior life. By giving birth to the 'inner man,' justification entails the sanctification of his whole being."[4] According to Catholicism, God only declares a person righteous (justified) who is practically righteous (sanctified). But how much practical sanctification is enough to know that one is justified? Mixing sanctification with justification makes salvation neither secure nor certain. While this conclusion may not come as a surprise with respect to Catholicism, it is astonishing to hear prominent "evangelical" leaders advocating essentially the same view.

---

[3] *Pillar of Fire, Pillar of Truth* (El Cajon, CA: Catholic Answers, 1997), 23.

[4] *Catechism of the Catholic Church* (Bloomingdale, OH: Apostolate for Family Consecration, 1994), 483, §1995.

At times, Reformed teachers and theologians sound virtually indistinguishable from their Roman Catholic counterparts. MacArthur, for example, confuses the imparted righteousness that occurs during the process of practical sanctification with the imputed, judicial declaration of righteousness that occurs at justification. Commenting on Romans 3:24, MacArthur says, "When a sinner believes in the Lord Jesus Christ, he is declared *to be* righteous, because he now possesses God's own righteousness as a gift of His grace. God does not *consider* a believer to be righteous; He *makes* him righteous."[5] If God only declares people to be righteous or justified because He makes them practically righteous, this results in requiring a certain level of practical righteousness to be saved. Although Reformed theology formally distinguishes justification from sanctification, practically it blends the two. One leading Reformed Baptist author and professor declares,

> Yes, works are necessary to be saved. No, this is not works righteousness, for the works are hardly meritorious. The grace of God is so powerful that it not only grants us salvation apart from our merits, but also transforms us. Christians are not only declared righteous but also experience observable and significant change in their lives.[6]

---

[5] John F. MacArthur, Jr., *The MacArthur New Testament Commentary, Romans 1–8* (Chicago: Moody Press, 1991), 208. In an earlier publication he stated that justification in Romans 3–4 includes both the imputation and impartation of righteousness. "Many people believe justified means 'just-as-if-I'd-never-sinned.' In other words, God says, 'I count you righteous even though you're really not.' It is true that God makes that declaration, but there is also a reality of righteousness. We are not only declared righteous; we are made righteous. There is not only imputation—the declaration of righteousness—but there is impartation—the granting of real righteousness. God is not guilty of some legal fiction. He is not play acting, that is, saying something is true that isn't" (John F. MacArthur, Jr., *Justified by Faith: Study Notes on Romans 3:20–4:25* [Panorama City, CA: Word of Grace Communications, 1984], 93-94. See also tape GC 45-33). He adds that righteousness in 2 Corinthians 5:21 involves "a genuine transformation" (ibid., 94). He concludes, "I'm convinced that the reason God can declare us righteous is that we are truly made righteous. Otherwise, God is saying something that isn't true about us. I know that there have been many people who have tried to teach that we are only declared to be righteous, and not actually made righteous. They then have this excuse: 'Since we are not made righteous, there doesn't have to be the result of righteousness in our lives.' But that is not the case" (ibid., 95).

[6] Thomas R. Schreiner, "Perseverance and Assurance: A Survey and a Proposal," *Southern Baptist Journal of Theology* 2 (Spring 1998): 53. For another example of a Reformed writer who practically conditions eternal salvation on grace-enabled good works in the believer's life see John F. MacArthur, Jr., *The Gospel according to Jesus: What Does Jesus Mean When He Says, "Follow Me"?* (Grand Rapids: Zondervan, 1988), 209, 219.

Yet claiming that God's grace enables good works in no way lessens the believer's personal responsibility to appropriate and act on that grace. The same author even states a few sentences later that we must actively keep ourselves in the love of God to stay saved. He says, "The imperative here reveals that this is our responsibility. To be spared from God's wrath on the last day we must keep ourselves in God's love, and yet such self-keeping is ultimately not our work but God's."[7] This is contradictory. If it is "self-keeping" then it is man's work and the "keeping" is not attributable to God. The same author goes on to conclude, "Though God undergirds all our effort, it is still the case that we must do what the scriptures command."[8] When final salvation is predicated on the believer's cooperation with God in a life of faithfulness and good works (even grace-enabled works), the result is a lack of certainty and security of salvation. Who can know whether they have done enough of "what the scriptures command"?

It is important to "rightly divide the word of truth" (2 Tim. 2:15) regarding these two scriptural issues, for a failure in a believer's practical sanctification does not negate his justification before God; otherwise, salvation is not solely by God's grace.[9]

#6: Because of a failure to distinguish being a member in the FAMILY OF GOD once for all and a believer's daily FELLOWSHIP WITH GOD.

Similar to the difference between justification before God and the believer's practical sanctification in time, this biblical distinction must be kept clear. Regarding the believer's entrance into the family of God, the Bible states,

> He came to His own, and His own did not receive Him. But as many as received Him, to them He gave the right to become children of God, to those who believe in His name: who were born, not of blood, nor of the will of the flesh, nor of the will of man, but of God. (John 1:11-13)

> For you are all sons of God through faith in Christ Jesus. (Gal. 3:26)

---

[7] Schreiner, "Perseverance and Assurance: A Survey and a Proposal," 53.

[8] Ibid., 54.

[9] For an excellent study on the subject of practical sanctification in the Christian life by God's grace, see Kurt Witzig, "Sanctification by God's Free Grace," in *Freely by His Grace: Classical Free Grace Theology*, ed. J. B. Hixson, Rick Whitmire, and Roy B. Zuck (Duluth, MN: Grace Gospel Press, 2012), 363-418.

This new birth, like a physical birth, is a once-for-all event that never needs to be repeated and cannot be undone, making the believer in Christ a child of God forever. However, when it comes to the believer's daily fellowship with God, 1 John 1 declares...

> That which we have seen and heard we declare to you, that you also may have fellowship with us; and truly our fellowship is with the Father and with His Son Jesus Christ. And these things we write to you that your joy may be full. This is the message which we have heard from Him and declare to you, that God is light and in Him is no darkness at all. If we say that we have fellowship with Him, and walk in darkness, we lie and do not practice the truth. But if we walk in the light as He is in the light, we have fellowship with one another, and the blood of Jesus Christ His Son cleanses us from all sin. If we say that we have no sin, we deceive ourselves, and the truth is not in us. If we confess our sins, He is faithful and just to forgive us our sins and to cleanse us from all unrighteousness. If we say that we have not sinned, we make Him a liar, and His word is not in us. (1 John 1:3-10)

Consider the following chart in clarifying these biblical concepts.

Family of God	Fellowship with God
1. entered at a *point of time* when born again (John 1:12-13; 3:1-18; 1 John 3:2)	1. enjoyed in the *present* if a believer walks in the light (1 John 1:3-7)
2. true of *all* genuine believers in Christ (Gal. 3:26; 1 Jn. 5:1)	2. *not* true of all believers . . . "if" (1 John 1:5-10)
3. sins are *positionally / judicially* forgiven (Eph.1:7; Col. 2:13; 1 John 2:12)	3. sins may be *parentally* forgiven (1 John 1:9)
4. *faith* alone required (John 1:12; Gal. 3:26)	4. *faith* and *confession of sin* required (Heb. 11:6; 1 John 1:9)
5. evidenced by a *new nature* (2 Pt. 1:3-4), God's *chastisement* (Heb. 12:6-8), and becoming a *new creation* (2 Cor. 5:17)	5. evidenced by *obedience* to God's will (1 John 2:3-6) and *love* for other believers (1 John 2:7-11)

While sin in believers' lives breaks fellowship with God, it does not change their status as children of God. And a failure to confess their sins to God in genuine repentance brings divine discipline into their lives. Yet it is important to remember that God only chastens His children, not the unsaved.

> And you have forgotten the exhortation which speaks to you as to sons: "My son, do not despise the chastening of the LORD, nor be discouraged when you are rebuked by Him; for whom the LORD loves He chastens, and scourges every son whom He receives." If you endure chastening, God deals with you as with sons; for what son is there whom a father does not chasten? But if you are without chastening, of which all have become partakers, then you are illegitimate and not sons. (Heb. 12:5-8)

Many of you who are reading this are parents. When your children disobey you, do they stop being your children? Of course not. Why not? It's because they were born into your family. And should your children remain in rebellion, you discipline them out of love. In the same way, because believers in Christ have been born again into the family of God, they will never cease to be God's spiritual children, even when they break fellowship with Him. Now I ask you, are you a better parent than God?

#7: Because of a failure to DISTINGUISH BETWEEN THE PRESENT GIFT OF ETERNAL LIFE which CAN NEVER BE LOST and FUTURE REWARDS which CAN BE FORFEITED.

Careless exegetes of the Scriptures with theologically driven interpretations have repeatedly failed to recognize this important biblical distinction. This has been especially true with the so-called "problem passages" which deniers of eternal security resort to in order to suggest that a believer can lose his salvation. In his classic study Bible, C. I. Scofield writes,

> God in the N.T. Scriptures offers to the lost, salvation; and for the faithful service of the saved, He offers rewards. These passages are easily distinguished by remembering that salvation is invariably spoken as a free gift (e.g. John 4:10; Rom. 6:23; Eph. 2:8-9), while rewards are earned by works (Matt. 10:42; Luke 19:17; 1 Cor. 9:24-25; 2 Tim. 4:7-

8; Rev. 2:10; 22:12). A further distinction is that salvation is a present possession (Luke 7:50; John 3:36; 5:24; 6:47), whereas rewards are a future attainment to be given at the rapture (2 Tim. 4:8; Rev. 22:12).[10]

When people fail to distinguish between salvation and rewards, they wrongly interpret certain biblical passages on Christian living and rewards and incorrectly understand them to be verses about salvation from Hell. This occurs when people fail to consider a passage's context and content and to compare Scripture with Scripture. While eternal salvation is the believer's present possession and can never be lost, future rewards will be given out at the Judgment Seat of Christ (2 Cor. 5:10). They will be given only to faithful believers (1 Cor. 4:1-2) who have lived by faith (Gal. 2:20) with perseverance (2 Tim. 4:7) and Christ-honoring motives (1 Cor. 4:5), being empowered by the Holy Spirit (Eph. 5:18) to do their deeds heartily as to the Lord (Col. 3:23–24) and for the glory of God (1 Cor. 10:31). A believer's potential reward may be forfeited or lost (1 Cor. 3:15a; 2 John 8; Rev. 3:11), yet his salvation is eternal and secure (1 Cor. 3:15b).[11]

The following chart and the Scriptures it cites will help you understand and clarify the important distinctions between salvation and rewards.

Salvation	Rewards
1. is offered to *unbelievers*.	1. are offered to *believers*.
2. is appropriated by *grace through faith alone in Christ alone apart from works*. (Rom. 3:28; Eph. 2:8-9)	2. are obtained by *grace through on-going faith resulting in Christ-honoring works*. (1 Cor. 3:5-13)
3. is the believer's *present possession*. (John 3:16-18, 36)	3. are the believer's possible *future attainment*. (1 Cor. 3:14).

---

[10] *The Scofield Study Bible, New King James Version*, ed. C. I. Scofield, et al. (Oxford: Oxford University Press, 2002), 1579.

[11] For further study on this subject, see Thomas L. Stegall, "Rewards and the Judgment Seat of Christ," in *Freely by His Grace: Classical Free Grace Theology*, ed. J. B. Hixson, Rick Whitmire, and Roy B. Zuck (Duluth, MN: Grace Gospel Press, 2012), 419-73.

Salvation	Rewards
4. is received the *moment of faith in Christ.* (John 5:24)	4. are given out at the *Judgment Seat of Christ after the Rapture.* (Rom. 14:10; 2 Cor. 5:10)
5. can *never* be lost. (1 Cor. 3:15)	5. *may be lost.* (1 Cor. 3:11-15)
6. solely involves *trusting in Christ.* (What do you think of Christ?)	6. involve . . . a. the *quality of one's post-justification works.* (1 Cor. 3:12-15; 2 Cor. 5:10-11) b. one's *faithfulness to God's will and Word.* (1 Cor. 4:2; 2 Tim. 4:7-8; James 1:12; 1 Peter 5:4; 2 John 8-11) c. one's *motives before God.* (Matt. 6:1-6; 1 Cor. 4:4; Col. 3:23-25)
7. determines one's *eternal destiny.* (1 John 5:11-13)	7. determine your *function and privilege in Heaven.* (Phil. 3:11-14; 2 Peter 1:11)
8. makes one *accepted before God.* (Eph. 1:6)	8. reflects that one's post-salvation life was *well-pleasing to God.* (2 Cor. 5:9)
9. will result in *praise to God.* (Rev. 5:8-14)	9. will result in *praise to God.* (Rev. 4:9-11)

#8:   Because of a failure to ACCEPT THE CLEAR AND OBVIOUS BIBLICAL PASSAGES that teach eternal security based on a MISUNDERSTANDING ABOUT SELECT PROOF TEXTS which opponents use to deny eternal security.

Sometimes when discussing this subject of eternal security, I will read a number of verses that very clearly demonstrate this wonderful truth. Instead of hearing "Hallelujah," I hear a response like, "But isn't there a verse in Hebrews 6, or Hebrews 10, or 2 Peter 2 that teaches that you *can* lose your salvation?" My first reaction to this query is utter disbelief. In the face of all these clear and simple verses that exalt the grace of God and teach the eternal security of the believer, why would anyone doubt or deny these marvelous truths just because some passages at first glance *seem* to contradict them? When addressing this objection we must grasp a basic principle of scriptural interpretation, namely, that *the Bible correctly understood never contradicts itself.* Therefore, any alleged contradiction to the biblical truth of eternal security is an *apparent* problem in *our* understanding of the passage which can be explained on closer examination of the verses involved. And that is exactly what chapters 22–31 will do. So read on!

> Blessed assurance, Jesus is mine!
> O what a fore-taste of glory divine!
> Heir of salvation, purchase of God,
> Born of His Spirit, washed in His blood!
>
> This is my story, this is my song,
> Praising my Savior all the day long.
> This is my story, this is my song,
> Praising my Savior all the day long.[12]

---

[12] Fanny J. Crosby, *Blessed Assurance.*

Part IV

The Consequences
of
Carnality

CHAPTER 20

If You Can't Lose Eternal Salvation, What Can You Lose? Part 1

The Bible contains an abundance of verses that communicate clearly the eternal and free gift of salvation that all believers receive the moment they place their trust in Jesus Christ alone as He is presented in the Gospel of grace (1 Cor. 15:1-4). Although the salvation that all believers possess is eternal and secure forever, there are many spiritual realities that believers can still lose through ongoing sin or carnality in their lives. In the next two chapters I will seek to highlight seven of these spiritual realities that may be lost or forfeited if a believer fails to live by faith through the power of the Holy Spirit to the glory of God.

THE CARNAL CHRISTIAN

The carnal Christian is a paradox of biblical proportions. While he is on his way to Heaven, he may live like he is going to Hell (2 Sam. 11–12). Though he is saved, he behaves just like the lost (1 Cor. 3:3). Instead of daily operating from a divine viewpoint on life, he functions out of human wisdom (1 Cor. 1:10-31). He possesses the Holy Spirit (1 Cor. 6:19), yet the flesh as a pattern still practically controls him (1 Cor. 3:3). Instead of growing in grace to spiritual maturity, he is retrogressing (Heb. 5:11-14) or stuck in immaturity (1 Cor. 3:2). Though Jesus Christ is his Lord/God, he is not voluntarily yielding to Him to direct his life (Rom. 6:12-13). Is it possible that these characteristics describe a Heaven-bound child of God? For the person who believes the Bible, the answer is an unequivocal and emphatic. "YES"!

> And I, brethren, could not speak to you as to spiritual
> people but as to carnal, as to babes in Christ. I fed you
> with milk and not with solid food; for until now you
> were not able to receive it, and even now you are still
> not able; for you are still carnal. For where there are
> envy, strife, and divisions among you, are you not
> carnal and behaving like mere men? For when one says,
> "I am of Paul," and another, "I am of Apollos," are you
> not carnal? (1 Cor. 3:1-4)

Dear readers, these Corinthian saints epitomized the old adage,
"Christians are not perfect, just forgiven." Though *justification* by
grace causes God to *declare* the believing sinner *righteous* in Christ,
practical *sanctification* is designed and desired by God to *make* the
believer increasingly *righteous* in his daily walk and practice until
the day that he arrives in Heaven and experiences *glorification* when
the Lord returns.

Yet a lack of practical and progressive sanctification and
spiritual growth does not negate the reality of the believer's past
justification before God, nor the Christian's future glorification in
Heaven. This is a wonder of God's grace. If you do not believe me,
ask the carnal Corinthian Christians!

7 TRUTHS ABOUT CARNALITY

1. Carnality hinders one's spiritual GROWTH but never his POSITION in Christ. (3:1)

2. Carnality affects one's DESIRE and ABILITY to take in and digest the Word of God. (3:2)

3. Carnality may be due to WEAKNESS or WILLFULNESS. (3:1-3)

4. Carnality is not automatically connected with TIME. (3:3)

5. Carnality is evidenced by the WORKS OF THE FLESH in your life. (3:3)

6. Carnality is oftentimes characterized by SELF-DECEPTION. (3:3-4)

7. Carnality in the believer's life causes him to walk like an UNBELIEVER. (3:3)

THE NATURAL MAN

God perceives people regarding their relationship to the Holy Spirit and responsiveness to His Word in three clearly defined categories. The first is the "natural" man, who is unsaved (1 Cor. 1:18; Rom. 8:9) and void of the indwelling of the Holy Spirit (Jude 19) to illuminate for him the deeper truths of the Word of God.

> But the natural man does not receive the things of the Spirit of God, for they are foolishness to him; nor can he know them, because they are spiritually discerned. (1 Cor. 2:14)

This "soulish" (*psychikos*) man may be uncultured or cultured, refined or coarse, educated or uneducated, moral or immoral, religious or agnostic, but he does not "receive" or welcome to himself by faith the Word of God. This is a description of the majority of mankind today (Matt. 7:13-14).

THE SPIRITUAL MAN

In stark contrast to the natural man, God also considers certain individuals to be "spiritual."

> But he who is spiritual judges all things, yet he himself is rightly judged by no one. For "who has known the mind of the LORD that he may instruct Him?" But we have the mind of Christ. (1 Cor. 2:15-16)

The Greek word for the spiritual man is *pneumatikos* which is a compound word consisting of *pneuma* which is the word for "spirit," and the suffix *-ikos* which refers to the dominating factor that characterizes a person. So the spiritual man is a believer in Jesus Christ who has the Holy Spirit indwelling and empowering him. In addition, the spiritual man is also allowing the Holy Spirit to teach him or her the Word of God and to transform his or her thinking. As a result of living by faith under the control of the Holy Spirit, the spiritual believer has unlimited capacity for growing spiritually. And the Spirit of God is allowed to take the Word of God and bring this person to right conclusions based on the Word of God ("judges all things" of God's Word in the context). While this Spirit-led believer is responding to the Lord and the Word of God, the unbeliever cannot properly figure him out ("yet he himself is rightly judged by no one"). The unbeliever can only think naturally while the Spirit-filled believer is thinking supernaturally. The unbeliever can only think in terms of time and earth, while the spiritual believer factors in God's viewpoint and living in light of eternity. Thus, the spiritual believer has "the mind of Christ" via the Word of God. However, there is a third option rather than the natural and spiritual man.

THE CARNAL MAN

> And I, brethren, could not speak to you as to spiritual people but as to carnal, as to babes in Christ. (1 Cor. 3:1)

The word "carnal" (*sarkinos/sarkikos*) means fleshly or dominated by the sin nature. These Christians' daily walk characterized them as carnal, yet Paul still addressed as "brethren" and "in Christ" (v. 1), which indicates that they were believers in Jesus Christ as Savior. They were indwelt by the Holy Spirit (6:19-20), but they were not yielding to the Lord and walking by faith in Him, and were instead yielding to their sin natures. Thus, they are called "carnal." In addition, they were operating mentally on the basis of human wisdom instead of the wisdom of God in His Word (1 Cor. 1–2).

Their spiritual condition of ongoing carnality indicates to us that the believer's sin nature is not eradicated when he is born again (though believers receive a new nature at new birth). In addition, though the sin nature has been stripped of its authority to legally rule in the believer's body because of his co-crucifixion with Jesus Christ (Rom. 6:6-7), it still wants to and is able to reign as king practically in the Christian's daily life if allowed. This is why Paul warned the Roman Christians, "Therefore do not let sin reign in your mortal body, that you should obey it in its lusts" (Rom. 6:12). But praise the Lord that God, by His grace, has provided everything necessary for practical victory over sin in the child of God's daily life due to his identification with Jesus Christ (Rom. 6:1-10), the enabling power of the Holy Spirit (Gal. 5:16), and the unfailing principles and promises of God (Ps. 119:9-11). Nevertheless, believers must daily appropriate by faith God's sufficient grace provisions and enabling power to enjoy this practical victory over sin that Christ purchased at Calvary for them (Rom. 6:11-14; 8:1-4; Gal. 2:20; Col. 3:1ff). Unfortunately, the carnal Corinthians were not doing so!

I find it amazing that those who teach Lordship Salvation deny the reality of the carnal Christian. They do this largely to fit their theological system instead of practicing sound exegesis of this pertinent passage. Notice again what the Bible clearly states:

> And I, brethren, could not speak to you as to spiritual people but as to *carnal*, as to babes in Christ. I fed you with milk and not with solid food; for until now you were not able to receive it, and even now you are still not able; for you are *still carnal*. For where there are envy, strife, and divisions among you, are you not *carnal* and behaving like mere men? For when one says, "I am of Paul," and another, "I am of Apollos," are you not *carnal*? (1 Cor. 3:1-4)

Apparently the apostle Paul had not read the writings of Lordship teachers, for he definitely believed in the reality of carnal Christians! Paul is writing under the direction of the Holy Spirit to these believers in Christ residing in Corinth whom he describes as *"sanctified in Christ Jesus"* (1:2), *"called saints"* (1:2), who *"were enriched in everything by Him"* (1:5), who *"come short in no gift"* (1:7), who were *"eagerly waiting for the revelation of Jesus Christ"* (1:7), and who *"were called into the fellowship of His Son, Jesus Christ the Lord"* (1:9). Furthermore, the apostle of grace distinguishes these believers in Christ from unsaved *"natural"* people who are devoid of the Holy Spirit (2:14), as well as from *"spiritual"* believers who are characterized by the control of the Holy Spirit and responsiveness to God's Word (2:15). Yet he does not go so far as to question the reality of their salvation (3:1; 6:19). He declares them to be *"brethren"* and *"in Christ"* (in union with Jesus Christ) regarding their *position* before God. Yet Paul then slaps the label "carnal" on them four times in four verses (3:1, 3 [2x], 4) as it relates to their spiritual *condition* in time. Were they Christians? YES! Were they spiritual Christians? NO! Were they carnal Christians? YES! Is there such a reality as a carnal Christian? YES!

If there was any group of believers who should have either lost their salvation (Arminianism) or were proof that they were never saved (Calvinism), this is the church! And yet God concludes a third option: they were genuine believers who were characterized by living in ongoing carnality enthralled with human wisdom. And true to God's Word, some of these believers had experienced divine discipline as children of God "for whom the Lord loves He chastens, and scourges every son whom He receives" (Heb. 12:6). This even involved maximum discipline for many by physical death.

> For this reason many are weak and sick among you, and many sleep. For if we would judge ourselves, we would not be judged. But when we are judged, we are chastened by the Lord, that we may not be condemned with the world. (1 Cor. 11:30-32)

It is important to remember that while God condemns the unsaved, He chastens or divinely disciplines His genuine children only.

The recognition of the carnal Christian, however, is not designed by God to discourage spiritual maturation but to encourage it. Nor is this to imply that carnality in the believer's walk does not have serious consequences both in time and eternity, for it does! So read along with me of no less than seven spiritual realities that children of God *can lose* through present or prolonged carnality in their daily walk.

Though believers in Christ can never lose their eternal salvation, they can still lose (through carnality) their future REWARDS IN HEAVEN.

> For no other foundation can anyone lay than that which is laid, which is Jesus Christ. Now if anyone builds on this foundation with gold, silver, precious stones, wood, hay, straw, each one's work will become clear; for the Day will declare it, because it will be revealed by fire; and the fire will test each one's work, of what sort it is. If anyone's work which he has built on it endures, he will receive a reward. If anyone's work is burned, he will suffer loss; but he himself will be saved, yet so as through fire. (1 Cor. 3:11-15).

Whether a believer is a spiritual or a carnal Christian, he has the same foundation to build his life and ministry upon, "For no other foundation can anyone lay than that which is laid, which is Jesus Christ" (1 Cor. 3:11). Using the analogy of a building, Paul reminds these believers of the great potential of allowing their lives to glorify God, fulfill His will in time, and then to receive a proper future reward. But they would not accomplish this by acting like the unsaved in rallying around human leaders (3:4) but by keeping in mind the proper place of God's servants and Christ's future evaluation of each one.

> Who then is Paul, and who is Apollos, but *ministers through whom you believed, as the Lord gave to each one?* I planted, Apollos watered, but God gave the increase. So then neither he who plants is anything, nor he who waters, but God who gives the increase. Now he who plants and he who waters are one, and each one will receive *his own reward* according to his own labor. For we are God's fellow workers; you are God's field, you are God's building. According to the grace of God which was given to me, as a wise master builder I have laid the foundation, and another builds on it. But *let each one take heed how he builds on it.* (3:5-10)

WHICH MATERIALS WILL YOU USE TO BUILD ON YOUR FOUNDATION?

What are your choices? They basically fall into two categories. They are those materials which are permanent—gold, silver, and precious stones, and three that are perishable—wood, hay, and straw (3:12). You as a believer must determine day-by-day and moment-by-moment the kind or quality of materials you are going to build with in your life and ministry. In this context, gold, silver, and precious stones obviously relate to utilizing divine wisdom from God's Word by faith (2:6-13) with the Spirit of God (2:15) enabling you to live your life as unto the Lord. In contrast, wood, hay, and straw are works done according to human wisdom via the flesh which then glorify man (3:18-23).

WHEN WILL IT ALL BE REVEALED?

While some individuals, pastors, or missionaries may have humanly impressive lives and ministries on earth, there is coming a day in which Jesus Christ at His Judgment Seat (2 Cor. 5:10) will put to the test and reveal the true quality or materials that they used. Paul makes it clear that "each one's work will become clear; for the Day will declare it, because it will be revealed by fire; and the fire will test each one's work, of what sort it is (1 Cor. 3:13). "The Day" is a reference to the return of Christ for His Church and the resultant divine evaluation ("revealed by fire") of believers' "works" (2 Cor. 5:10), as well as the motives and thinking behind the works they did on earth.

> Therefore judge nothing before the time, until the Lord comes, who will both bring to light the hidden things of darkness and reveal the counsels of the hearts. Then each one's praise will come from God. (1 Cor. 4:5)

WHAT IS AT STAKE?

> If anyone's work which he has built on it [the foundation of Jesus Christ] endures, he will receive a reward. If anyone's work is burned, he will suffer loss. (3:14-15a)

This passage makes it clear that a believer may receive a reward from Jesus Christ for a life and ministry built with the permanent materials of God's wisdom. This is not the same as the gift of eternal life (Rom. 5:16; 6:23) which is the believer's present possession (John 3:16) given freely by God's grace based upon the redemptive work of Jesus Christ (Rom. 3:24) and received by faith alone in Christ alone apart from human works (Rom. 4:4-5; Eph. 2:8-9). Instead, this passage refers to a future reward which will be given to faithful believers who have walked by faith according to the Word of God under the Spirit's enablement resulting in Christ-honoring works to the glory of God. Now you may be thinking, "Isn't Heaven enough? Why do I need a reward?" While Heaven will be great and glorious, the numerous references to the truth of rewards in Scripture underscore their importance, and your rewards will determine whether and how you will rule and reign with Christ in the future.

WHAT IS NOT AT STAKE?

When fire is put to wood, hay, and straw, they are consumed; they go up in smoke. If your life's work as a believer goes up in smoke, you will suffer loss. Loss of what? The loss of a reward you could have had if you had built upon the foundation with God's materials instead of yours. But will a believer ever lose his eternal salvation? NEVER! "What saith the Scriptures?"

> If anyone's work is burned, he will suffer loss; but he himself will be saved, yet so as through fire. (3:15)

Though wood, hay, and straw burn up, the foundation remains. The same is true for every believer in Christ, whether carnal or spiritual, immature or mature. You can lose your reward as a believer, but you can never lose your eternal salvation because your salvation is not based on your faithfulness or works but on Christ's finished work on your behalf on the cross—your foundation! Verse 15 assures believers that even if God judges everything they have done in their life after salvation as worthless, they will still be saved by God (passive voice) in the future (future tense) and that's a guarantee (indicative mood)! This is a wonderful picture and promise of the eternal security of the believer.

DOES IT REALLY MATTER HOW YOU LIVE YOUR LIFE AS A BELIEVER?

Coupled with this absolute assurance of eternal salvation and security is an important reminder that how you live your life after receiving the gift of salvation is still very important and will one day be evaluated by Jesus Christ Himself!

> For many deceivers have gone out into the world who do not confess Jesus Christ as coming in the flesh. This is a deceiver and an antichrist. *Look to yourselves, that we do not lose those things we worked for, but that we may receive a full reward.* (2 John 7-8)

The Scriptures refer to these rewards with various metaphors including the concept of "crowns." At least three crowns are distinguished in the New Testament:

1. **The CROWN OF LIFE for believers persevering and being faithful to God unto death in trials.**

   > Blessed is the man who endures temptation; for *when he has been approved, he will receive the crown of life* which the Lord has promised to those who love Him. (James 1:12)

Do not fear any of those things which you are about to suffer. Indeed, the devil is about to throw some of you into prison, that you may be tested, and you will have tribulation ten days. *Be faithful until death, and I will give you the crown of life.* (Rev. 2:10)

2. **The CROWN OF RIGHTEOUSNESS for believers persevering and being faithful in doing God's will.**

I have fought the good fight, I have finished the race, I have kept the faith. Finally, *there is laid up for me the crown of righteousness, which the Lord, the righteous Judge, will give to me* on that Day, and not to me only but also to all who have loved His appearing. (2 Tim. 4:7-8)

3. **The CROWN OF GLORY for pastors persevering and being faithful in their ministry.**

The elders who are among you I exhort, I who am a fellow elder and a witness of the sufferings of Christ, and also a partaker of the glory that will be revealed: Shepherd the flock of God which is among you, serving as overseers, not by compulsion but willingly, not for dishonest gain but eagerly; nor as being lords over those entrusted to you, but being examples to the flock; *and when the Chief Shepherd appears, you will receive the crown of glory that does not fade away.* (1 Peter 5:1-4)

If genuine believers can lose their reward but never their eternal salvation, it should not surprise us then to hear the Lord Jesus Christ herald to the believers in the church at Philadelphia,

Behold, I am coming quickly! Hold fast what you have, *that no one may take your crown.* (Rev. 3:11)

Though the gift of eternal salvation can never be lost, forfeited, or returned, genuine believers in Christ can lose a reward, a full reward, or a crown which Jesus Christ desires to give them at the Judgment Seat of Christ for their faithful service to their Savior.

Therefore we make it our aim, whether present or absent, *to be well pleasing to Him. For we must all appear*

> *before the judgment seat of Christ,* that each one may
> receive the things done in the body, according to what
> he has done, whether good or bad. (2 Cor. 5:9-10)

A key issue in living the Christian life is walking by faith in Christ
as your life through the power of the Holy Spirit in order to be
faithful to the Lord which results in a future reward, not salvation
from Hell. This is because a believer's final destiny is already settled
the moment he puts his trust in Jesus Christ to save him. But if he
faithfully finishes the race God has for him, he will also receive a
reward. But for those who quit along the way, who stop walking
with and serving the Lord or who choose to live for themselves and
this present world, they will fail to receive a reward. Every believer
is in a spiritual battle (Eph. 6:10-18) with a race to run and finish in
doing the will of God (Acts 20:24). Some, like Paul, succeed (2 Tim.
4:6-8); some, like Demas, don't (2 Tim. 4:10). How about you? By
God's grace, will you fight the good fight of faith? Will you finish
your race? Will you keep the faith? For not only did Paul receive a
crown or reward, but so can you!

Let's remember the words of our Lord who promised,

> Blessed are you when they revile and persecute you,
> and say all kinds of evil against you falsely for My sake.
> *Rejoice and be exceedingly glad, for great is your reward in*
> *heaven,* for so they persecuted the prophets who were
> before you. (Matt. 5:11-12)

May these truths cause us to bow in humility and yieldedness to our
Savior and Lord and sing…

> Take my life and let it be
> Consecrated, Lord, to Thee.
> Take my moments and my days—
> Let them flow in ceaseless praise;
> Let them flow in ceaseless praise.
>
> Take my hands and let them move
> At the impulse of Thy love.
> Take my feet and let them be
> Swift and beautiful for Thee,
> Swift and beautiful for Thee.

Take my voice and let me sing
Always, only, for my King.
Take my lips and let them be
Filled with messages from Thee,
Filled with messages from Thee.

Take my silver and my gold—
Not a mite would I withhold.
Take my intellect and use
Every power as Thou shalt choose,
Every power as Thou shalt choose.

Take my will and make it Thine—
It shall be no longer mine.
Take my heart—it is Thine own;
It shall be Thy royal throne;
It shall be Thy royal throne.

Take my love—my Lord, I pour
At Thy feet its treasure store.
Take myself and I will be
Ever, only, all for Thee,
Ever, only, all for Thee.[1]

---

[1] Frances R. Havergal, *Take My Life, and Let It Be Consecrated.*

CHAPTER 21

If You Can't Lose Eternal Salvation, What Can You Lose? Part 2

In the previous chapter, we saw that though believers in Christ can never lose eternal salvation, there are still some things they can lose. First, believers can still lose through carnality their future rewards in heaven and even suffer loss during their present lives on earth. This chapter will show that there are at least six other things believers can lose through carnality.

2. **Though the believer in Christ can never lose his eternal salvation, you can still lose (through carnality) your daily FELLOWSHIP WITH GOD in time.**

> That which was from the beginning, which we have heard, which we have seen with our eyes, which we have looked upon, and our hands have handled, concerning the Word of life—the life was manifested, and we have seen, and bear witness, and declare to you that eternal life which was with the Father and was manifested to us—that which we have seen and heard we declare to you, *that you also may have fellowship with us; and truly our fellowship is with the Father and with His Son Jesus Christ.* And these things we write to you that your joy may be full. (1 John 1:1-4)

There are those who teach that 1 John is a series of tests to determine if you are a genuine believer or not. That is a misunderstanding of the book. Those of this persuasion then encourage you to determine your salvation by getting your eyes off Jesus Christ and His finished work (Gal. 3:1) and placing them instead upon your daily fluctuating walk by asking yourself questions like: "Do I confess my sins? Do I obey God? Do I love the brethren? Do I do this or that?" And if I do these things (they allege), I can be assured that I am truly saved and one of God's elect. One of many problems with this way of thinking is that by the time you honestly examine your life in all these areas, you will have lost all assurance of your salvation unless you are arrogant enough to think that your spiritual batting average cuts it. You are looking at yourself and thinking, "What if I don't confess all my sins? How do I know if I am doing this? What if I get bitter or irritated with the brethren instead of loving them? Am I faithfully serving the Lord? And how do I know that my perception of my walk is in keeping with God's as I am prone to self-deception?" What is the core problem in all of this? First of all, you are looking for the assurance of your salvation based on your walk and works instead of on what Christ did for you and the promises of God.

Second, the epistle of 1 John is not about how to enter the family of God and have eternal life, for John already explained this in the Gospel of John. (See John 1:12-13; 3:14-16; 3:36; 5:24; etc., as John states in 20:31, "These are written that you may believe that Jesus is the Christ, the Son of God, and that believing you may have life in His name.") Instead, the purpose statement for 1 John occurs right at the beginning where John writes, "that which we have seen and heard we declare to you, that you also may have *fellowship* with us; and truly our *fellowship* is with the Father and with His Son Jesus Christ. And these things we write to you that *your joy may be full*" (1 John 1:3-4). These introductory verses tell us that John is writing to believers about having fellowship with God. God wants you to have fellowship with Him and His Son with the result that your joy may be overflowing. This is also why the word "fellowship" is used so predominantly in the following verses:

> This is the message which we have heard from Him and declare to you, that God is light and in Him is no darkness at all. If we say that we have *fellowship* with Him, and walk in darkness, we lie and do not practice the truth. But if we walk in the light as He is in the light, we have *fellowship* with one another, and the blood of Jesus Christ His Son cleanses us from all sin. (1 John 1:5-7)

IS 1 JOHN 1 FOR UNBELIEVERS OR BELIEVERS?

Now some argue that the first chapter of 1 John is for unbelievers while the latter chapters are for believers. They even argue that "fellowship" in this chapter is a positional term that communicates to unbelievers that they may enter in "the fellowship of His Son, Jesus Christ" (1 Cor. 1:9). However, this erroneous interpretation can be dismissed when one observes that John includes himself as a believer in the five "if *we*" statements of 1:6-10. Second, the apostle John is not addressing positional truth ("the fellowship") in this chapter as he utilizes a verb, "have fellowship" (1:6-7), instead of a definite article and noun, "the fellowship" as Paul did in 1 Corinthians 1:9. Third, the five statements of 1:6-10 are all third class subjunctive conditional clauses (you might or might not), not positional, indicative realities that are settled possessions and true of every believer. Next, would you instruct unbelievers to walk in the light in order to be saved when it's impossible for them to walk in the light until they are, indeed, saved? Last, would you tell unbelievers to confess their sins to have eternal life? Or would you tell them to simply believe in Jesus Christ alone as presented in the Gospel to possess eternal life right now and forever (John 3:16)? The epistle of 1 John does not instruct the unsaved on how to enter the family of God; instead, it instructs God's children about how to have fellowship with God!

Fellowship is a relational term, whether in reference to fellowship with God or with others. For though a couple may be married, this does not guarantee that they will always enjoy fellowship with one another. In fact, estrangement can occur in a marriage instead of fellowship. And when believers walk in the darkness of sin and falsehood instead of walking in the light of God's holiness and truth, they do not have fellowship with God (1:5-7). The same is true when they cover their sins instead of confessing them to God (1:9-10). Yet a willingness to walk by faith in the light of God's Word (v. 7a) combined with a willingness to confess one's sins to God when the Holy Spirit convicts (v. 9) produces fellowship with God and practical cleansing of sin, resulting in progressive sanctification in a believer's life (vv. 7b, 9b).

However, it is important to note that these wonderful provisions of God's grace are not designed to encourage irresponsibility or sin in the Christian's life. Should believers abuse or misuse these truths as a license to sin? NEVER!

> My little children [a term for believers], *these things I*
> *write to you, so that you may not sin.* (1 John 2:1a)

Victory over sin is God's perfect will, as God does not want Christians to sin and has made abundant provision to prevent (1:7) and correct sin (1:9) in believers' lives. But John then moves from the ideal to the real and the permissive will of God when he adds, "And if anyone sins…" (1 John 2:1b).

Too often believers fail to draw upon God's daily grace provisions and seek to live their lives independent of the Lord resulting in personal sin in thought, word, or deed. But God, who knows our needs and anticipates our failures, directed the apostle John to write that,

> We have an Advocate with the Father, Jesus Christ the
> righteous. And He Himself is the propitiation for our
> sins, and not for ours only but also for the whole world.
> (1 John 2:1c-2)

Jesus Christ is both the *"advocate"* of believers, along with being the *"propitiation"* (satisfactorily payment) for the sins of the whole world. Praise the Lord! This debunks the idea that some believers have that God is on a swivel chair. They wrongly conclude that when you sin as a believer, God swivels away from you; and when you confess your sins, He swivels back. No, that is not what the Bible teaches at all. God the Father has been satisfied forever by the substitutionary sacrifice of Jesus Christ on the cross (Rom. 3:25; 1 John 4:9-10). He offers grace to us freely (Rom. 3:24). His mercies are new every morning (Lam. 3:23). If God has been satisfied, He has no cause to swivel when we sin after being saved and forgiven. Instead, the reality is that believers are the ones who swivel and turn their backs on God and act independently with no regard for or reliance on God. Believers are the ones who cease having fellowship with God. What then is the solution? We are to confess our sins with an attitude that seeks to yield to the Lord and to live in dependence on Him instead of independent of Him, for *"without Me, you can do nothing"* (John 15:5).

THE PRODIGAL SON

The prodigal son in Luke 15:11-24 is a perfect example of a believer who sins, squanders his wealth in carnal living, breaks fellowship with his father, and lives for the pleasures of sin. But when he returns to his father with a willingness to confess his sin and live under his father's terms, his father is waiting with open arms to restore him to fellowship, and there is joy.

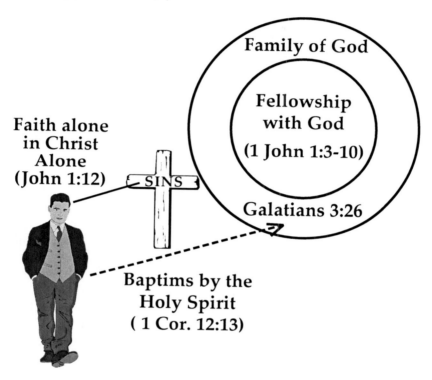

One thing is abundantly evident from the story of the prodigal son. Even in his rebellion towards his father, he remained a *son* and *his father never stopped loving him.* Even if he would have died in the pig pen, he would have died a *son whom his father loved.* His sonship position never changed, but his fellowship with his father changed. This acts as a great illustration of God's unchanging love despite the believer's failures and fluctuating fellowship with God. Although believers can lose fellowship with God, they can never, ever stop being a child of God in God's forever and forgiven family. Believer, are you rejoicing in your eternal security in Christ and walking in the light of God's Word so that you can have fellowship with your gracious and loving heavenly Father? If not, why not stop right now and confess your sins to Him (1 John 1:9a), thank Him for His guaranteed promise of familial forgiveness (1 John 1:9b), forget those things that are behind, and reach for those things that are before you (Phil. 3:13-14) by enjoying the Father's fellowship again?

3. **Though believers in Christ can never lose their eternal salvation, they can lose (through carnality) their JOY and the FRUIT OF THE HOLY SPIRIT in their daily walk.**

> Restore to me the joy of Your salvation (Ps. 51:12).

Notice the heading of Psalm 51: "A Psalm of David when Nathan the prophet went to him, after he had gone in to Bathsheba." This psalm was written after the events of 2 Samuel 11–12 when David committed adultery with Bathsheba and had her husband Uriah murdered. For a long time after these tragic events, David covered his sins until the Lord sent Nathan the prophet to David to point out his sin to him (2 Sam. 12:1-12). Finally, David was brought to repentance and admitted his own sin to the Lord (2 Sam. 12:12-15). Psalm 51 records his thoughts after he was brought to confession and repentance about his sins and carnality.

> Have mercy upon me, O God, according to your lovingkindness; according to the multitude of your tender mercies, blot out my transgressions. Wash me thoroughly from my iniquity, and cleanse me from my sin. For I acknowledge my transgressions, and my sin is always before me. Against You, You only, have I sinned, and done this evil in Your sight—that You may be found just when You speak, and blameless when You judge. (Ps. 51:1-4)

David finally confessed his sin to the Lord and acknowledged, "Against You, You only, have I sinned" (v. 4). When we sin, we ultimately sin against God. David sinned against God and he was miserable. He had lost his fellowship with God and had no inner joy in his life, which is the by-product of fellowship with God (1 John 1:3-4). So what does David consequently pray? "Restore to me the *joy* of Your salvation" (Ps. 51:12). Notice that what David lost during his days of carnality and hard-heartedness was his joy, not his salvation. He did not lose the reality, security, or assurance of his salvation, but the joy of his salvation.

Salvation means deliverance. When we trust in Jesus Christ as Savior, we are delivered from the *penalty* of sin, so that day-by-day we now have the opportunity to enjoy deliverance from the *power* of sin in our lives until the day we go home to be with the Lord in Heaven and are ultimately delivered from the very *presence* of sin in our lives. The phrase, "Restore unto me" indicates that he had lost his joy, for you don't restore something you still have, but you restore something you have lost. When a believer lives in carnality, quits having fellowship with God, and remains in this condition for a period of time, he is capable of anything in the catalogue of sins (see David's actions), and he will lose the joy of his salvation. But when there is honest confession of sin instead of covering it (Prov. 28:13), God is merciful and willing to restore David's fellowship, adjust his thinking, and then even use him again in some spiritual capacity toward others. So now that he was responding to the Lord and having fellowship with God, his concern and vision appropriately turned from himself to others. For notice how Psalm 51 goes on to say in verse 13, "Then I will teach transgressors Your ways, and sinners shall be converted to You."

What is to be your primary concern as a Christian? It should be a vertical relationship with God that consists of a walk of faith and fellowship with Him. After you are experientially forgiven and the joy of your salvation has been restored, only then can God use you for effective ministry to others. Sometimes believers think, "I have been carnal for so long. I don't see how God could ever use me again." While believers do reap what they sow, and it may take time to regain a credible testimony toward others, they need to remember that the Christian life is a grace operation from beginning to end. We all sin at times, and by God's grace when we confess our sins and are restored to fellowship again, God can and will use us afresh to be a testimony and a servant for Jesus Christ. This is part of God's amazing grace and to His glory.

As we consider "joy," Galatians 5:22-23 states, "But the fruit of the Spirit is love, joy, peace, longsuffering, kindness, goodness, faithfulness, gentleness, self-control. Against such there is no law." How is this spiritual fruit produced in the believer's life? Is it by struggle? Is it by self-effort? Is it by making resolutions? Is it by promise-keeping? Is it by trying harder? No! This fruit is only produced by the enabling power of the Holy Spirit as you faith-rest in the Lord. God does not need your help, though He wants to work in and through you by His divine power to do His will and works (2 Cor. 3:5-6)!

Jesus Christ taught His disciples how spiritual fruit is produced—not by the branches, but by the Vine through the branches as they abide in yielded dependence in the Vine (John 15:4-5). It is the fruit of the Holy Spirit; and it is not produced through the believer's efforts in his own strength. (See Paul's failure and trying to do this in Romans 7:14-25.)

> Abide in Me, and I in you. As the branch cannot bear fruit of itself, unless it abides in the vine, neither can you, unless you abide in Me. I am the vine, you are the branches. He who abides in Me, and I in him, bears much fruit; for without Me you can do nothing. (John 15:4-5)

But what occurs when a believer fails to abide in a yielded dependence on the Lord?

> If anyone does not abide in Me, he is cast out as a branch and is withered; and they gather them and throw them into the fire, and they are burned. (John 15:6)

When Jesus Christ made this statement to His disciples, only genuine believers were present, for Judas had already departed to betray Jesus Christ (John 13:21-30). The context is clearly not the believer's eternal salvation but instead the believer's fruit bearing (15:2, 4, 5, 8, 16). Verse 6 makes it clear that a believer can fail to abide in Christ, which is the prerequisite for fruitfulness. The result is not the loss of salvation (which is never stated in this passage) but a lack of fellowship with God, fruitfulness for God, and usefulness to others. For what do people do to unfruitful branches? They gather and burn them. The "fire" mentioned in this verse is not referring to Hell, for not only is this contrary to the context of this passage on fruit bearing, but this verse would then indicate that men could cast other men into Hell, which is absurd! In contrast, our Lord encourages every believer,

> If you abide in Me, and My words abide in you, you will ask what you desire, and it shall be done for you. By this My Father is glorified, that you bear much fruit; so you will be My disciples. (John 15:7-8)

Are you learning to abide daily in dependence on the Lord so that He can produce His fruit through you by means of the Holy Spirit's enablement in your life? Remember what Jesus Christ declared: "Without me you can do nothing" (v. 5c).

Dear believer, these verses teach us that believers can lose their joy and the fruit of the Holy Spirit in their lives, but never their eternal salvation.

4. **Though believers in Christ can never lose their eternal salvation, they can still lose (through carnality) their DIRECTION, PURPOSE, and CAPACITY in life.**

> "Vanity of vanities," says the Preacher; "Vanity of vanities, all is vanity." What profit has a man from all his labor In which he toils under the sun? (Eccl. 1:2-3)

This is the human viewpoint perspective of Solomon, an Old Testament believer who had lived in prolonged carnality. "Vanity" in these verses refers to the emptiness and futility of life, for the basic axiom of the book of Ecclesiastes simply stated is this:

> Apart from a right vertical fellowship with God, man is miserable and life is meaningless.

Solomon, as the king of Israel, had unlimited freedom to indulge his flesh. Yet, when he lived under the control of his sin nature, he discovered afresh,

> All things are full of labor; man cannot express it. The eye is not satisfied with seeing, nor the ear filled with hearing. (Eccl. 1:8)

Our flesh is never satisfied. So when believers walk according to the flesh, they seek to find happiness and meaning in life by running down the dead-end streets of this world's pursuits and pleasures. In doing so, they lose God's direction and purpose for their lives as they seek to wring out happiness from the details of this ungodly world system. This, indeed, is vanity and never ultimately satisfies. Have you ever known believers who have been saved and yet have totally lost their divine direction in life? They are no longer living for things above (Col. 3:1-2); instead they are living for the things on earth which they are commanded not to love (1 John 2:15-17). Perhaps they were saved at a young age, grew up in a Christian home, but during college seriously lost their desire and direction in living for Jesus Christ (Phil. 1:21). They have lost their real meaning in life, while perhaps a few years ago they were growing in the Lord, learning the Word of God, joyously fellowshipping with other believers, and witnessing to the lost. Yet now you would not know by their actions that they were even saved. Perhaps in some cases they never clearly understood the Gospel and never trusted in Christ alone. Perhaps they repented of their sins, asked Jesus into their hearts, surrendered supposedly to Christ's Lordship, and said the sinner's prayer, but they never trusted in Jesus Christ and His work on Calvary alone. Or perhaps they were saved by God's grace in the past but now have strayed from the truth (James 5:19), and are living in temporal death apart from God's fellowship (James 1:13-16). This can happen in our lives. And while the Arminians may be convinced that these people lost their salvation, and the Lordship Calvinists may declare that they were never elect or saved in the first place, is there another explanation that Scripture offers?

> When He had called the people to Himself, with His disciples also, He said to them, "Whoever desires to come after Me, let him deny himself, and take up his cross, and follow Me. For whoever desires to save his life will lose it, but whoever loses his life for My sake and the gospel's will save it. For what will it profit a man if he gains the whole world, and loses his own soul? Or what will a man give in exchange for his soul? For whoever is ashamed of Me and My words in this adulterous and sinful generation, of him the Son of Man also will be ashamed when He comes in the glory of His Father with the holy angels." (Mark 8:34-38)

It is important to note that the Greek word translated "soul" (*psychē* in vv. 36-37) is also translated as "life" (*psychē* in v. 35). Verse 37 is normally used as a reference to an unbeliever with the sense of "What does it profit a man if he gains everything in the whole world and ends up going to Hell?" This is indeed a true scriptural principle, for what value is it to succeed in life and gain riches, fame, and more, yet end up going to Hell forever? However, the context of Mark is addressed to a believer. Jesus does not call on these individuals to "come to Me" for eternal life as He does on other occasions where the context deals with salvation (see Matt. 11:28; John 5:39-40; 6:35-40, 44; 7:37). Instead, this passage is a call for believers to become faithful disciples of Jesus Christ and to "come after Me" (v. 35).

3 TENSES OF SALVATION

PAST TENSE	PRESENT TENSE	FUTURE TENSE
Saved from the **PENALTY** of sin (in Hell)	Saved from the **POWER** of sin (in your life)	Saved from the **PRESENCE** of sin (in Heaven)
Titus 3:5 Ephesians 2:8-9 John 3:17, 10:9 2 Timothy 1:9	2 Corinthians 7:10 1 Timothy 4:16 James 1:21, 2:14, 5:20 Philippians 2:12-13	Romans 5:9-10 Romans 13:11 1 Corinthians 3:15
JUSTIFICATION	**SANCTIFICATION**	**GLORIFICATION**
Happens at a **POINT OF TIME** (When you trust in Christ alone.)	Happens over a **PROCESS OF TIME** (While you walk by faith in the Spirit.)	Happens at a **POINT OF TIME** (When you die or are raptured.)
By God's grace alone through faith alone in Christ alone. (Acts 16:31)	By God's grace through daily dependence on the Lord via the Holy Spirit. (Romans 6:1-14; 8:1-4)	By death (2 Cor. 5:10) or by Rapture. (1 Thess. 4:13-18)

What does it profit a man if he gains everything that this life has to offer but in the process loses his inner capacity for what life is really all about, namely, to enjoy fellowship with and live for Jesus Christ and to do the will of God (Phil. 1:21; Rom. 12:1-2)? He won't hear "Well done thou good and faithful servant" when the Lord returns. Instead, Jesus Christ is ashamed of him for not losing his life in service to Him and the Gospel (Mark 8:38). This carnal believer ends up losing his direction, meaning, purpose, and capacity in life. He loses the wonderful reality that as a believer in Christ he can enjoy daily fellowship with God, and that God has an eternal purpose for his life that far exceeds any of the wealth, riches or duration of this life. What will it profit you if you gain everything this world has to offer and yet you are a spiritual blowout for Jesus Christ? What does it matter?

Consider the example of Demas. If you trace chronologically the few comments in Scripture regarding Demas's life, you will observe that he was viewed as a believer and a trusted companion of Paul. He accompanied Paul on his missionary journeys (Col. 4:14). He was a useful servant of the Lord who was worthy to be noted as a fellow-laborer in the Gospel (Philem. 1:24). Yet there came a point in his Christian life when he lost his God-given direction in life and went back to loving the world (possibly because of the fear of persecution, as Paul wrote about him from a prison cell, "for Demas has forsaken me, having loved this present world" [2 Tim. 4:10]).

What a sad tragedy. Does this prove that Demas was never saved? No! Are we to conclude from the Scriptures that every back-slidden believer was never truly born again? No! Are we to perceive that every believer who fails to stand for Jesus Christ at a time of persecution was never saved to begin with? No! So did Demas lose his salvation? No! But he did lose his direction and purpose in life, and he did lose rewards in Heaven. Later in 2 Timothy 4, the same chapter that describes Demas as "having loved this present world" (v. 10), he stands in stark contrast to the apostle Paul who was soon to die for Jesus Christ by way of martyrdom. What did Paul, by the grace of God, look forward to receiving for persevering in the race and not quitting like Demas? A future reward from the Lord!

> For I am already being poured out as a drink offering, and the time of my departure is at hand. I have fought the good fight, I have finished the race, I have kept the faith. Finally, there is laid up for me the crown of

> righteousness, which the Lord, the righteous Judge,
> will give to me on that Day, and not to me only but also
> to all who have loved His appearing. (2 Tim. 4:6-8)

While Demas chose to "love this present world" and quit following
Jesus Christ in discipleship, Paul chose instead to "love His appearing." We learn from this a basic axiom: love the world now and
lose your future reward later, or love His appearing now and gain
a future reward later. But keep in mind that you can't do both! So
which will it be in your life? If you as a believer choose to live for
yourself and the things of this world, not only will you lose now in
this life, but you also will lose out later.

> For whoever is ashamed of Me and My words in this
> adulterous and sinful generation, of him the Son of Man
> also will be ashamed when He comes in the glory of His
> Father with the holy angels. (Mark 8:38)

Though the context of Mark 8 is Christ's Kingdom teaching to His
disciples, years later John warns Church-age believers in Christ
about the same principle of Mark 8:38 in 1 John 2:28:

> And now, little children, abide in Him, that when He
> appears, we may have confidence and not be ashamed
> before Him at His coming. (1 John 2:28)

Paul also challenged and warned believers about their direction in
life when the Holy Spirit directed him to write:

> Now godliness with contentment is great gain. For we
> brought nothing into this world, and it is certain we can
> carry nothing out. And having food and clothing, with
> these we shall be content. But those who desire to be rich
> fall into temptation and a snare, and into many foolish
> and harmful lusts which drown men in destruction and
> perdition. For the love of money is a root of all kinds of
> evil, for which some have strayed from the faith in their
> greediness, and pierced themselves through with many
> sorrows. But you, O man of God, flee these things and
> pursue righteousness, godliness, faith, love, patience,
> gentleness. (1 Tim. 6:6-11)

Echoing the concepts our Lord taught about "losing your life" in Mark 8, the epistle of James exhorts believers about the daily salvation from sin's power that is available through the Word of God to "save your souls" or save your life from the damaging effects of sin through a life lived apart from divine purposes for the glory of God.

> So then, my beloved brethren, let every man be swift to hear, slow to speak, slow to wrath; for the wrath of man does not produce the righteousness of God. Therefore lay aside all filthiness and overflow of wickedness, and receive with meekness the implanted word, which is able to save your souls. (James 1:19-21)

As believers in Christ, we can lose sight of the very purpose for which God saved us — to glorify Him. We can lose the privilege He gives us to fellowship with Him and the capacity He gives us to be witnesses for Him. When this is true, we not only lose now, but we lose our reward when we stand before the Lord and give an account of our lives at the Judgment Seat of Christ. Instead, we will be ashamed and Jesus Christ will be ashamed of us.

Dear believers, what will be true of you when Christ appears? Will you be confident before the Lord because you repeatedly abided in Christ, or will you be ashamed before your Lord and Savior? And though God's grace and not our guilt should motivate us, we need to take these encouraging or sobering realities to heart! Notice again, while a believer can lose his direction, purpose, and capacity in life, he can never lose his eternal salvation.

5. **Though believers in Christ can never lose their eternal salvation, they can still lose (through carnality) their TESTIMONY and MINISTRY to others.**

> Blessed are those who are persecuted for righteousness' sake, for theirs is the kingdom of heaven. Blessed are you when they revile and persecute you, and say all kinds of evil against you falsely for My sake. Rejoice and be exceedingly glad, for great is your reward in heaven, for so they persecuted the prophets who were before you. You are the salt of the earth; but if the salt loses its flavor, how shall it be seasoned? It is then good for nothing but to be thrown out and trampled underfoot

by men. You are the light of the world. A city that is set
on a hill cannot be hidden. Nor do they light a lamp
and put it under a basket, but on a lampstand, and it
gives light to all who are in the house. Let your light so
shine before men, that they may see your good works
and glorify your Father in heaven. (Matt. 5:10-16)

During the Sermon on the Mount, Jesus Christ gave many clear
and convicting instructions to the Jews who heard Him that were
consistent with His offer to these covenanted people that "the
kingdom of heaven is at hand" (Matt. 4:17). His instructions included
the reality of severe persecution, the opportunity for "reward in
heaven," and the place and importance of good works in the lives
of His disciples. They were to be faithful to their Lord and act as
salt and light, having godly impact and influence in the world. But
the whole implication of the "salt" that "loses its flavor" means that
believers can indeed lose their godly testimony and influence in
the world. Furthermore, a lit lampstand that is put under a basket
does not cease being a lampstand but loses its light and influence
upon others. No wonder our Lord ended by declaring, "Let your
light so shine before men, that they may see your good works and
glorify your Father in heaven." You must never underestimate the
importance of your testimony for Jesus Christ to others by your life
and lip as a blood bought child of God.

Underscoring also the importance of being a godly testimony to
others, Paul (from a prison cell) encourages the Philippian believers
in Christ with these words:

For it is God who works in you both to will and to do for
His good pleasure. Do all things without complaining
and disputing, that you may become blameless and
harmless, children of God without fault in the midst of
a crooked and perverse generation, among whom you
shine as lights in the world, holding fast the word of
life. (Phil. 2:13-16)

Paul challenges these believers about the importance of their godly
life and their testimony to the unsaved world around them, which
he describes as a "crooked and perverse generation." And Paul, like
Jesus Christ in Matthew 5, refers to these believers as "lights in the
world." If you want to be different from the unbelievers you rub

elbows with, and not give them legitimate handles to criticize the Savior you represent, simply be thankful instead of complaining at your place of employment or in your community and cease disputing over trivial, non-doctrinal matters at your local church. How practical the Word of God can be! And how sad that too often the testimony of Jesus Christ toward unbelievers has been soiled by complaining believers, churches filled with foolish division, pastors in moral ruin, and other sins in the lives of God's children. Yet this need not be the case in your life as "it is God that works in you both to will and to do for His good pleasure" (2:13)!

God wants to use you as a light in this dark world. Light exposes darkness. Jesus Christ is the Light of the world, and as we walk by faith in yielded dependence upon Him as our Life, the power of the Holy Spirit and the Word of God will transform our thinking, resulting in a definite difference in what we say, how we think, and how we act compared to the unsaved. And God alone is the One who can transform our lives so that we can have a credible platform by our good works to then preach the Gospel of grace to others.

So again we observe that while a believer can lose his testimony for Christ and ministry to others, he can never lose his eternal salvation.

6. **Though believers in Christ can never lose their eternal salvation, they can still lose (through carnality) their SPIRITUAL EYESIGHT and ETERNAL PERSPECTIVE.**

> For he who lacks these things is shortsighted, even to blindness, and has forgotten that he was cleansed from his old sins. (2 Peter 1:9)

In its context, this verse indicates that believers (1:1) can lose sight of their divine resources in grace (1:2-4), the spiritual growth and fruitfulness that God can produce in their lives (1:5-8), and the fact that life is short and only what is done for Jesus Christ will last in light of eternity (1:9-11). We can lose our spiritual eyesight. We can become short-sighted and lose our eternal perspective.

Every believer has an equal position in Christ and equal blessing from God. The question is whether or not we are going to respond to the Lord and draw upon these grace resources on a daily basis. Are we going to walk by faith with the Lord? Are we going to spiritually grow in the Lord? Will we be fruitful believers or not?

> But also for this very reason, giving all diligence, add to
> your faith virtue, to virtue knowledge, to knowledge self-
> control, to self-control perseverance, to perseverance
> godliness, to godliness brotherly kindness, and to
> brotherly kindness love. For if these things are yours
> and abound, you will be neither barren nor unfruitful in
> the knowledge of our Lord Jesus Christ. (2 Peter 1:5-8)

Every believer is susceptible to spiritual short-sightedness. We can
either daily walk by faith or walk by sight (2 Cor. 5:7). We can either
walk moment by moment by means of the Spirit or fulfill the lusts
of the flesh (Gal. 5:16). We can be diligent in spiritual matters or
become complacent (2 Peter 1:5-8). We can either let the Word of
Christ dwell in us richly or stop spending time in God's Word (Col.
3:16), and when we choose the latter, we start living for today and
the things on the earth so as to lose our heavenly and eternal perspective (Col. 3:1-2).

When I think of this sad possibility, I cannot help but think
of Samson in the Old Testament, who was a strong he-man with a
serious she-weakness. Eventually, through ongoing carnality, he not
only lost his hair and his strength, but the Philistines plucked out his
eyes. Samson temporarily lost his spiritual perspective, but in spite
of his failures, he never lost his eternal salvation and even made the
Hall of Fame of Faith, namely, Hebrews chapter 11 (v. 32). In the
same way, we as believers can lose our spiritual eyesight and eternal
perspective if we walk according to the flesh.

> Therefore, brethren, be even more diligent to make your
> call and election sure, for if you do these things you will
> never stumble. (2 Peter 1:10)

God wants you to know that He has a great purpose for your life. In
keeping with what we have noted in Matthew 5:10-16, Philippians
2:13-16, and James 2:14-26, every believer needs to be diligent in
daily abiding by faith in Christ so as to make his "call and election
sure" or evident to others. Obviously, God knows His elect, and the
believer likewise has the assurance of eternal salvation, but only the
growing and fruitful believer demonstrates his calling and election
by God to others through a clear, godly testimony of life and lip.
And should this be true in an ongoing manner, he will never stumble
into unfruitfulness, a lack of eternal perspective, and disuse in this

context. Will it really be worth it all? Yes, again it will be worth it now as well as in eternity, "For so an entrance will be supplied to you abundantly into the everlasting kingdom of our Lord and Savior Jesus Christ" (2 Peter 1:11).

A key word to observe in this verse is "abundantly," for it means richly or in full measure. While all believers will one day enter "the everlasting kingdom of our Lord and Savior Jesus Christ," some will have an abundant or rich entrance by way of reward! God tells us in verse 11 that every believer in Christ will not only graduate to Heaven one day, but that some will graduate with honors and be rewarded at the Judgment Seat of Christ. Why? Because by God's grace they walked with the Lord, grew in the Lord, bore fruit for the Lord, and served the Lord as a good and godly testimony to others.

Once again we see the Scriptures beautifully harmonize when you "rightly divide the word of truth" (2 Tim. 2:15) so as to conclude that while a believer can lose his spiritual eyesight and eternal perspective, he can never lose his eternal salvation.

7.   **Though believers in Christ can never lose their salvation, they can still lose (through carnality) their spiritual and doctrinal STABILITY and even their FAITH.**

> You therefore, beloved, since you know this beforehand, beware lest you also fall from your own steadfastness, being led away with the error of the wicked. (2 Peter 3:17)

Is it possible for believers ("beloved") to "fall" from their own "steadfastness"? Absolutely! That's what this verse warns against! In the context of 2 Peter, this warning was necessary because of the inroads of false teaching which the epistle repeatedly exposes (read chapter 2–3). The reality of such potential damage caused by false teaching explains why the apostle Paul rejoiced in the Colossian believers "to see your good order and the steadfastness of your faith in Christ" (Col. 2:5). Yet knowing that the danger of false teachers lurked in their midst, he warned the Colossians: "Beware lest anyone cheat you through philosophy and empty deceit, according to the tradition of men, according to the basic principles of the world, and not according to Christ" (Col. 2:8).

Can believers fall from their salvation? No. Can they fall from their steadfastness personally and doctrinally? Yes! Thus, in order not to fall, what is necessary? "But grow in the grace and knowledge of our Lord and Savior Jesus Christ. To Him be the glory both now and forever. Amen" (2 Peter 3:18).

The word "but" forms an important contrast from verse 17. Peter is warning believers to be on guard regarding false teachers; otherwise, they could fall from their own steadfastness. Unfortunately, this describes too many believers in our day. Peter exhorts these believers to instead "grow in the grace and knowledge of our Lord and Savior Jesus Christ." The word "grow" denotes choosing (active voice) the path for ongoing (present tense) and necessary (imperative mood) spiritual progress in one's Christian life in contrast to falling from one's steadfastness. This commanded spiritual growth is "in [not 'into'] the grace and knowledge" of our wonderful "Lord and Savior Jesus Christ." And why should we grow and be occupied with Him? It is because "to Him [belongs] the glory both now and forever." And all God's people said, "Amen!" In keeping with Peter's exhortation, Paul also wrote and warned,

> I charge you therefore before God and the Lord Jesus Christ, who will judge the living and the dead at His appearing and His kingdom: Preach the word! Be ready in season and out of season. Convince, rebuke, exhort, with all longsuffering and teaching. For the time will come when they will not endure sound doctrine, but according to their own desires, because they have itching ears, they will heap up for themselves teachers; and they will turn their ears away from the truth, and be turned aside to fables. But you be watchful in all things, endure afflictions, do the work of an evangelist, fulfill your ministry. (2 Tim. 4:1-5)

This important passage highlights every pastor and teacher's serious responsibility and accountability before God to faithfully preach the Word of God in both a doctrinal and practical way. Is this not desperately needed in the pulpits and churches of our day? If you are a pastor or teacher, the bottom line is not, "Did the people like my message today?" but "Was the Lord pleased with my message today?" So you can be either popular or faithful—take your pick! But this is not to imply that the people in the pew always want to hear sound doctrine that is filled with reproof, rebuke, and exhortation. In fact, verses 3 and 4 make it clear that there comes a time "when they will not endure sound doctrine, but according to their own desires, because they have itching ears, they will heap up for themselves teachers; and they will turn their ears away from the truth, and be turned aside to fables." But to whom does the "they" in these verses refer? In that Timothy was involved in pastoral ministry in the church of Ephesus, the "they" in these verses refers to believers. Paul predicts that there would come a time when these believers no longer wanted to hear sound doctrine. So did they quit assembling with others? No, instead they heaped to themselves teachers that would tickle their ears instead of challenging their hearts with sound doctrine and practical applications!

In addition, Paul had demonstrated in his first letter to Timothy the reality of believing teachers shifting doctrinally and even requiring serious church discipline.

> This charge I commit to you, son Timothy, according to the prophecies previously made concerning you, that by them you may wage the good warfare, having faith and a good conscience, which some having rejected, concerning the faith have suffered shipwreck, of whom are Hymenaeus and Alexander, whom I delivered to Satan that they may learn not to blaspheme. (1 Tim. 1:18-20)

You cannot wreck a ship that doesn't exist. In the same way you cannot shipwreck a faith that never was personally embraced or possessed. Paul mentions these saved yet false teachers by name (Hymenaeus and Alexander) and their church discipline in the form of excommunication from the local church which is clearly spelled out, "whom I delivered to Satan" (cf. 1 Cor. 5:1-5). But while this needed action was designed to protect believers from their false teaching, this church discipline also had a personal benefit or goal for these teachers who had strayed from the truth. What was it? Verse 20 states, "that they may learn not to blaspheme." The word "learn" is used of child-training or divine discipline of Christians, indicating that believers, not unbelievers, are in view in this verse.

The sad but stark reality of how false teaching can overthrow a believer's biblical beliefs is further delineated earlier in 2 Timothy.

> Be diligent to present yourself approved to God, a worker who does not need to be ashamed, rightly dividing the word of truth. But shun profane and idle bab-

blings, for they will increase to more ungodliness. And their message will spread like cancer. Hymenaeus and Philetus are of this sort, who have strayed concerning the truth, saying that the resurrection is already past; and they *overthrow the faith of some.* (2:15-18)

Several observations are necessary regarding this passage. Two of the divine prescriptions for staying faithful to the Lord and sound scriptural doctrine are to study and accurately handle the word of truth (v. 15), and avoid false teachers (v. 16). Unfortunately, the Church of Jesus Christ is lacking in sound exegesis and proper biblical separation in our day because many people view them as "unloving." But a failure to apply these biblical principles will result in false teaching slowly affecting believers like gangrene (translated "cancer" in v. 17) for which the cure in the first century was amputation (Paul's directive as well). Again, Paul names some of these false teachers, such as Hymenaeus and Philetus. This is the same Hymenaeus mentioned in 1 Timothy 1:20, which indicates that church discipline is not always effective in bringing a false teacher to repentance and sound doctrine, yet it is still needed to protect others. What was the standard for determining a pastor or teacher's accuracy or lack thereof? "Who have strayed concerning *the truth*" (v. 18a). What was the specific indictment against these men? "Saying that *the resurrection is already past*" (v. 18b). And how did this false teaching affect others? "And they *overthrow the faith* of some" (v. 18c). Can one overthrow the faith of another if that faith doesn't already exist? Are we to somehow conclude that their false teaching only affected unbelievers and that these were the non-elect? While some theologies teach this, the context and content of this passage strongly argues that those affected were believers whose faith was "overthrown." Should a Christian's faith be overthrown? No! Can a believer's faith or doctrinal beliefs be overthrown? The Scriptures emphatically say, YES!

In fact, do we not all know some believers to whom this has unfortunately happened? Perhaps you know someone who trusted in Jesus Christ by faith but later went astray doctrinally or practically while in college, or after a divorce, or by attending an apostate church, or in some other circumstance. I read a few years ago that the Mormon Church (which denies the unique and absolute deity of Jesus Christ and preaches "another gospel") claims that forty percent of their converts come from Baptist backgrounds. If this is even remotely true, are we to conclude that none of these converts to Mormonism were ever saved? Are we to believe that all of them were just "counterfeit" Christians and "non-elect"? Or perhaps, even if *many* were not genuine believers in Jesus Christ alone as presented in the Gospel, could it be that *some* were truly saved but became like those of Paul's day whose faith was overthrown or whose faith had become shipwrecked?

While a believer can lose his biblical, doctrinal moorings, is his eternal salvation ever in jeopardy? Never! Why? The answer occurs earlier in this same chapter of 2 Timothy: "If we are faithless, He remains faithful; He cannot deny Himself" (2 Tim. 2:13). Praise the Lord! Yet may we take these warnings and examples seriously, for 1 Corinthians 10:12 says, "Therefore let him who thinks he stands take heed lest he fall."

May we also take to heart the admonitions to guard the truths we have come to understand from the Scriptures and to personally separate from false teaching when necessary.

> O Timothy! Guard what was committed to your trust, avoiding the profane and idle babblings and contradictions of what is falsely called knowledge—by professing it some have strayed concerning the faith. Grace be with you. Amen. (1 Tim. 6:20-21)

Let's Summarize:

Carnality has its price and it is costly. While it will not cost you as a child of God your eternal salvation, which is eternally secure by God's grace and power, it can cost you:

1. your REWARD in Heaven.

2. your FELLOWSHIP with God

3. your JOY and the FRUIT OF THE HOLY SPIRIT in your walk.

4. your DIRECTION, MEANING, PURPOSE, and CAPACITY in life.

5. your TESTIMONY and MINISTRY to others.

6. your SPIRITUAL EYESIGHT and ETERNAL PERSPECTIVE.

7. your spiritual and doctrinal STABILITY and even your FAITH.

Dear friends, while we should not give a false sense of the assurance of salvation to those who have never trusted in Jesus alone as Savior, nor should we crush the assurance of salvation of those who are struggling and failing in their Christian lives. While the former need a clear explanation and invitation to trust in Christ alone for their eternal salvation, the latter need to know that they are forever secure in God's love and family. Only then can they come to understand their position in Christ and how He has freed them from the reigning power of sin through their identification with Him (Rom. 6:1-7), and now makes available to them the opportunity to daily "walk in newness of life" (Rom. 6:4) by yielded dependence upon the Lord (Rom. 6:11-14) and through the power of the Holy Spirit (Rom. 8:1-4). Pulling the rug of assurance out from under these believers in Christ who may be struggling with life-dominating sins is not God's solution to enable them to escape these deep struggles.

While you as a believer can lose any or all of these seven spiritual realities covered in the last two chapters, you must keep in mind that this is not God's will for your life. God has saved you by His grace, and God will one day bring you to Heaven to be with Him forever. In the meantime, God has a definite purpose for your life, namely, to glorify Him; and He wants to fellowship with you, mature you into Christ-likeness, and enable you to be useful for Him in impacting and ministering to others for His glory. Are you willing? Will you be able to say with Paul that you have fought the good fight, finished the race, and kept the faith (through God's power), and that as a result there is laid up for you the reward of a crown at the Judgment Seat of Christ? By God's grace and to His glory may this be true of you!

Where He leads me I must follow
Without Him I'd lose my way
I will see a bright tomorrow
If I follow Him today

Like a lamb who needs the Shepherd
At His side I'll always stay
Through the night His strength I'll borrow
Then I'll see another day

Life is like a winding pathway
Who can tell what lies ahead?
Will it lead to shady pastures,
Or to wilderness instead?

Like a lamb who needs the Shepherd
When into the night I go
Help me find the path that's narrow
While I travel here below

Though you walk through darkest valleys
And the sky is cold and gray
Though you climb the steepest mountains
He will never let you stray

Like a lamb who needs the Shepherd
By your side He'll always stay
'Til the end of life's long journey
He will lead you all the way[1]

---

[1] Ralph Carmichael, *Like a Lamb Who Needs the Shepherd.*

Part V

Probing the
Perplexing Passages

CHAPTER 22

By Their Fruits You Will Know Them
(Matthew 7:15-23)

As a new believer, I rejoiced greatly in my eternal salvation and security in Christ. And with great enthusiasm I began to read the Bible and "desire the pure milk of the Word" as a "newborn babe" (1 Peter 2:2). However, I began to find certain verses that were perplexing to me, which, at first glance, seemed to contradict the wonderful truth of salvation by grace and the reality of my eternal security in Christ. Since I believed that the Bible correctly understood never contradicts itself, I was convinced that there were reasonable and contextual explanations for each of these perplexing verses. And there are! Perhaps as you have read this book you find yourself in the same boat as me in the past. You may be thinking, "This sounds really good, but what about that verse in . . . ?" In the next several chapters, I will interact scripturally and contextually with many of the so-called "problem passages" that people raise to deny or call into question the biblical doctrines of eternal security and assurance. I will devote a significant amount of space to several major passages that are often brought up when discussing the issue of eternal security since they require more in-depth explanations. To many of the lesser known passages that are twisted to seek to disprove this wonderful biblical doctrine, I devote less space. May you again be challenged to be like the Bereans of old (Acts 17:10-12) and search the Scriptures carefully with me by considering the context, examining the content, and comparing Scripture with Scripture to arrive at sound, scriptural conclusions. May God bless you as you do so and may the Holy Spirit grant you His illumination of the text in its context (2 Tim. 2:7).

BEWARE OF FALSE PROPHETS

> Beware of false prophets, who come to you in sheep's clothing, but inwardly they are ravenous wolves. You will know them by their fruits. Do men gather grapes from thorn bushes or figs from thistles? Even so, every good tree bears good fruit, but a bad tree bears bad fruit. A good tree cannot bear bad fruit, nor can a bad tree bear good fruit. Every tree that does not bear good fruit is cut down and thrown into the fire. Therefore by their fruits you will know them. Not everyone who says to Me, "Lord, Lord," shall enter the kingdom of heaven, but he who does the will of My Father in heaven. Many will say to Me in that day, "Lord, Lord, have we not prophesied in Your name, cast out demons in Your name, and done many wonders in Your name?" And then I will declare to them, "I never knew you; depart from Me, you who practice lawlessness!" (Matt. 7:15-23)

This passage is often used to support the idea that the reality of someone's faith can be tested by the amount and kind of fruit in that person's life, since "by their fruits you will know them." Allegedly, those who do not have enough practical righteousness will hear Christ say at the final judgment, "I never knew you; depart from Me, you who practice lawlessness!" Does this mean that Christ will reject a person for not having done enough righteous works even though that person has supposedly trusted in Jesus Christ alone as his only hope of salvation? Is this passage teaching that a life of obedience to the lordship of Christ is needed to prove the genuineness of a person's "saving relationship" with Christ? Such an interpretation totally misses the point of Christ's teaching. In the context, the false prophets by their lifestyle were externally indistinguishable from the true believers since they looked like sheep (v. 15). The "fruit" which would reveal their true spiritual status (vv. 16-20) would be the profession and teaching that came from their mouths, not the externals of their lifestyles. Remember, these are *false prophets*!

This is also how Christ Himself defines fruit in Matthew 12:33-37, which is a parallel passage: "For a tree is known by its fruit. Brood of vipers! How can you, being evil, speak good things? For out of the abundance of the heart the mouth speaks" (vv. 33b-34). "For by your words you will be justified, and by your words you will be condemned" (v. 37). In the context of Matthew 12, the Jewish leaders professed with their own mouths that the Holy Spirit was not the power source for Jesus' miracles and teaching. Therefore, they stated that He was not the Messiah but was instead a demonically indwelt imposter (vv. 18-32).

The context and point of Matthew 7:13-23 is similar. Christ summarizes the "fruit" coming from the lips of the unsaved false prophets (vv. 15–20) in the verses that follow: "Not everyone who says to Me, 'Lord, Lord,' shall enter the kingdom of heaven, but he who does the will of My Father in heaven. Many will say to Me in that day, 'Lord, Lord, have we not prophesied in Your name, cast out demons in Your name, and done many wonders in Your name'" (vv. 21-22). Such people plead their own works before Christ (prophesied, cast out demons, done many wonders) as the basis on which He should accept them. Jesus Christ stated twice to emphasize that these people even profess His lordship: "Lord, Lord"! Yet they were never saved and never had a relationship with Christ ("I never knew you") because they depended still on their own religious works as the basis for God's acceptance, rather than trusting in the sufficiency of Christ (see Rom. 9:30–10:4). It is impossible to be justified before God on the basis of our own deeds and righteousness (Matt. 5:20; 19:16-30; Luke 18:9-14; Isa. 64:6). Justification before God is a gift of God by faith in His Son (Matt. 21:21-32; Phil. 3:8-9). To all who have refused to trust in Christ alone but instead rely on their own righteousness and good works as the basis for eternal life, Christ will say, "I *never* knew you" (Matt. 7:23). Christ will not say to them, "I *once* knew you but you lost salvation because you didn't have enough good works." This passage is not addressing the loss of eternal salvation but how to (and not to) obtain it in the first place.

Dear reader, is your faith in Christ *plus* or Christ *period*? For to truly know Jesus Christ by faith is to have eternal life (John 17:3)!

> I know not why God's wondrous grace
> To me He hath made known,
> Nor why, unworthy, Christ in love
> Redeemed me for His own.
>
> I know not when my Lord may come,
> At night or noonday fair,
> Nor if I walk the vale with Him,
> Or meet Him in the air.

But "I know Whom I have believed,
And am persuaded that He is able
To keep that which I've committed
Unto Him against that day."[1]

---

[1] Daniel W. Whittle, *I Know Whom I Have Believed*.

CHAPTER 23

Have You Committed the Unpardonable Sin?
(Matthew 12:31-32)

Many who are uncertain of their salvation or who deny the eternal security of the believer in Christ will raise the inquiry or objection, "But what about the blasphemy against the Holy Spirit?" In response I've asked, "What exactly is the blasphemy against the Holy Spirit?" And with a look of confusion on their faces they've replied in essence, "I don't know, but whatever it is, DON'T DO IT!" To answer this question biblically, we need to examine the *context* in Matthew 12:22-32:

> Then one was brought to Him who was demon-possessed, blind and mute; and He healed him, so that the blind and mute man both spoke and saw. And all the multitudes were amazed and said, "Could this be the Son of David?" Now when the Pharisees heard it they said, "This fellow does not cast out demons except by Beelzebub, the ruler of the demons." But Jesus knew their thoughts, and said to them: "Every kingdom divided against itself is brought to desolation, and every city or house divided against itself will not stand. If Satan casts out Satan, he is divided against himself. How then will his kingdom stand? And if I cast out demons by Beelzebub, by whom do your sons cast them out? Therefore they shall be your judges. But if I cast out demons by the Spirit of God, surely the kingdom of God has come upon you. Or how can one enter a strong man's house and plunder his goods, unless he first binds

the strong man? And then he will plunder his house. He who is not with Me is against Me, and he who does not gather with Me scatters abroad. Therefore I say to you, every sin and blasphemy will be forgiven men, but the blasphemy against the Spirit will not be forgiven men. Anyone who speaks a word against the Son of Man, it will be forgiven him; but whoever speaks against the Holy Spirit, it will not be forgiven him, either in this age or in the age to come.

This event occurred during Jesus Christ's earthly ministry. Prior to this in the book of Matthew, it is recorded that Jesus' fame and followers were steadily increasing. Yet this passage highlights a dramatic and definitive change in direction. It all started with Christ's instantaneous, total, and undeniable healing of a demoniac that clearly displayed and demonstrated His miraculous power over both the spiritual world of demons and the physical world of disease (v. 22). This caused the people to be amazed and to repeatedly utter the claim, "Is this not the son of David?" (v. 23), a rhetorical question that perceived and proclaimed Jesus to be their rightful Messiah. Unable to deny the obvious reality of the demoniac's exorcism and healing, the Pharisees reacted quickly and resorted to denying that the Holy Spirit's power accomplished the miracle by attributing the healing to the power of Beelzebub or Satan (v. 24). Jesus then toppled the flimsy foundation of their denial by disclosing that their claim was illogical (vv. 25-26) and biased (v. 27).

Our Lord then raised another possibility for the Pharisees to evaluate when he stated, "But if I cast out demons by the Spirit of God, surely the kingdom of God has come upon you" (v. 28). In other words, Jesus is the Messiah and this miracle proves and proclaims His power is from the Holy Spirit. Then, to reinforce this conclusion, Jesus reasoned that to overcome Satan requires someone stronger than Satan, which leaves only one possibility: God (v. 29)! This irrefutable argument allows for no argument or alternative and no further debate (v. 30).

Having observed the *context* of this passage, let's now examine its *content*.

Therefore I say to you, every sin and blasphemy will be forgiven men, but the blasphemy against the Spirit will not be forgiven men. Anyone who speaks a word against the Son of Man, it will be forgiven him; but whoever speaks against the Holy Spirit, it will not be forgiven him, either in this age or in the age to come. Either make the tree good and its fruit good, or else make the tree bad and its fruit bad; for a tree is known by its fruit. (Matt. 12:31-33)

The Bible abounds with statements of God's amazing and awesome forgiveness to undeserving sinners. He gives this divine forgiveness regardless of the severity, amount, or kind of sin(s) that have been committed because of His character and the once and for all payment for sins that Christ made on the cross for the whole world. So why would God refuse forgiveness on this occasion? To understand this, we need to answer five key questions.

What exactly is the "blasphemy against the Holy Spirit"?

The word "blasphemy" means to speak against someone, to slander, or to insult. It is clear that this is a verbal sin that emanates or emerges from a sinful heart. Thus, to claim that Jesus performed this miracle through the power of Beelzebub seriously slandered and insulted the Holy Spirit, the real source of power behind Jesus' miracles. Thus the religious leaders' conclusion about Jesus was that He most definitely was not the Son of David, and He was not even a good man. This clear rejection of Jesus as the Messiah was publicly done by these religious leaders who represented the nation as a whole.

Who committed the "blasphemy against the Holy Spirit"?

Was it genuine believers in Jesus Christ who had known the joy of their sins totally forgiven but had now somehow undone (no forgiveness) what God had previously done for them (forgiven them)? NO! It was the unsaved Pharisees who rejected Jesus as the Messiah and who were trusting their religious works instead of Christ's to receive the righteousness of God. On another occasion, Jesus would say to these Pharisees, "You search the Scriptures, for in them you think you have eternal life; and these are they which testify of Me. But you are unwilling to come to Me that you may have life" (John 5:39-40). The Lord Jesus reserved His most scathing words of condemnation for these unsaved, religious Pharisees (read Matthew 23). As unbelievers, rather than believers who lost their salvation, Jesus Christ states in a parallel account of this event, "Assuredly, I say to you, all sins will be forgiven the sons of men, and whatever blasphemies they may utter; but he who blasphemes against the Holy Spirit never has forgiveness, but is subject to eternal condemnation" (Mark 3:28-29).

What did the verbal sin of "blasphemy against the Holy Spirit" reveal?

This slanderous claim laid bare a hard heart of unbelief in the face of revealed truth. The Pharisees did not sin because they lacked sufficient information about Jesus Christ. They had heard His teaching, and never a man taught like Him. They had also witnessed numerous displays of miraculous power in keeping with the Old Testament predictions regarding Israel's promised Messiah, so that some proclaimed, "It was never seen like this in Israel" (Matt. 9:33). The core issue was these religious rulers' unbelief — plain and simple. And what did they conclude in their unbelief? "He has an unclean spirit" (Mark 3:30). Instead of receiving Him as their Redeemer, they rejected Him and falsely determined that He was demon-indwelt and empowered. Their words divulged their hard hearts of unbelief.

> Either make the tree good and its fruit good, or else make the tree bad and its fruit bad; for a tree is known by its fruit. Brood of vipers! How can you, being evil, speak good things? For out of the abundance of the heart the mouth speaks. (Matt. 12:33-34)

So why did they reject Jesus as the Messiah. Because he exposed their inability of trying to keep the Law to save them (Rom. 9:30-34), Jesus just didn't fit their own perceptions of what the Messiah was supposed to say and do (Luke 7:30-35), and they wanted to protect their religious system (John 11:47-48). Are these still not problems that hinder people today from humbling themselves and placing their faith in Jesus Christ alone as their Savior?

Why can't the sin of the "blasphemy against the Holy Spirit" be forgiven?

Is this a sin that is beyond God's forgiveness? Is this a sin that the blood of Christ somehow misses? No! The reason for the lack of divine forgiveness is almost so simple and obvious that it's easy to miss. For what is the one biblical condition that God places on sinners in order to have their sins forgiven? It is simple child-like faith in Jesus Christ alone. And what were these Pharisees unwilling to do even after repeatedly receiving the convincing and convicting revelation of truth regarding Jesus Christ? They would not put their trust in Him and acknowledge Him for Who He is and for what His miracles demonstrated about Him. They would not believe He was the genuine Messiah who would save them from their sins by simple faith in Him. Therefore, Jesus Christ declared that "it will not be forgiven him, either in this age or in the age to come" (v. 32). This is consistent with such verses as,

> He who believes in Him is not condemned; but he who does not believe is condemned already, because he has not believed in the name of the only begotten Son of God. (John 3:18)

> To Him all the prophets witness that, through His name, whoever believes in Him will receive remission of sins. (Acts 10:43)

> Therefore I said to you that you will die in your sins; for if you do not believe that I am He, you will die in your sins. (John 8:24)

Though there was a personal rejection of Jesus Christ through unbelief, the breadth of this sin reaches far beyond any individual. The blasphemy against the Holy Spirit revolves around the Jewish national rejection of Jesus as the Messiah by their leaders and God then laying aside of His offer of the long awaited kingdom which would now be postponed but not cancelled (see Romans 11). This passage has strong national overtones in light of Matthew's flow of thought, argument, and clumping of significant events in this book. All of these are designed to communicate the significance of this specific event in which the religious leaders of Israel make a representative and hardened decision to once and for all reject Jesus as the Christ/Messiah. Observe the progression of events in the following chart.

The Basic Outline of Matthew

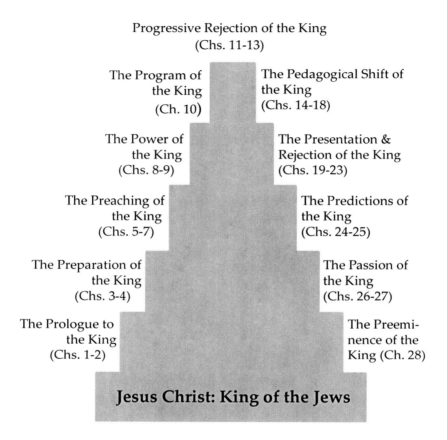

Progressive Rejection of the King
(Chs. 11-13)

The Program of
the King
(Ch. 10)

The Pedagogical Shift of
the King
(Chs. 14-18)

The Power of
the King
(Chs. 8-9)

The Presentation &
Rejection of the King
(Chs. 19-23)

The Preaching of
the King
(Chs. 5-7)

The Predictions of
the King
(Chs. 24-25)

The Preparation of
the King
(Chs. 3-4)

The Passion of
the King
(Chs. 26-27)

The Prologue to
the King
(Chs. 1-2)

The Preemi-
nence of the
King (Ch. 28)

Jesus Christ: King of the Jews

Can the "blasphemy against the Holy Spirit"
still be committed today?

This event chronicles a change in the book of Matthew as the religious
leaders' rejection of Jesus as the Messiah or Christ sealed the fate
and future judgment of this generation in the nation of Israel. This
is indicated a few chapters later when we hear from the lips of the
Lord Jesus for the first time the prediction,

> And I also say to you that you are Peter, and on this
> rock *I will build My church,* and the gates of Hades shall
> not prevail against it. (Matt. 16:18)

A few verse later we then read for the first time,

> *From that time Jesus began* to show to His disciples that
> He must go to Jerusalem, and suffer many things from
> the elders and chief priests and scribes, and be killed,
> and be raised the third day. (Matt. 16:21)

In addition, Jesus Christ would later announce divine judgment on
this generation of Jews that had rejected Him by stating,

> "Therefore, indeed, I send you prophets, wise men,
> and scribes: some of them you will kill and crucify, and
> some of them you will scourge in your synagogues and
> persecute from city to city, that on you may come all
> the righteous blood shed on the earth, from the blood
> of righteous Abel to the blood of Zechariah, son of
> Berechiah, whom you murdered between the temple
> and the altar. Assuredly, I say to you, *all these things will
> come upon this generation.* O Jerusalem, Jerusalem, the
> one who kills the prophets and stones those who are
> sent to her! How often I wanted to gather your children
> together, as a hen gathers her chicks under her wings,
> *but you were not willing!* See! Your house is left to you
> desolate; for I say to you, you shall see Me no more till
> you say, 'Blessed is He who comes in the name of the
> LORD!'" (Matt. 23:34-39)

God's description of this generation of unbelieving Jews and His
lack of forgiveness is reinforced by Peter on the day of Pentecost
(though there was a way out) when he proclaimed,

> And with many other words he testified and exhorted
> them, saying, *"Be saved from this perverse generation."*
> Then those who gladly received his word were baptized;
> and that day about three thousand souls were added to
> them. (Acts 2:40-41)

Arnold Fruchtenbaum states it well when he writes,

> In verses 30-37, [Jesus] pronounced a judgment on
> the Jewish generation of that day. That generation
> had committed the unpardonable sin; the blasphemy

against the Holy Spirit. The unpardonable sin was not an individual sin but a national sin. It was committed by that generation of Israel in Jesus' day and cannot be applied to future generations. The content and definition of the unpardonable sin is the national rejection of the Messiahship of Jesus by Israel while He was physically present on the basis that He was demon possessed. This sin is unpardonable, and judgment was set. The judgment came in the year A.D. 70 with the destruction of Jerusalem and the Temple and the worldwide dispersion of the Jewish people. It was a national sin committed by the generation of Jesus' day and for that generation, the sin was unpardonable.[1]

It is interesting to note that after this event the Bible never again utilizes the phrase, "blasphemy against the Holy Spirit" to describe a future event or to underscore a person's rejection of Jesus Christ. This phrase is limited to Israel's national rejection of Jesus Christ in these events recorded during Christ's earthly ministry. It is also important to note that this sin was not done by genuine believers, resulting in the loss of their eternal salvation. In contrast, it was done by unbelieving religious sinners who were unwilling to put their trust in Jesus Christ alone. Lastly, while the Scriptures indicate that believers can "lie to the Holy Spirit" (Acts 5:3), "grieve the Holy Spirit" (Eph. 4:30), "quench the Spirit" (1 Thess. 5:19), "walk in the Spirit" (Gal. 5:16), and "be filled with the Spirit" (Eph. 5:18) in their daily walk with the Lord, the Bible NEVER TEACHES that believers in Christ (or even unbelievers today) can ever technically blaspheme the Holy Spirit or lose their eternal salvation. Praise the Lord!

Let's Summarize

The blasphemy against the Holy Spirit was the sin of attributing the miracles of Jesus Christ to the power of Satan or Beelzebub instead of the power of the Holy Spirit, thus blaspheming the Holy Spirit. Because this sin was spawned by hardhearted unbelief against the divine revelation of Jesus Christ's miracles that demonstrated His deity and Messiahship (Matt. 8–11), this sin could not be forgiven since one must believe in Him to be forgiven (Acts 10:43). This sin

---

[1] Arnold G. Fruchtenbaum, *Israelology: The Missing Link in Systematic Theology* (Tustin, CA: Ariel Ministries, 1993), 617.

committed by unbelieving Jewish leaders marks the official national rejection of Jesus Christ which culminated later in His crucifixion. From this point forward, Christ withdraws His previous offer of the kingdom of Heaven being "at hand" and then begins to announce that He would "build His church" (Matt. 16:18) and would suffer, die, and be raised from the dead (Matt. 16:21). This passage does not teach that a believer in Christ can lose his eternal salvation since these Jewish religious leaders were unbelievers and never saved.

So do you need to fear that you may have blasphemed the Holy Spirit? No! It was a Jewish national sin in rejecting their Messiah. And need you fear that your sins are so great that they are beyond the forgiveness of God's mercy and grace? Not true! Consider carefully the following statement by Saul of Tarsus, who had been a Jewish unbeliever and persecutor of Christians but later became the apostle Paul, the great defender of the Gospel of Jesus Christ:

> And I thank Christ Jesus our Lord who has enabled me, because He counted me faithful, putting me into the ministry, although I was formerly a blasphemer, a persecutor, and an insolent man; but I obtained mercy because I did it ignorantly in unbelief. And the grace of our Lord was exceedingly abundant, with faith and love which are in Christ Jesus. This is a faithful saying and worthy of all acceptance, that Christ Jesus came into the world to save sinners, of whom I am chief. However, for this reason I obtained mercy, that in me first Jesus Christ might show all longsuffering, as a pattern to those who are going to believe on Him for everlasting life. (1 Tim. 1:12-16)

If God by His grace and mercy could save the chief of sinners, He can also save you. How? Through simple faith in Him Jesus Christ and His finished work alone! Are you "going to believe on Him for eternal life" or not? Why not do it right now and settle this crucial issue forever?

O Lord my God! When I in awesome wonder
Consider all the works Thy hand hath made,
I see the stars, I hear the mighty thunder,
Thy power throughout the universe displayed;

And when I think that God His Son not sparing,
Sent Him to die – I scarce can take it in,
That on the cross my burden gladly bearing,
He bled and died to take away my sin:

When Christ shall come with shout of acclamation
And take me home what joy shall fill my heart!
Then I shall bow in humble adoration
And there proclaim, my God, how great Thou art!

Then sings my soul, my Savior God, to Thee,
How great Thou art, how great Thou art!
Then sings my soul, my Savior God, to Thee,
How great Thou art, how great Thou art![2]

---

[2] Stuart K. Hine, *How Great Thou Art*.

CHAPTER 24

Can a Believer Fall Away?
(Hebrews 6:4-6)

"For it is impossible for those who were once enlightened, and have tasted the heavenly gift, and have become partakers of the Holy Spirit, and have tasted the good word of God and the powers of the age to come, if they fall away, to renew them again to repentance, since they crucify again for themselves the Son of God, and put Him to an open shame."

Who Are the Recipients of This Epistle?

This epistle addresses believers in Christ (3:1, 12; 4:14-16; 5:13; 6:1, 9-12, 19; 10:10, 14, 19-25, 32-39; 12:1-15; 13:20-21) who had experienced persecution in the past from their Jewish community (10:32-34). They could also expect more in the future if they continued to follow Jesus Christ (13:12-13). Thus, this epistle urges them to persevere in faith (10:35-39) by recognizing that Jesus Christ is superior ("better") in His person (1:1–4:13) and His work (4:14–10:18) than the angels, Moses, the Levitical priesthood, and its sacrifices. Therefore, the writer encourages theses believers to "hold fast the confession of our hope without wavering, for He who promised is faithful" (10:23).

What Was Their Condition and Problem?

In explaining the superiority of Christ's priesthood (4:14–7:28), the writer temporarily stops his teaching on this subject to exhort some of these believers about their present spiritual retrogression. He states that they were "dull of hearing" (5:11); they needed basic remedial teaching "again" (v. 12); they had slipped backwards in their growth into babyhood ("babe") and could only handle the "milk" of the Word (v. 13) because of their failure to actively hear and "use" the Word of God by faith (v. 14). Thus, he challenges them to face this retrogression seriously and to "go on to perfection" or spiritual maturity (6:1). This is a clarion call and plea to renewed spiritual growth in maturity ("perfection" 6:1).

What Is the Historical Context of This Epistle?

This exhortation would be appropriate only *for a believer*, since an unbeliever lacks spiritual birth and is thus incapable of spiritual growth. But for this growth to occur in the lives of these believers,[1] they needed to realize that it was "impossible" (v. 4) "to renew them to repentance"[2] (v. 6) "if they fall away" (v. 6) from following the Lord by going back to Judaism and its bankrupt but still functioning sacrificial system. One must keep in mind that this epistle was written before the destruction of the temple by the Roman general Titus in A.D. 70, while the temple was still in full operation. This places the time of writing around A.D. 68. Thus, if they succumbed to the pressure and persecution they faced, it would result in these believers participating in animal sacrifices which served in the past as a picture of Christ's final sacrifice (10:1-4). In doing so, they would then "crucify the Son of God afresh, and put Him to an open shame" (6:6), contradicting their past confession of faith and the reality of Christ's once-for-all sacrifice on the cross (10:12). No wonder the writer of Hebrews devotes chapters 9 and 10 to defend the truth that the final and finished sacrifice of Christ is "better" than any Old Testament sacrifice. The preceding context of Hebrews 5, along with the content of Hebrews 6:4-5, provides overwhelming evidence that genuine believers in Christ are in view in Hebrews 6.

Is It Possible for a Genuine Believer to Fall Away?

What do the Scriptures say? "Therefore let him who thinks he stands take heed *lest he fall*" (1 Cor. 10:12). "Let us therefore be diligent

---

[1] Hebrews 6:4-5 contains a series of participles that can only describe genuine possessors of salvation.

[2] The phrase in verse 6, "to renew them again to repentance," refers not to salvation but to an ongoing change of mind associated with spiritual growth as in Romans 12:2 which also refers to being "transformed by the renewing of your minds." For biblical evidence that repentance means a change of mind, see G. Michael Cocoris, *Repentance: The Most Misunderstood Word in the Bible* (Milwaukee: Grace Gospel Press, 2010).

to enter that rest, *lest anyone fall* according to the same example of disobedience" (Heb. 4:11). However, while a believer may fall, he does not fall away from his eternal salvation. "The steps of a good man are ordered by the LORD, and He delights in his way. *Though he fall,* he shall not be utterly cast down; for the LORD upholds him with His hand" (Ps. 37:23-24).

What might cause a Christian to fall? Though various reasons exist, Jesus' parable of the soils and the seed highlights one particular reason: the problem of persecution (which is parallel to the dilemma in the book of Hebrews). Luke 8:12-13 states, "Those by the wayside are the ones who hear; then the devil comes and takes away the word out of their hearts, lest they should believe and be saved. But the ones on the rock are those who, when they hear, *receive the word with joy;* and these have no root, *who believe* for a while and *in time of temptation fall away.*"

In light of this possibility, these Hebrew believers, who originally heard this epistle read, had two options. Being the very word of God to them, the epistle of Hebrews was likened to "the rain that comes often upon the earth" (6:7; cf. Isa. 55:8-11). These believers could either respond by faith to this epistle, bear fruit, and receive blessing from God (v. 7); or they could disregard this teaching and "bear thorns and briers" that would be "rejected"[3] and become "near to being cursed, whose end is to be burned" (v. 8). However, the ground (i.e., the believer) is not burned; instead, the thorns and briers (i.e., what is produced in the believer's life who is disobedient and falling away) are burned.

Was It Impossible Now to Ever Renew Them Again to Repentance in Order to Spiritually Grow?

To answer this pertinent question it is helpful to closely observe the participial phrase: "Since they crucify again for themselves the Son of God, and put Him to an open shame." The phrase "since they crucify again" is just one word in the Greek text *anastauroō*. It is a present active temporal participle which is contemporaneous in time to the action of the main verb and that carries the idea of *while doing,* especially when it is related to the main verb.[4] This could then

---

[3] The word "rejected" (*adokimos*) is elsewhere translated "disqualified" (1 Cor. 9:27), as in a race, with the result being a failure to receive a crown (i.e., reward).

[4] Daniel B. Wallace, *Greek Grammar beyond the Basics* (Grand Rapids: Zondervan, 1995), 623, 625.

be translated, "If they fall away, [it is impossible] to renew them again to repentance, *while* they crucify again for themselves the Son of God, and put Him to an open shame." The writer of Hebrews is not shutting the door forever upon these believers experiencing spiritual growth again. But he is making it clear that this spiritual renewal will not occur *while at the same time* they persist in going back to the defunct Temple and its needless sacrifices.

Is Hebrews 6:6 Describing a Falling Away from Eternal Salvation?

Such an erroneous conclusion would completely violate the context and be contrary to many other verses in Scripture that clearly teach eternal security. Such an interpretation would amount to sheer eisegesis. So what is Hebrews 6:6 actually teaching?

This passage is a serious warning to some slothful believers about the danger of falling away from following the Lord by faith. To do so would involve ongoing spiritual retrogression that would only lead to worse and worse practical results in their lives. Thus, if believers in Christ capitulated to the pressure to return to Judaism, they would certainly become involved in the inappropriate sacrificing of lambs that were intended before the cross to picture or illustrate the Lamb of God (Jesus Christ) who came to take away the sins of the world (John 1:29). To turn back to these pictures and shadows when the reality had already come would be putting their Savior to an open shame. However, the writer of Hebrews has a gracious optimism and confidence in God's amazing power, so he closes this section with words of encouragement to these struggling Christians.

> But, beloved, we are confident of better things concerning you, yes, things that accompany salvation, though we speak in this manner. For God is not unjust to forget your work and labor of love which you have shown toward His name, in that you have ministered to the saints, and do minister. And we desire that each one of you show the same diligence to the full assurance of hope until the end, that you do not become sluggish, but imitate those who through faith and patience inherit the promises. (Heb. 6:9-12)

Does Hebrews 6 teach that a believer can lose his eternal salvation? No! But it does teach the propensity for believers to become dull of hearing, to spiritually retrogress, to need to be taught again biblical basics, and the possibility of returning to religious systems that teach and practice that which is contrary to the Word of God because of pressure and persecution. On the other hand, we learn that believers need not cave in to the pressure to compromise their faithfulness to God and His Word because God still grants them the possibility of growing spiritually and becoming fruitful for Christ. Believer, will you be faithful or popular? Take your pick!

When peace, like a river, attendeth my way,
When sorrows like sea billows roll;
Whatever my lot, Thou has taught me to say,
It is well, it is well, with my soul.

Though Satan should buffet, though trials should come,
Let this blest assurance control,
That Christ has regarded my helpless estate,
And hath shed His own blood for my soul.

My sin, oh, the bliss of this glorious thought!
My sin, not in part but the whole,
Is nailed to the cross, and I bear it no more,
Praise the Lord, praise the Lord, O my soul!

And Lord, haste the day when my faith shall be sight,
The clouds be rolled back as a scroll;
The trump shall resound, and the Lord shall descend,
Even so, it is well with my soul.

It is well, with my soul,
It is well, it is well, with my soul.[5]

---

[5] Horatio G. Spafford, *It Is Well with My Soul.*

CHAPTER 25

The Warning of the Consequences of Willful Sin
(Hebrews 10:26-30)

"For if we sin willfully after we have received the knowledge of the truth, there no longer remains a sacrifice for sins, but a certain fearful expectation of judgment, and fiery indignation which will devour the adversaries. Anyone who has rejected Moses' law dies without mercy on the testimony of two or three witnesses. Of how much worse punishment, do you suppose, will he be thought worthy who has trampled the Son of God underfoot, counted the blood of the covenant by which he was sanctified a common thing, and insulted the Spirit of grace? For we know Him who said, 'Vengeance is Mine, I will repay,' says the Lord. And again, 'The LORD will judge His people.' It is a fearful thing to fall into the hands of the living God."

What Is the Immediate Context of This Passage?

In this section, the writer of Hebrews presents a series of practical exhortations to his Christian readers (vv. 19-25) in light of the completed, once-for-all, substitutionary sacrifice of Jesus Christ (vv. 1-18) that provided for them a secure, eternal salvation (vv. 10-14). The writer of Hebrews calls them "brethren" (v. 19) and also utilizes plural pronouns that include himself in these practical exhortations—"let *us* draw near" (v. 22), "let *us* hold fast" (v. 23), "let *us* consider one another" (v. 24). This indicates that his readers were believers in Christ like himself. Thus, there is no reason to falsely assume that the writer of Hebrews has anyone but believers in mind when he goes on to say, "For if *we* sin willfully after *we* have received the knowledge of the truth."

What Is This Willful Sin?

In Hebrews 10:26-30 we have the fourth warning to believers in the book of Hebrews (2:1-4; 3:7-19; 6:6-8) regarding their possible slippage back into Judaism because of a failure to faith-rest in the Lord who is "better" (chap. 4). While in one sense all sin is willful or voluntary, here the writer of Hebrews has in mind the deliberate sin of turning away from the truths of Jesus Christ set forth in this epistle ("for if we sin willfully *after we have received the knowledge of the truth*") and thus returning to the animal sacrifices of the spiritually defunct but still operating temple system. This is why he had just exhorted them, "Let us hold fast the confession of our hope without wavering, for He who promised is faithful." But if they still chose apostasy over "holding fast," the writer warns that "there no longer remains a sacrifice for sins." Why? This is because this same chapter has declared in no uncertain terms that Jesus Christ's sacrifice was the last sacrifice for sins (Heb. 10:10, 12, 14, 18). To turn away from following Christ, the last sacrifice, left no other sacrifice as the basis for forgiveness between God and the sinning, apostatizing believer.

What Can a Believer Expect if He Persists in This Sin?

The answer: serious divine discipline—"a certain fearful expectation of judgment, and fiery indignation which will devour the adversaries" (v. 27). This verse is a direct allusion to Isaiah 26:11 where God's judgment refers to physical death, not Hell. So what kind of divine judgment or discipline will this involve? Hebrews 10:28-30 says,

> Anyone who has rejected Moses' law dies without mercy on the testimony of two or three witnesses.[1] Of how much worse punishment [in light of the truths and grace blessings of Jesus Christ in this present day], do you suppose will he be thought worthy who has trampled the Son of God underfoot, counted the blood of the covenant by which he was sanctified a common thing, and insulted the Spirit of grace? For we know Him who said, "Vengeance is Mine, I will repay," says the Lord. And again, "The LORD will judge His people."[2]

---

[1] This is an allusion to Deuteronomy 17:6 and the death penalty for certain serious sins by either believers or unbelievers.

[2] Both quotations here are references to Deuteronomy 30.

Is This Passage Describing Believers or Unbelievers?

Seven evidences support the conclusion that the people in view are genuine believers in Christ who are in danger of serious divine discipline through apostatizing.

1. The use of the plural pronoun "we" (v. 26) and the flow of thought from the preceding context and exhortations clearly have believers ("let us") in view (vv. 19-25) who are described as "brethren" (v. 19).

2. The phrase "he *was sanctified*" (v. 29) describes a believer who at a point of time in his past (aorist tense) was sanctified by God (passive voice) in fulfillment of His promises (v. 10) and it is a fact (indicative mood).

3. The phrase, "the Lord shall judge *His people*" (v. 30), points to these individuals being Jewish believers.

4. The following passage (v. 32ff) indicates that no change of audience (from believers to unbelievers) is in view and that they had been illuminated to the truth of the Gospel (i.e., saved, "But recall the former days in which, after *you were illuminated*" [v. 32a]).

5. In keeping with their faith in Jesus Christ, there was even some fruit in their lives following their salvation—"*you endured a great struggle with sufferings*: partly while you were made a spectacle both by reproaches and tribulations, and partly while you became companions of those who were so treated" (vv. 32b-33).

6. According to some Greek texts, the readers of this epistle had a lasting possession *in Heaven*. The writer of Hebrews says to his readers, "You had compassion on me in my chains, and joyfully accepted the plundering of your goods, knowing that you have a better and an enduring possession for yourselves *in heaven*" (v. 34). This could only be stated of a believer in Christ.

7. They were then exhorted in light of the present pressure and persecution: "Therefore do not cast away your confidence, which has *great reward*" (v. 35). Rewards are given only to faithful believers, not to unbelievers (1 Cor. 3:11-15).

In addition, the following verses set forth to these believers the options of either pleasing God via walking by faith and doing His will or facing divine displeasure (10:36-39). The similar pattern found in the following chapters of Hebrews 11 (the great "faith" chapter) and Hebrews 12 (the great "divine discipline" chapter) reinforces these two options.

What Is the "Worse Punishment"?

But this leaves a vital question unanswered, namely, what is the "worse punishment" described in verse 29? It clearly is not eternal Hell since this passage is describing believers who "have been sanctified" (v. 10) and "perfected forever" (v. 14) through the once-for-all sacrifice of Jesus Christ. But if they do apostatize and "draw back" because of their present persecution, they could anticipate God's displeasure (v. 38) and serious divine discipline (v. 29). This would involve physical death (v. 28) with the loss of a great present opportunity (v. 39b) and future reward (v. 35) at the Judgment Seat of Christ. But this could involve realities worse than physical death, since to simply die is an easier option than facing certain consequences in this life.

This passage also appears to have national overtones regarding the pending destruction of Jerusalem (A.D. 70). Because of Israel's backsliding, this judgment constituted God's predicted fifth cycle of discipline (Lev. 26; Deut. 28), resulting in massive death and worse (e.g., starvation, mothers eating their children, mass crucifixion, and so forth).[3] Church historians note that there were those believers who took to heart the exhortations of this epistle to the Hebrews and escaped this divine judgment on Jerusalem by specifically heeding Hebrews 13:12-14: "Therefore Jesus also, that He might sanctify the people with His own blood, suffered outside the gate. Therefore let us go forth to Him, outside the camp, bearing His reproach. For here we have no continuing city, but we seek the one to come."

Some Concluding Thoughts

With clear exegetical and Jewish insight, Arnold Fruchtenbaum writes,

> The author moves towards giving his fourth warning and begins with a principle for those who reject the

---

[3] Josephus, *Jewish Wars*, 5:420-572 and 6:1-219.

truth (10:26). In light of the nearness of the coming judgment, they must be warned against willful sin on their part. Now that they have received full knowledge of the truth, if they willfully choose to apostasize from the faith and once and for all go back into Judaism, there remains no more sacrifice for their sin. The Messiah is the final sacrifice, and if He is rejected, there is no other sacrifice for sin available. Since for the believer all sin is dealt with for eternity, the question is: what is this sin that the cross of the Messiah does not cover in time? In this context, it is a voluntary sin which a believer wills to commit after he has been saved and has been warned of the consequences. It involves a repudiation of one's previous confession of the Messiahship of Jesus.

What the sin is becomes evident by comparing verses 23-25 with verses 26-29. It involves a separation of the believer from other believers permanently and the return to Judaism, the Temple and all that it entails in order to escape persecution. The sin involves a denunciation of the three elements of verse 29: the work of the Son, the work of the Father, and the work of the Holy Spirit. For this kind of sin, there is no more sacrifice for sin, but the guilty become subject to judgment (10:27). The judgment is the only result of rejecting the only way, and there is no other sacrifice for this sin. The nature of the judgment is threefold: physical death (10:28, 29); the A.D. 70 judgment being the time of death (10:25, 27); and the loss of rewards (10:35-36). The Old Testament teaches the fact of judgment (10:28). Under the Law of Moses, one was punished by physical death at the word of two or three witnesses. By the same token, physical death, not spiritual, will fall upon them as well, for punishment is greater under the Law of Christ than under the Law of Moses (10:25). The author spells out what is involved in the willful sin, and that is a rejection of the work of the Trinity. It means *treading underfoot the Son of God,* and this is a rejection of God the Father who declared Him to be the Son of God. It means *considering the blood of the covenant an unholy thing,* and this is a rejection of God the Son whose blood it is, because it means to consider the blood of the Messiah no different than the blood of other men, common blood rather than better blood; and in this way implying that Jesus suffered justly for His own sins. It means doing *despite unto the Spirit of grace*, and this is a rejection of God the Holy Spirit. It identifies them with those guilty of the unpardonable sin: the blasphemy of the Holy Spirit. The reason judgment is necessary is because of the character of God (10:30-31). The author quotes from Deuteronomy 32:35-36 (10:30) to show that vengeance is the sole prerogative of God, and that God will judge His people. The author then draws his conclusion (10:31): it is a fearful thing to fall into the hands of the living God. For this reason, they must heed this fourth warning.[4]

Does this passage teach that a believer can lose eternal salvation if he sins willfully? Not at all! But what a serious warning of divine discipline and pending judgment should they persist in this willful sin of apostasy. What was the "better" choice to make regarding their "better" Lord and Savior?

But recall the former days in which, after you were illuminated, you endured a great struggle with sufferings: partly while you were made a spectacle both by reproaches and tribulations, and partly while you became companions of those who were so treated; for you had compassion on me in my chains, and joyfully accepted the plundering of your goods, knowing that you have a better and an enduring possession for yourselves in heaven. Therefore do not cast away your confidence, which has great reward. For you have need of endurance, so that after you have done the will of God, you may receive the promise: For yet a little while, And He who is coming will come and will not tarry. Now the just shall live by faith; But if anyone draws back, My soul has no pleasure in him. But we are not of those who draw back to perdition, but of those who believe to the saving of the soul. (Heb. 10:32-39)

---

[4] Arnold G. Fruchtenbaum, *Israelology: The Missing Link in Systematic Theology,* rev. ed. (Tustin, CA: Ariel Ministries, 2001), 971-72.

'Tis so sweet to trust in Jesus,
Just to take Him at His Word,
Just to rest upon His promise,
Just to know: "Thus saith the Lord."

Jesus, Jesus, how I trust Him!
How I've proved Him o'er and o'er!
Jesus, Jesus, precious Jesus!
O for grace to trust Him more![5]

---

[5] Louisa M. R. Stead, *'Tis So Sweet to Trust in Jesus.*

CHAPTER 26

The Latter End Is Worse Than the Beginning
(2 Peter 2:20)

"For if, after they have escaped the pollutions of the world through the knowledge of the Lord and Savior Jesus Christ, they are again entangled in them and overcome, the latter end is worse for them than the beginning."

An Important Distinction to Keep Clear

The first key to arriving at the proper interpretation of this passage is distinguishing between the *unsaved false teachers* (vv. 1, 17) and the *vulnerable new believers* (v. 18).

> For when they [the unsaved false teachers] speak great swelling words of emptiness, they [the unsaved false teachers] allure through the lusts of the flesh, through lewdness, the ones who have actually escaped [new believers who have recently been saved] from those who live in error. While they [unsaved false teachers] promise them [new believers] liberty, they [the unsaved false teachers] themselves are slaves of corruption; for by whom a person is overcome, by him also he is brought into bondage. For if, after they have escaped [the new believers] the pollutions of the world through the knowledge of the Lord and Savior Jesus Christ, they [the new believers] are again entangled in them and overcome, the latter end is worse for them [the new believers] than the beginning. For it would have been

better for them [the new believers] not to have known
the way of righteousness, than having known it, to turn
from the holy commandment delivered to them [the
new believers]. But it has happened to them [the new
believers] according to the true proverb: "A dog returns
to his own vomit," and, "a sow, having washed, to her
wallowing in the mire."

Verses 20-22 have in view the effects of false teaching on these
recent converts ("the ones who have actually [recently] escaped").
In comparing 2 Peter 1 (which everyone agrees refers to believers in
Christ) with these new believers in chapter 2, three observations are
important.

a. The words "they *have escaped*" (v. 20) also occur in 1:4, "by which
have been given to us exceedingly great and precious promises,
that through these you may be partakers of the divine nature,
having escaped the corruption that is in the world through lust."
Clearly, genuine believers are in view.

b. The phrase "the pollutions of the world" (v. 20) is similar to 1:4,
"having escaped *the corruption that is in the world* through lust."

c. The words "through the *knowledge* of the *Lord* and *Savior, Jesus
Christ*" (2:20) are related to the description of these believers in
1:1-3:

Simon Peter, a bondservant and apostle of *Jesus Christ*,
to those who have obtained like precious faith with us
by the righteousness of our God *and Savior Jesus Christ*:
Grace and peace be multiplied to you in the *knowledge*
of God and of *Jesus* our *Lord*, as His divine power has
given to us all things that pertain to life and godliness,
through the *knowledge* of Him who called us by glory
and virtue.

Also the phrase "*again* entangled" indicates these new believers had
temporarily enjoyed deliverance from the enslaving effects of the
world after their salvation, but were "*again* entangled" because they
were heeding these false teachers of corruption.

In What Way Would It Have Been Better to Have Never Known the Way of Righteousness?

What, however, is meant by, "For it would have been better for them [the new believers] not to have known the way of righteousness" which was delivered to them? This cannot be referring to the Gospel since it would never be better for a sinner not to have known the plan of salvation, which would have resulted in their eternal destiny being Hell instead of Heaven. Rather, Peter is using this term ("way of righteousness") to refer to the Christian life by grace through faith which results in practical holiness or righteousness in a believer's life. This is in keeping with his reference to the "holy commandment" (v. 21) that he mentioned in 1 Peter 1:13-16:

> Therefore gird up the loins of your mind, be sober, and rest your hope fully upon the grace that is to be brought to you at the revelation of Jesus Christ; as obedient children, not conforming yourselves to the former lusts, as in your ignorance; but as He who called you is holy, *you also be holy in all your conduct*, because it is written, *"Be holy, for I am holy."*

In What Sense is "the Latter End Worse for Them Than the Beginning"?

The two illustrations of verse 22 highlight the answer: "But it has happened to them according to the true proverb: 'A dog returns to his own vomit,' and, 'a sow, having washed, to her wallowing in the mire.'" When originally eating some bad food, a dog doesn't know any better and so he vomits. That's understandable. But then to eat the vomit is *worse than the beginning* because the dog now knows better. The same is true of the hog that was accustomed to wallowing in the mire. The sow did not know any better until it had been washed. But then to go back to her wallowing in the mire is *worse than the beginning* because she has experienced freedom from the mire and now knows better. In the same way these new believers had come to faith in Christ and had escaped the pollutions of the world to some degree. For them to now return to their previous bondage to the world because of the influence of false teachers is *worse than the beginning* since they now know better, having "escaped the pollutions of the world" and now knowing "the way of righteousness."

Does this passage teach that a believer can lose his eternal salvation if he returns to the pollutions of the world? No! Does this teach that you were never truly saved if you, like the dog and hog, return to your sinful ways? Never! In addition, this passage does not address "false professors" of salvation; but instead, it addresses new believers who become entangled again with the corruption of the world because of false teaching that has affected their progressive sanctification. If you have been saved by God's grace, don't forsake sound doctrine, nor believe every so-called Bible teacher that comes peddling his doctrine to you (2 Cor. 4:2). Otherwise, will you be like the dog who returns to the vomit of the world after Christ has set you free. What a miserable existence and worthless life! Instead, listen carefully and respond by faith to Peter's closing exhortation in this epistle:

> You therefore, beloved, since you know this beforehand, beware lest you also fall from your own steadfastness, being led away with the error of the wicked; but grow in the grace and knowledge of our Lord and Savior Jesus Christ. To Him be the glory both now and forever. Amen. (2 Peter 3:17-18)

All my life-long I had panted
For a drink from some cool spring
That I hoped would quench the burning
Of the thirst I felt within.

Feeding on the husks around me
Till my strength was almost gone,
Longed my soul for something better,
Only still to hunger on.

Poor I was, and sought for riches,
Something that would satisfy;
But the dust I gathered round me
Only mocked my soul's sad cry.

Well of water, ever springing,
Bread of Life, so rich and free,

Untold wealth that never faileth,
My Redeemer is to me.

Hallelujah! I have found Him—
Whom my soul so long has craved!
Jesus satisfies my longings;
Thro' His blood I now am saved.[1]

---

[1] Clara T. Williams, *Satisfied*.

CHAPTER 27

Do You Fear Your Name Being Blotted Out?
(Revelation 3:5)

"He who overcomes shall be clothed in white garments, and I will not blot out his name from the Book of Life; but I will confess his name before My Father and before His angels."

Who Is the Overcomer?

Those who deny eternal security (Arminian view) claim that this passage about the church at Sardis teaches that if you do not live a victorious, overcoming life as a believer, you are in danger of losing your salvation and having your name blotted out of God's register of the redeemed. Others teach that if you are truly one of God's elect, then you will live an overcoming life as proof of your salvation, or else you were never really saved to begin with (consistent Calvinist view). Still others teach (new Free Grace view) that this passage has nothing to do with salvation but is a rewards passage for believers who lead a victorious Christian life. But the classical Free Grace view (the view espoused here) interprets the overcomers as a reference to all believers in Christ, just as the same writer (John) previously described the overcomer in his first epistle. "For whatever is born of God overcomes [*nika*] the world. And this is the victory that has overcome [*nikēsasa*] the world—our faith. Who is he who overcomes [*ho nikōn*] the world, but he who believes that Jesus is the Son of God?" (1 John 5:4-5).

Why are all believers viewed as overcomers in Christ? It is because of their wonderful position and blessings in Christ by God's grace. Romans 8:37 calls all believers not just overcomers but literally "superovercomers" because of our position in Christ! "Yet in all these things we are more than conquerors [*hypernikōmen*] through [*en*] Him who loved us" (Rom. 8:37). This is in keeping with what our Lord stated when it came to overcoming the world: "These things I have spoken to you, that in Me you may have peace. In the world you will have tribulation; but be of good cheer, I have overcome [*nenikēka*] the world" (John 16:33).

What Is This Verse Promising to Believers?

Thus, since Jesus Christ has overcome the world, God views every believer as an overcomer in union with Him (Rom. 8:37).[1] In light of this, Revelation 3:5 is not a warning of the loss of salvation or even of reward for the believer. Rather, this verse acts as a great motivator to respond to the Lord's admonition of Revelation 3:3 in light of His wonderful promise, "He who overcomes [i.e., the believer in Christ] shall be clothed in white garments, and I will not [*ou mē*, "never"] blot out his name from the Book of Life." Thus, do you realize that this passage actually confirms eternal security rather than denying it?!

> What a wondrous message in God's Word!
> My sins are blotted out, I know!
> If I trust in His redeeming blood,
> My sins are blotted out, I know!
>
> Once my heart was black, but now what joy;
> My sins are blotted out, I know!
> I have peace that nothing can destroy;
> My sins are blotted out, I know!
>
> I shall stand some day before my King;
> My sins are blotted out I know!
> With the ransomed host I then shall sing:
> My sins are blotted out, I know!
>
> My sins are blotted out, I know:
> My sins are blotted out, I know!
> They are buried in the depths of the deepest sea:
> My sins are blotted out, I know![2]

---

[1] For further biblical evidence that all believers in Christ are overcomers positionally in Christ, see Thomas L. Stegall, *Who Is the Overcomer?* (Duluth, MN: Grace Gospel Press, forthcoming 2013).

[2] Merrill Dunlop, *My Sins Are Blotted Out I Know.*

CHAPTER 28

Will You Have an Inheritance in the Kingdom of God? (1 Corinthians 6:9-11)

"Do you not know that the unrighteous will not inherit the kingdom of God? Do not be deceived. Neither fornicators, nor idolaters, nor adulterers, nor homosexuals, nor sodomites, nor thieves, nor covetous, nor drunkards, nor revilers, nor extortioners will inherit the kingdom of God." (1 Cor. 6:9-10)

> For this you know, that no fornicator, unclean person, nor covetous man, who is an idolater, has any inheritance in the kingdom of Christ and God. (Eph. 5:5)

> Idolatry, sorcery, hatred, contentions, jealousies, outbursts of wrath, selfish ambitions, dissensions, heresies, envy, murders, drunkenness, revelries, and the like; of which I tell you beforehand, just as I also told you in time past, that those who practice such things will not inherit the kingdom of God. (Gal. 5:20-21)

Depending on what theological eyeglasses you might have on, you may interpret these same verses in a variety of ways. If you are Roman Catholic, you may read these verses to be saying that you must avoid these sins in order to be saved and go to Heaven—salvation by faith plus works. (Read Ephesians 2:8-9.)

If you are Arminian in conviction, you may interpret these verses to be teaching that if you practice these sins, then you will lose your salvation—salvation by faith and works requiring a holy life. (Read John 10:27-30.)

If you are a Lordship Salvationist Calvinist, you may interpret these verses to be explaining that a person who claims to be saved but has this kind of lifestyle was never really born again—salvation by faith followed by a lifestyle of godly works as ultimately necessary to go to Heaven. (Read 2 Peter 2:7-8; 1 Cor. 3:1-4.)

If you believe in Free Grace, you may interpret these verses to be teaching that believers who live unrighteously will enter the Kingdom of God but not "inherit" the reward of reigning with Christ in the Kingdom.

But could there be another explanation that is exegetically sound and consistent with the context and content of these passages, along with the balance of the Scriptures? I would like to propose to you an interpretation of these passages that has been held by grace-oriented, dispensational expositors of the past but seems to be shelved by many in the present. Let's examine afresh each of these passages.

> Do you not know that the unrighteous will not inherit the kingdom of God? Do not be deceived. Neither fornicators, nor idolaters, nor adulterers, nor homosexuals, nor sodomites, nor thieves, nor covetous, nor drunkards, nor revilers, nor extortioners will inherit the kingdom of God. And such were some of you. But you were washed, but you were sanctified, but you were justified in the name of the Lord Jesus and by the Spirit of our God. (1 Cor. 6:9-11)

Who Are the "Unrighteous" in This Context?

Our first exegetical clue to properly interpreting this passage is the word "unrighteous." It is critical to note that Paul uses this exact Greek word when referring to the unsaved in stark contrast to believers earlier in this same chapter:

> Dare any of you, having a matter against another, go to law before the unrighteous, and not before the saints? (1 Cor. 6:1)

> But brother goes to law against brother, and that before unbelievers! (1 Cor. 6:6)

The "unrighteous" in this context are not "saints"; nor are they "brothers" but "unbelievers."

Secondly, verse 9 begins with the personal address of "you" which is referring to these believers whom Paul has previously described as...

> The church of God which is at Corinth, to those who are sanctified in Christ Jesus, called to be saints, with all who in every place call on the name of Jesus Christ our Lord, both theirs and ours. (1 Cor. 1:2)

> And I, brethren, could not speak to you as to spiritual people but as to carnal, as to babes in Christ. (1 Cor. 3:1)

Paul recognizes the Corinthians as genuine believers in Christ in spite of their carnality and fleshly lifestyles which he confronts them about throughout this epistle. Can one be carnal and yet a genuine believer in Christ? Paul certainly declared it!

Thus, verses 9-11 do not refer to believers who are living unrighteously and will lose out on the reward of "inherit[ing] the kingdom of God" as some have supposed. The "unrighteous" in this context refers to the unsaved unbelievers whom God still sees in their sins (fornicators, idolaters, adulterers, homosexuals, sodomites, thieves, covetous, drunkards, revilers, extortioners) since they have never believed and have never been totally forgiven by God. This verse is not saying that if you ever commit one of these sins you cannot be saved or that you are not saved. Otherwise, *who could be saved?* Not even the Corinthians, for "such were some of you" (6:11). Nor is this teaching that if you ever have a pattern of sins in your life as a believer you lose your salvation (Armininan view) since all sin was fully paid for at Calvary (Hebrews 10:12) and is completely forgiven when one believes in Christ alone (Col. 2:13). Nor is this passage stating that you never really possessed salvation (Lordship Salvation, Calvinistic view) if you have committed any of these sins or a pattern of them, for the Corinthians were guilty of these very sins (ongoing fornication [1 Cor. 5:1-5]; drunkenness, even in church [1 Cor. 11:21]) yet Paul still called them "saints" (1 Cor. 1:2). Also, if the Lordship Salvation, Calvinist view is correct, it leaves one in a terrible quandary wondering, "How many sins constitute a pattern?" How many times must you fornicate before you are a fornicator? Usually the answer would be *once*.

A second observation to note is that these Corinthian "saints" (6:1) "were washed" (from their sins), "were sanctified" (set apart unto God), and "were justified" (declared righteous) "in the name of the Lord Jesus and by the Spirit of our God" (6:11). It is interesting to observe that all three verbs ("washed," "sanctified," "justified") indicate a completed action in these believers' pasts (aorist tense, at the moment of salvation). This means being washed, sanctified, and justified were not progressive processes which were ongoing; but rather these were now a fact of reality for them (indicative mood), not a mere hope-so possibility. The emphasis in these verses is on the Christian's position in Christ and possessions by God's grace, not on his daily walk. For, if Paul was stating that the "unrighteous" were actually genuine believers who were living unrighteously and therefore would "not inherit the kingdom of God" as a reward for godly living in time as some Free Grace expositors teach, then his contrast in verse 11 misses the mark. Would not the appropriate contrast to unrighteous behavior among believers be a conditional statement, such as, "But you are spiritual, faithful, and godly and are on your way to inheriting the Kingdom of Heaven *as a reward for your perseverance*"? Instead, Paul contrasts the unbelievers' position before God ("unrighteous") followed by their practice ("fornicators, idolaters," etc.) with the believers' position before God ("washed," "sanctified," "justified") followed by an appeal for their practice to become consistent with their position in Christ (6:18-20).

A third exegetical clue that must be discovered and discerned is that in contrast to the "unrighteous" (*adikoi*) who "will not" inherit the Kingdom of God, these believers had been "justified" (*adikaioō*) or "declared righteous" in the courtroom of Heaven. Paul appears to use an inclusio here that completes the circle of thought from the unsaved or "unrighteous" (v. 9) to these believers who were "justified." This further confirms that the contrast Paul is establishing is between a believer in Christ versus an unbeliever.

What then Is Paul's Appeal to These Believers?

Therefore, in light of their position and blessings in Christ, God then appeals for these Christians to live a holy life befitting their identity with Jesus Christ.

> Flee sexual immorality. Every sin that a man does is outside the body, but he who commits sexual immorality sins against his own body. (1 Cor. 6:18)

The implication of this imperative for these believers to "flee sexual immorality" is that some were either still involved in sexual sin or at least could potentially be. In fact, 1 Corinthians 5:1 indicates that ongoing sexual immorality was a definite problem in this Christian assembly.

> It is actually reported that there is sexual immorality among you, and such sexual immorality as is not even named among the Gentiles—that a man has his father's wife! (1 Cor. 5:1)

No wonder Paul goes on to appeal to these believers in Christ:

> Or do you not know that your body is the temple of the Holy Spirit who is in you, whom you have from God, and you are not your own? For you were bought at a price; therefore glorify God in your body and in your spirit, which are God's. (1 Cor. 6:19-20)

It is imperative to note that even these believers who were "justified" before God in their position before God and were "doing wrong" (v. 8, *adikeō*—doing unrighteously) in their practice were exhorted as those whose bodies were "the temple of the Holy Spirit." Paul differentiated between justification and sanctification issues, and so must you!

This interpretation of 1 Corinthians 6 is further reinforced when comparing this passage of Scripture with other related Scriptures. For the same author, Paul, addressing the same issue (practical sanctification), using the same phraseology ("inherit the kingdom of God"), and making the same appeal for holy living (in light of believers' position in Christ and in contrast to the unsaved), addresses these same matters in Ephesians 5 and Galatians 5.

Ephesians 5:1-7

> Therefore be imitators of God as dear children. And walk in love, as Christ also has loved us and given Himself for us, an offering and a sacrifice to God for a sweet-smelling aroma. But fornication and all uncleanness or covetousness, let it not even be named among you, as is fitting for saints; neither filthiness, nor foolish talking,

nor coarse jesting, which are not fitting, but rather giving of thanks. For this you know, that no fornicator, unclean person, nor covetous man, who is an idolater, has any inheritance in the kingdom of Christ and God. Let no one deceive you with empty words, for because of these things the wrath of God comes upon the sons of disobedience. Therefore do not be partakers with them. (Eph. 5:1-7)

Who Are Paul's Readers?

Paul addressed this passage to the Ephesian believers (1:1) whom he previously informed earlier in this epistle that they were all "blessed with all spiritual blessings in heavenly places in Christ" (1:3) which included an "inheritance" in Christ.

In Him also we have obtained an inheritance, being pre-destined according to the purpose of Him who works all things according to the counsel of His will. (Eph. 1:11)

Just three verses later, Paul explains that the guarantee of this inheritance which all believers possess is the sealing of the Holy Spirit.

In Him you also trusted, after you heard the word of truth, the gospel of your salvation; in whom also, having believed, you were sealed with the Holy Spirit of promise, who is the guarantee of our inheritance until the redemption of the purchased possession, to the praise of His glory. (Eph. 1:13-14)

So it should not surprise us that four verses later in Ephesians 1, we observe the apostle Paul praying for these believers and asking God that,

The eyes of your understanding being enlightened; that you may know what is the hope of His calling, what are the riches of the glory of His inheritance in the saints. (Eph. 1:18)

This was not a prayer for select saints who were especially godly in their walk but for all believers in Christ who had all obtained an inheritance by God's grace when they were born again. This is important to note as most New Testament passages address the believer's inheritance as a gift of God's grace lavished upon all believers in Christ (Col. 1:12), while only a few verses communicate that certain faithful believers can receive "the reward of the inheritance" which God gives over and above the gift of the inheritance.

Let's Illustrate the Difference

To illustrate this difference between a gift and a reward, let's imagine for a moment a rich father who has three sons. Upon the father's death, his last will and testament is read out loud in the sons' presence. It reveals that this gracious father bequeathed to *all* his sons a great but equal inheritance that they receive as a *gift* merely because of the Father's generosity and their birth into his family. But in addition to the *gift*, this same father gave as a *reward* certain additional blessings to *one* of his sons who faithfully served him night and day for many years while he was in poor health before he died. In the same way, the Scriptures set forth the fact that *all* believers in Christ have received the gracious blessings of God's *inheritance* merely because they are God's children through being born again.

> Blessed be the God and Father of our Lord Jesus Christ, who according to His abundant mercy has begotten us again to a living hope through the resurrection of Jesus Christ from the dead, to an inheritance incorruptible and undefiled and that does not fade away, reserved in heaven for you, who are kept by the power of God through faith for salvation ready to be revealed in the last time. (1 Peter 1:3-5)

On the other hand, there will be *some* believers who will receive a *reward* for their faithful service to Jesus Christ.

> And whatever you do, do it heartily, as to the Lord and not to men, knowing that from the Lord you will receive the reward of the inheritance; for you serve the Lord Christ. (Col. 3:23-24)

In light of the previous context and usage of "inheritance" in Ephesians (1:11, 14, 18), it stands to reason that Paul is designating that those who have NO "'inheritance in the kingdom of God and Christ" are UNBELIEVERS, especially since Paul so dogmatically states that "NO fornicator . . . has ANY INHERITANCE" (Eph. 5:5) while previously explaining that ALL BELIEVERS have an inheritance by God's grace. But let's be clear that the reason these unbelievers have NO INHERITANCE is not because they have committed these sins individually or as a pattern, but because while Jesus Christ died for their sins, they have never trusted in Him alone in order to be justified and forgiven.

> Being justified freely by his grace through the redemption that is in Christ Jesus: Whom God hath set forth to be a propitiation through faith in his blood. (Rom. 3:24-25a)

> To Him all the prophets witness that, through His name, whoever believes in Him will receive remission of sins. (Acts 10:43)

More Exegetical Clues

To further support this interpretative conclusion that this passage is referring to unbelievers, there are several other exegetical clues that we need to observe. Paul goes on to state,

> Let no one deceive you with empty words, for because of these things the wrath of God comes upon the sons of disobedience. (Eph. 5:6)

The "you" of verse 5 is referring to all the believers in Christ at Ephesus, not just a select few. This stands in contrast to the phrase "sons of disobedience" who will experience God's "wrath." The Ephesian believers would understand these terms in light of Paul's previous usage of this phrase in this same epistle when he described their previous *unregenerate condition* before they were saved by God's grace through faith in Jesus Christ (2:8).

> And you He made alive, who were dead in trespasses and sins, in which you once walked according to the course of this world, according to the prince of the power of the air, the spirit who now works in the sons of

> disobedience, among whom also we all once conducted ourselves in the lusts of our flesh, fulfilling the desires of the flesh and of the mind, and were by nature children of wrath, just as the others. (Eph. 2:1-3)

Ephesians 5:6 is not referring to disobedient Christians who would experience the wrath of God due to their carnality, as some suppose. What a ludicrous thought in light of Christ's work, God's grace, and the believer's position and possessions in Christ; for even God's discipline is done out of love, not wrath (Heb. 12:6-8). Instead, Ephesians 5:6 refers to the *unsaved* who die *unforgiven* because of their rejection of Jesus Christ as Savior!

Another significant exegetical clue supporting this interpretation is the striking contrast in verses 6 and 7 between *them* (the unsaved) and *you* (believers).

> Let no one deceive you [not just some believers but all the believers at Ephesus] with empty words, for because of these things the wrath of God comes upon the sons of disobedience [the unsaved]. Therefore do not be partakers with them [the unsaved].

To hammer one more nail in the interpretative coffin of Ephesians 5:1-7, the following verse states,

> For you were once darkness, but now you are light in the Lord. Walk as children of light. (5:8)

"You" is in the plural and is referring again to all the believers in Christ at Ephesus. Furthermore, Paul's targeted audience is "you" (v. 8, all believers) which he again sets in contrast to the "them" (unsaved) of verse 7. This passage is *not* contrasting obedient believers with disobedient believers, as some claim, but instead contrasts the children of God with the children of wrath.

Once again we see the logic of grace. The appeal to godly Christian living by God's grace is based on what Christ has done for us (Eph. 4:32–5:7) and the believer's position in Him as "children of light" (5:8). Ephesians 5:3 is another example of such an appeal. "But fornication and all uncleanness or covetousness, let it not even be named among you, as is fitting for saints." Thus, Paul exhorts Christians to live in a way that is consistent with and commensurate to their new identity and destiny in Christ with a walk that should be distinctly different from the unsaved around them whose destiny is not the "kingdom of God."

Galatians 5:19-21

A third passage of Scripture that echoes the same train of thought with similar wording is found in Galatians 5:

> I say then: Walk in the Spirit, and you shall not fulfill the lust of the flesh. For the flesh lusts against the Spirit, and the Spirit against the flesh; and these are contrary to one another, so that you do not do the things that you wish. But if you are led by the Spirit, you are not under the law. Now the works of the flesh are evident, which are: adultery, fornication, uncleanness, lewdness, idolatry, sorcery, hatred, contentions, jealousies, outbursts of wrath, selfish ambitions, dissensions, heresies, envy, murders, drunkenness, revelries, and the like; of which I tell you beforehand, just as I also told you in time past, that those who practice such things will not inherit the kingdom of God. But the fruit of the Spirit is love, joy, peace, longsuffering, kindness, goodness, faithfulness, gentleness, self-control. Against such there is no law. And those who are Christ's have crucified the flesh with its passions and desires. If we live in the Spirit, let us also walk in the Spirit. Let us not become conceited, provoking one another, envying one another. (Gal. 5:16-26)

Once again we observe the apostle Paul exhorting believers to live in a manner consistent with their blessings and position in Christ in glaring contrast to the unsaved world around them.

In Galatians, Paul defends the Gospel and teachings of grace in declaring that the Law cannot justify the sinner (2:16) nor sanctify the saint (2:20; 3:1-5). Both spiritual blessings (justification and sanctification) are all by God's grace through faith in Jesus Christ, not through some form of legalism which is to be avoided at all cost. But Paul then shifts in Galatians 5 to address another imbalance that can plague believers and occurs when grace is misunderstood or abused — namely the opposite ditch of license. Thus, believers are exhorted to walk by faith in Christ (2:20) in or by means of the Holy Spirit with the result being they shall not fulfill the lusts of the flesh in the midst of a very real spiritual battle daily fought within them (5:16-17). And "if" all believers have the Holy Spirit to lead them and enable them to live a holy life under grace (and they do—"if" is in the first class condition assuming a reality), they are not under the Law in any way as a means of sanctification in their daily walk (5:18).

However, by virtue of the reality that believers in Christ still possess a sin nature and may choose to yield to it with its passions and temptations instead of walking in the Spirit, Paul reminds these believers that they are capable of fulfilling the lusts of the flesh and producing the works of the flesh in their lives (5:19-21). To live in license would betray their real identity (in Christ), real authority (Jesus Christ), real destiny (the kingdom of God), and real power source for living (the Holy Spirit), and would cause them to live like "those . . . who will not inherit the kingdom of God."

This verse is not teaching that if a believer ever commits these sins or has a pattern of these sins that he loses his salvation (Arminian view), or that he was never saved (Calvinistic view), for the Scriptures set forth several examples of believers who committed these very sins (it does happen) and how they lost their testimony, fellowship with God, joy, and possibly more, but *never their salvation* (John 10:27-30; Rom. 8:31-39)! In fact, if you are honest with yourself, you know that too often you have committed such mental attitude sins as jealousy and envy (mentioned in Gal. 5:19-21), let alone the more overt sins also mentioned in this list of the works of the flesh.

But notice again, like 1 Corinthians 6 and Ephesians 5, the stark contrast between the "YOU" in reference to all the Galatian BELIEVERS and the "THOSE" of the UNSAVED who "will not inherit the kingdom of God."

> But if you [all the Galatian believers] are led by the Spirit, you are not under the law. Now the works of the flesh are evident, which are: adultery, fornication, uncleanness, lewdness, idolatry, sorcery, hatred, contentions, jealousies, outbursts of wrath, selfish ambitions, dissensions, heresies, envy, murders, drunkenness, revelries, and the like; of which I tell you [all the Galatian believers] beforehand, just as I also told you [all the Galatian believers] in time past, that those [the unsaved] who practice such things will not inherit the kingdom of God. (5:18-21)

In addition, when you compare 1 Corinthians 6:9-11 and Ephesians 5:1-8 and their usage of "will not inherit the kingdom of God," there is no reason to assume that Paul has a different referent in mind than *unbelievers* who remain unforgiven and whom God still sees as spiritually dead in their sins.

Lastly, Paul's grace logic and flow of thought remain similar here to 1 Corinthians 6 and Ephesians 5 as he sets forth how believers are to walk distinctly different from the unregenerate around them with the fruit of the Spirit manifested in their lives (5:22-23) based upon their position in Christ (5:24). Thus, Paul commands believers to walk in a manner consistent with and commensurate to their new identity and destiny in Christ by exhorting them, "If we live in the Spirit [positionally], let us also walk in the Spirit [practically]" (Gal. 5:25).

Again the "if" is in the first class condition assuming the reality that these believers are alive spiritually by means of the Spirit and now are to walk by means of the very same Holy Spirit. Through His divine enablement, every child of God can have victory over the flesh and manifest the fruit of the Spirit apart from a law-oriented, legalistic orientation to daily living.

Once again we have underscored the importance of basking in the riches of God's amazing grace and our identity in Christ as a basis for godly living through divine enablement for the glory of God. We need not threaten believers in Christ with some kind of millennial exclusion or Protestant purgatory to motivate them or appeal to them to live according to their high calling of God in Christ. Instead, let's point them to Jesus Christ, the riches of God's grace, their position in Christ, and encourage them to walk worthy of their high calling in Christ through living by faith in Christ empowered by the Holy Spirit.

> I therefore, the prisoner of the Lord, beseech you to walk worthy of the calling with which you were called. (Eph. 4:1)

> For the love of Christ compels us, because we judge thus: that if One died for all, then all died; and He died for all, that those who live should live no longer for themselves, but for Him who died for them and rose again. (2 Cor. 5:14-15)

Far dearer than all that the world can impart
Was the message came to my heart.
How that Jesus alone for my sin did atone,
And Calvary covers it all.

The stripes that He bore and the thorns that He wore
Told His mercy and love evermore
And my heart bowed in shame as I called on His name,
And Calvary covers it all.

How matchless the grace, when I looked in the face
Of this Jesus, my crucified Lord;
My redemption complete I then found at His feet,
And Calvary covers it all.

How blessed the thought, that my soul by Him bought,
Shall be His in the glory on high;
Where with gladness and song, I'll be one of the throng
And Calvary covers it all.

Calvary covers it all,
My past with its sin and stain;
My guilt and despair
Jesus took on Him there,
And Calvary covers it all.[1]

---

[1] Ethel R. Taylor, *Calvary Covers It All.*

CHAPTER 29

Will God Take Away Your Part in the Book of Life?
(Revelation 22:17-19)

"The Spirit and the bride say, 'Come!' And let him who hears say, 'Come!' And let him who thirsts come. Whoever desires, let him take the water of life freely. For I testify to everyone who hears the words of the prophecy of this book: If anyone adds to these things, God will add to him the plagues that are written in this book; and if anyone takes away from the words of the book of this prophecy, God shall take away his part from the Book of Life, from the holy city, and from the things which are written in this book."

An Important Observation to Note

This passage begins with an offer of salvation and an invitation *to unbelievers* to "come" (v. 17, twice) to faith in Christ as Savior and to "take the water of life freely" that Jesus paid for in full. God offers eternal salvation "freely" without further obligation, pledges, surrender, and so forth. Verses 18-19 follow with a grave warning *to unbelievers* who would add to or subtract from the words of this book. Either adding to or taking away from the Word of God is characteristic of unbelievers who cannot simply accept by faith what God says in His Word. When God speaks, the response of the believing heart is simply "Amen." But the unbeliever does not accept what God says at face value, and so he must change the Word to suit himself.

A Contrast to Observe

To unbelievers who reject God's Word and the salvation invitation in verse 17, a warning ensues in verse 18: "If anyone adds to these things, God will add to him the plagues that are written in this book." A common characteristic of cults and religions that profess to be "Christian" is that they invariably add other books, creeds, council decisions, or "inspired" writings of their founder or leaders to the Bible, and they put these on a par with God's Word. To unbelievers who would add to God's Word in this fashion, the Lord promises to "add to him the plagues that are written in this book." The plagues spoken of in the book of Revelation occur during that future period of God's judgment on the earth known as the Tribulation. If anyone reading Revelation accepts the invitation of verse 17 and becomes a believer in Christ prior to the Tribulation, that person will experience the pretribulational Rapture of the saints (1 Thess. 4:13-18) rather than the plagues of the Tribulation (1 Thess. 5:1-3). Therefore, the warning of Revelation 22:18 applies only to unbelievers. This is not a warning to believers to stay saved or to be rewarded for their perseverance.

Another Warning to Heed

Similarly, verse 19 warns unbelievers that if they take away from the words of this book, God will take away their "part" in, or right to, certain future blessings reserved only for the saved to experience (access to the holy city [21:23-27] and to the tree of life [22:2]). Verse 19 does not teach the possibility of losing one's salvation during this present lifetime since a person cannot lose something he has yet to possess or experience. The same word "part" (*meros*) appears elsewhere in Revelation to explain future experiences in which people have yet to take part (20:1; 21:8). Verse 19 warns unbelievers that God will not give them a part in the blessings reserved only for believers. This promise of blessing and/or cursing is consistent and in keeping with common contractual language of that day, appropriately placed at the end of the book of Revelation.[1]

An Encouraging Hope to Remember

After addressing unbelievers in verses 17-19, the book of Revelation shifts back to *believers* and ends with the promise of Christ's coming

---

[1] Hal Harless, *How Firm a Foundation: The Dispensations in the Light of the Divine Covenants* (New York: Peter Lange, 2004). Harless devotes 3 chapters to covenant/ contractual structure and language in the Bible that seems to apply to the ending of Revelation in light of its counterpart in Genesis.

and a note of grace: "He who testifies to these things says, 'Surely I am coming quickly.' Amen. Even so, come, Lord Jesus! The grace of our Lord Jesus Christ be with you all. Amen" (Rev. 22:21-22).

Does this passage teach that the believer in Christ can lose his eternal salvation? Not at all! But God places at the end of the Bible one more invitation to the thirsty unbeliever to "take the water of life freely" which will forever quench his soul (John 4:13-14). But mindful of those who reject God's Word, there is also a serious warning of the results of not believing the Word of God but adding or taking away from it. To you who are thirsty without Jesus Christ, is it not time to "taste and see that the Lord is good. Blessed is the man that trusts in Him"? (Ps. 34:8).

The love of God is greater far
Than tongue or pen can ever tell;
It goes beyond the highest star,
And reaches to the lowest hell;
The guilty pair, bowed down with care,
God gave His Son to win;
His erring child He reconciled,
And pardoned from his sin.

When years of time shall pass away,
And earthly thrones and kingdoms fall,
When men who here refuse to pray,
On rocks and hills and mountains call,
God's love so sure, shall still endure,
All measureless and strong;
Redeeming grace to Adam's race—
The saints' and angels' song.

Could we with ink the ocean fill,
And were the skies of parchment made,
Were every stalk on earth a quill,
And every man a scribe by trade;
To write the love of God above
Would drain the ocean dry;
Nor could the scroll contain the whole,
Though stretched from sky to sky.

Oh, love of God, how rich and pure!
How measureless and strong!
It shall forevermore endure—
The saints' and angels' song.[2]

---

[2] Frederick M. Lehman, *The Love of God.*

CHAPTER 30

Can a Believer Practice Sin and Be Truly Born Again? (1 John 3:9)

"Whoever has been born of God does not sin, for His seed remains in him; and he cannot sin, because he has been born of God."

For many passages considered in this book, Bible teachers offer various interpretations—some doctrinally correct and allowable, and others doctrinally wrong and unacceptable. First John 3:9 is another example of a passage with widely varying views. Some interpreters see this passage as teaching that a person who sins at all is not born again. This is an extreme view held by only a few who are self-deceived and fail to realize that we all still sin as believers in Christ. And they fail to read and grasp what John wrote two chapters earlier: "If we say that we have not sinned, we make Him a liar, and His word is not in us" (1:10).

Then there is the view held both by those who reject Lordship Salvation (yet seem to adopt some of its tenets) and those who embrace the false teaching of Lordship Salvation who interpret this verse to mean that believers still sin but not as a pattern. If people continually sin as a pattern, then this supposedly means that they have never been born again. Those who hold this view appeal to the present tense of the phrases "does [poieō] sin" and "cannot sin [hamartanein]," claiming that this refers to habitually sinning or practicing sin. However, almost all recent major Greek commentaries on 1 John over the last fifty years reject the interpretation that the born again person does not habitually sin. This is because Greek grammarians recognize that the present tense verb can be used in a variety of ways and can refer to current action (a present or progressive present) and not necessarily to habitual, continual action (habitual present), depending on its context and the presence or absence of qualifying words. Also, if people have been reading through 1 John verse by verse, they would have previously read in chapter one of the practice of confessing their sins as needed to have fellowship with God (1:3-9), as verse 9 declares, "If we confess [present tense] our sins, He is faithful and just to forgive [present tense] us our sins and to cleanse us from all unrighteousness." In addition if they keep reading on in 1 John, they will read in chapter 5: "If anyone sees his brother [a fellow-believer] sinning [present tense] a sin which does not lead to death, he will ask, and He will give him life for those who commit sin not leading to death. There is sin leading to death. I do not say that he should pray about that." Thus, these two verses (1 John 1:9 and 5:16) act as two bookends to clarify that those who are truly born again can commit (present tense) sin.

Also, from a practical standpoint, one Greek commentator wisely remarks,

> A popular interpretation of these verses distinguishes between occasional sin (which every Christian commits) and a continuing lifestyle of sin, which a genuine Christian cannot pursue. Appeal is usually made to the present tense to support this view. The Greek present tense describes ongoing action (action in progress). The problem with this view is that the author of 1 John does not appear to distinguish anywhere else between a lifestyle of sin and occasional acts of sin. Also, to make such a significant interpretative point on the basis of the Greek tense alone is extremely subtle. One can only wonder whether John's readers would have gotten the point.[1]

In addition, the view that claims "born again people don't habitually sin" doesn't hold water logically. From a practical standpoint, how many times must you sin a particular sin before it can be considered habitual or a pattern and then conclude that you are not born again? This view leaves one floating in a sea of subjectivity since it undermines the absolute assurance of one's salvation (which is scriptural). Those who embrace this view subjectively evaluate how much sin

---

[1] W. Hall Harris III, *1, 2, 3 John: Comfort and Counsel for a Church in Crisis* (n.p.: Biblical Studies Press, 2003), 143.

they are committing or not committing to determine whether or not they are truly born again. What an endless spiritual squirrel cage! And if God can prevent most sin in their lives so that sin is not a "pattern," why doesn't God prevent all sin in their lives? Obviously, there is a human element of choosing daily whether or not to appropriate God's grace resources in the process of sanctification, and such choices and patterns can fluctuate in one direction or the other.

Furthermore, what about godly believers in the Bible who sinned in flagrant disobedience against God, like David (adultery and murder), Abraham (lying), Peter (denying the Lord and hypocrisy with legalists), Moses (uncontrolled anger), and more? Were they not truly saved men? Again, how many sins constitute a pattern? How many times can you commit adultery before you are an adulterer? Or how many times can you murder before you are a murderer? Or steal before you are a thief?

Now, some will retort, "But they later repented of their sins." Yes, some did (thank God), but *not all did.* For what proof exists that Solomon ever repented of his idolatry and worshipping of false deities? There is no record of any repentance in 1 Kings 11 which records his idolatry in later life, God's chastening rebuke, and his physical death. And what about the ongoing sins of the carnal Corinthian believers? The Scriptures clearly indicate that God disciplined "many" by physical death ("sleep") and took them home to Heaven because they were *not* repenting of their unfaithfulness and sins (11:30-32)? Others, like David, eventually repented of their sins to be restored to fellowship with God, but it took them many months (read 2 Samuel 11–12).

Thus, we should reject the habitual sin view based on Greek grammar, other verses in 1 John, numerous biblical examples, logical deduction, and its undermining of the scriptural doctrine of the absolute assurance of one's eternal salvation. So what is 1 John 3:9 actually teaching?

I appeal again to the *context* of the passage, the *content* of the verse, and to *comparing Scripture with Scripture* to arrive at *biblical conclusions.* The context of 1 John centers on the truths of fellowship with God (1:3-4) with the sanctification concept of "abiding" being prevalent in this epistle. Note the following observations:

- The usage of "believe" in the Gospel of John: 99x
- The usage of the word "abide" in 1 John: 21x
- The usage of "believe" in 1 John: 6x

Why is this pattern of usage noteworthy? Because while the book of John is designed primarily for unbelievers to believe in Jesus Christ and receive eternal life (John 20:31), the book of 1 John is designed for believers to learn how to walk in the light and fellowship with Jesus Christ (1:1-7), resulting in obedience to God's will and love for one another (2:3-11). Note the usage of "abide" in 1 John:

- 1 John 2:6, 10, 14, 17, 19, 24 (2x), 27, 28
- 1 John 3:6, 14, 15, 17, 24 (2x), 27
- 1 John 4:12, 13, 15, 16 (2x)

Remember that the apostle John was present when Jesus Christ spoke these truths of the importance of "abiding" in John 15, and he never forgot them:

> Abide in Me, and I in you. As the branch cannot bear fruit of itself, unless it abides in the vine, neither can you, unless you abide in Me. I am the vine, you are the branches. He who abides in Me, and I in him, bears much fruit; for without Me you can do nothing. (John 15:4-5)

With these verses in mind, it should not surprise us then to read in 1 John 2:28: "And now, little children, abide in Him, that when He appears, we may have confidence and not be ashamed before Him at His coming."

John addresses his readers as genuine believers in Christ ("little children") and commands them to "abide in Him." Why? Is it so they would not lose their salvation and arrive in Heaven? No! But so "that when He appears, we [the apostle John includes himself with these believers] may have confidence [having abided in Christ and been faithful and fruitful for Him] and not be ashamed [the opposite of confidence] before Him [at the Judgment Seat of Christ – 1 Cor. 4:5; 2 Cor. 5:10] at His coming." And when believers abide in Christ and bear fruit through the power of the Holy Spirit, others then will know that they are born of God because "everyone who practices righteousness is born of Him" (2:29).

First John 2:29 begins a section of Scripture that uses Jesus Christ as the Christian standard and how believers reflect their abiding fellowship with Him by:

- manifesting practical righteousness to others since Jesus Christ is righteous (2:29)
- purifying themselves with the hope of His appearing and being like Christ since He is pure (3:2-3)
- living victoriously over sin by abiding in Christ since Christ came to take away our sins and in Him there is no sin (3:4-6)

So it should not shock us to read in 1 John 3:6 that "Whoever abides in Him does not sin. Whoever sins has neither seen Him nor known Him."

In an epistle about the believer's fellowship with God and its practical outworking in obedience and love (2:3-11), we should not be surprised to read from an original apostle of our Lord about the importance of abiding in Christ. When believers are abiding in yielded dependence on the Vine, they are not at the same time guilty of sin (see also Galatians 5:16) though they still have much spiritual maturation to experience. Now, this present victory over sin is not because they have lost their sin nature through the new birth, for 1 John 1:8 declares, "If we say that we have no sin, we deceive ourselves, and the truth is not in us." Note that "sin" is both singular and a noun, in reference to the sin nature. Thus, to claim that we have no sin nature is to "deceive ourselves [not others like our spouse and kids], and the truth [regarding this issue] is not in us." One writer precisely observes,

> The habitual sin view is also ruled out by the context. In verse 5 John said that there is no sin in Christ. He clearly meant that there is absolutely no sin in Him. Then in the very next sentence he said that those who abide in Christ do not sin. He could hardly have meant that Christ sins not at all and those who abide in Him sin but not a lot. John's point is clearly that sin is never an expression of abiding in Christ. When we abide we do not sin at all.[2]

In contrast, 1 John 3:6 communicates that the believer who "sins has neither seen nor known Him." Both "seen" and "known" are in the perfect tense as state of being verbs that communicate intensity. This

---

[2] Bob Wilkin, "Do Born Again People Sin?" *The Grace Evangelical Society News* (March 1990).

indicates intimately seeing and knowing a person. For example, the statement, "I'm seeing someone special," means more than visually observing someone with the naked eye. It speaks of a more intimate fellowship. The same is true of the biblical term "known" which can be used of possessing objective information (1 John 5:13) or of personal, intimate sexual or spiritual intercourse (Gen. 4:1; 1 John 4:8).

The apostle John next goes on to distinguish between the practical manifestations of righteousness to others by those believers who are abiding in Christ and those individuals who are not. He writes, "Little children, let no one deceive you. He who practices righteousness is righteous, just as He is righteous" (3:7). This sounds very similar to 1 John 2:29 and how walking in the light and having fellowship with the Lord gives a practical manifestation to others of a believer practicing righteousness. Who, again, is the standard? Verse 7 reminds us "just as He is righteous." And who could potentially deceive the believers whom John addresses? The answer is false teachers who embraced an early form of Gnosticism from which they falsely concluded that physical matter was evil (1 John 1:1-3; 4:1-3) and that sin and God could somehow coexist in fellowship with one another (1:5). Therefore, the apostle John uses repeated absolute terminology throughout this epistle to expose this rank heresy so that believers would not be deceived.

In contrast to an abiding believer who practices righteousness, we then read, "He who sins is of the devil, for the devil has sinned from the beginning" (1 John 3:8). Obviously, the contrast between the manifestation to others of sin and righteousness in a person's life is striking.

Why does the believer who is abiding in Christ not sin at the same time he is abiding? Why does the child of God who abides in Christ live in obedience to God's will (i.e., practice righteousness)? The answers are found in his spiritual birth and the new nature that he has received from God.

> Whoever has been born of God does not sin, for His seed remains in him; and he cannot sin, because he has been born of God. (3:9)

Through being born again ("Whoever has been born of God"), the believer does not sin (he need not sin; in the context this is true when abiding in Christ, v. 6), "for His seed [the new nature which comes from God through the new birth] remains in Him; and he [as a born again, new creation in Christ] cannot sin [as an expression of his new nature], because he is born of God." No believer ever commits sin as an expression of his new nature ("His seed") but still does sin when he yields to his sin nature, which still desires to reign as king in his life (Rom. 6:12). The sin nature reigns when believers fail to appropriate by faith (Rom. 6:11) Christ's victory over the sin nature at Calvary (Rom. 6:10) which they can claim because of their identification with Him in His death, burial, and resurrection (Rom. 6:1-6).

First John 3:9 obviously is a difficult passage regardless of what interpretation one embraces. It clearly cannot contradict the multitude of clear passages in Scripture that teach the eternal security of the believer. As I studied the epistle of 1 John, I found it interesting that one commentator states that John sometimes uses "ubiquitous shorthand."[3] Ubiquitous means that it exists everywhere. Another commentator states that John's text is sometimes "obscure," "difficult," and "awkward."[4] Why might John use "shorthand" and make statements of this nature? Hiebert addresses the reason when he writes, "While the Fourth Gospel is not without its difficulties of interpretation, it is well known that 1 John contains its due share of obscurities and ambiguities. . . . The fact that the epistle was addressed to readers familiar with the writer's teachings, as well as that the work was prompted by a sense of urgency in view of the crisis facing the readers, would help to account for these obscurities of expression."[5]

If at times John does use "shorthand" as he assumes that his audience is familiar with his teachings and has read what he wrote earlier in the book or passage, many passages could be greatly cleared up without this interpreter being guilty of adding to the Word of God. Frankly, we all make these assumptions and non-verbal insertions often in normal conversation when we assume or insert a statement in light of the context or a previous statement. For example, we might say, "We would like you to join us for a meal at 6 pm tonight. So do you think you can join us at 6 pm?" What was assumed but not stated in the second sentence in light of the previous statement? "So do you think you can join us at 6 pm *for a meal.*" This phrase is parenthetically and mentally inserted though

---

[3] Robert W. Yarbrough, *1, 2, and 3 John,* Baker Exegetical Commentary on the New Testament (Grand Rapids: Baker, 2008), 202.

[4] Harris, *1, 2, 3 John,* 229-30.

[5] D. Edmond Hiebert, *The Epistles of John: An Expositional Commentary* (Greenville, SC: Bob Jones University Press, 1991), 9.

not actually stated because it is assumed "shorthand." It appears that John's epistle often contains this kind of contextual assumption and statement-insertion.

Perhaps in the epistle of 1 John the apostle John is actually following the stylistic example of the Master teacher regarding this same concept of "abiding" when our Lord emphatically stated "Abide in Me, and I [will abide – inserted and assumed] in you. As the branch cannot bear fruit of itself, unless it abides in the vine, neither can you, unless you abide in Me" (John 15:4).

Note the following verses in 1 John that appear to beg for an assumed insertion without the actual statement included.

> Now by this we know that we know Him [by fellowship, 1:1–2:2], if we keep His commandments. He who says, "I know Him," and does not keep His commandments, is a liar, and the truth is not in him. But whoever keeps His word, truly the love of God is perfected in him. By this we know that we are in [fellowship with, 1:3-7] Him. (1 John 2:3-5)

> Brethren, I write no new commandment to you, but an old commandment which you have had from the beginning. The old commandment is the word which you heard from the beginning. Again, a new commandment I write to you, which thing is true in Him and in you, because the darkness is passing away, and the true light is already shining. He who says he is [walking/abiding, 1:7] in the light, and hates his brother, is [walking/abiding, 1:6] in darkness until now. He who loves his brother abides in the light, and there is no cause for stumbling in him. But he who hates his brother [a fellow-believer] is [abiding, 2:10] in darkness and walks in darkness [1:6], and does not know where he is going, because the darkness has blinded his eyes. (1 John 2:7-11)

> Whoever abides in Him does not sin. Whoever sins has neither seen Him nor known Him. Little children, let no one deceive you. He who practices righteousness is righteous, just as He is righteous. He who sins is of the devil, for the devil has sinned from the beginning.

> For this purpose the Son of God was manifested, that He might destroy the works of the devil. Whoever has been born of God [and abides in Him, 3:6] does not sin, for His seed remains in him; and he cannot sin [when abiding in Christ, 3:6], because he has been born of God [with a new nature]. (1 John 3:6-9)

> Now he who keeps His commandments abides in Him, and He [abides, John 15:4] in him. And by this we know that He abides in us, by the Spirit whom He has given us. (1 John 3:24)

> By this we know that we abide in Him, and He [abides] in us, because He has given us of His Spirit. (1 John 4:13)

> Whoever confesses that Jesus is the Son of God, God abides in him, and he [abides] in God. (1 John 4:15)

> And we have known and believed the love that God has for us. God is love, and he who abides in love abides in God, and God [abides] in him. (1 John 4:16)

Thus, it is possible and even appropriate for us to understand John using the same stylistic shorthand and contextual assumptions in 3:9 in light of his prior statement in 3:6 so as to interpret verse 9,

> Whoever has been born of God does not sin [when abiding in Him], for His seed [the new nature] remains in him; and he cannot sin [when he is abiding in Him], because he has been born of God [with a new nature].

In summary,

- When believers abide in Christ, will they have confidence before the Lord when He returns? YES!

- When believers fail to abide in Christ, will they be ashamed before Christ at His coming? YES!

- When believers walk by faith in fellowship with the Lord, do they practice righteousness toward others, reflecting Christ who is righteous? YES!

- When believers do not walk by faith in fellowship with the Lord, do they practice righteousness toward others and reflect Christ who is righteous? NO!

- When believers have the hope of Christ's appearing abiding in them, do they purify themselves as Christ is pure? YES!

- When believers do not have the hope of Christ's appearing abiding in them, do they purify themselves as Christ is pure? NO!

- When believers abide in yielded dependence upon the Lord as His life, do they at the same time sin? NO! Why? Because Christ has come to take away sin and in Christ there is no sin.

- When believers fail to abide in Christ, do they fail to see and know Christ in intimate fellowship with Him? YES!

- When believers who are born again abide in Christ, do they sin? NO! Why? Because they have God's seed remaining in them (the new nature) via the new birth which is incapable of sin.

- Does 1 John 3:9 teach that a sinner who is born again is incapable of practicing sin? NO!

- Does 1 John 3:9 teach that if a so-called believer does practice sin that he was never truly born again at all? NO!

- Does 1 John 3:9 teach that believers can ever lose their eternal salvation? NO!

- Does 1 John 3:9 teach that all genuine born-again believers will persevere in faith and holiness all the days of their lives or they were never truly born again? NO!

- Is 1 John 3:9 a difficult verse to interpret? YES!

- Is it possible that John used "shorthand" at times in this epistle and that he assumed his readers would understand verses in light of context, previous statements, and appropriate insertions? YES!

- Does the Bible correctly understood ever contradict itself? NO! Nor does it here! Praise the Lord!

His robes for mine: O wonderful exchange!
Clothed in my sin, Christ suffered 'neath God's rage.
Draped in His righteousness, I'm justified.
In Christ I live, for in my place He died.

His robes for mine: what cause have I for dread?
God's daunting Law Christ mastered in my stead.
Faultless I stand with righteous works not mine,
Saved by my Lord's vicarious death and life.

His robes for mine: God's justice is appeased.
Jesus is crushed, and thus the Father's pleased.
Christ drank God's wrath on sin, then cried "'Tis done!"
Sin's wage is paid; propitiation won.

His robes for mine: such anguish none can know.
Christ, God's beloved, condemned as though His foe.
He, as though I, accursed and left alone;
I, as though He, embraced and welcomed home!

I cling to Christ, and marvel at the cost:
Jesus forsaken, God estranged from God.
Bought by such love, my life is not my own.
My praise—my all—shall be for Christ alone.[6]

---

[6] Chris Anderson, *His Robes for Mine.*

CHAPTER 31

What about That Verse in . . . ?

Permit me to just briefly comment on a variety of other passages that people often use to call into question or outrightly deny the eternal security of the believer in Christ.[1]

1. Matthew 24:13 and "he who endures to the end shall be saved."

This verse is part of the Olivet Discourse (Matt. 24–25) where Christ answers the disciples' questions of Matthew 24:3. "Now as He sat on the Mount of Olives, the disciples came to Him privately, saying, 'Tell us, when will these things be? And what will be the sign of Your coming, and of the *end of the age?*'" The "end" (v. 13) in this context is not perseverance to the end of one's life but to the "end of the age" (vv. 3, 6, 14) in relationship to Christ's second coming. The salvation in view is not spiritual salvation from Hell but *physical deliverance* through the Great Tribulation preceding Christ's return. For this reason, Jesus concludes, "For then there will be great tribulation, such as has not been since the beginning of the world until this time, no, nor ever shall be. And unless those days were shortened, *no flesh would be saved*; but for the elect's sake those days will be shortened" (24:21-22).

2. John 15:6 and a failure to "abide" in Christ.

This verse is part of Christ's Upper Room Discourse to His *believing* disciples on the night before His death, as Judas Iscariot (an

---

[1] These verses were selected from a list of verses compiled by Jimmy Swaggart to deny eternal security in his booklet, *What Is the Doctrine of Unconditional Eternal Security?* (Baton Rouge, LA: Jimmy Swaggart Ministries, 1982).

unbeliever) had already departed to betray Him (John 13:30). John 15 is not about eternal salvation but about bearing "fruit" for the Lord as a believer (15:2, 4, 5, 8, 16) by "abiding" in fellowship and ongoing dependence on Him and His Word (vv. 4-5, 7): "for without Me you can do nothing" (v. 5b). John 15 is about our communion or fellowship with Christ, not our union with Christ or status as a child of God.[2] What if a believer ("branch" vv. 2, 5) fails to abide or remain in fellowship with Christ? "If anyone does not abide in Me, he is cast out as a branch and is withered; and they gather them and throw them into the fire, and they are burned" (v. 6). Jesus Christ explains that a believer's failure to abide in fellowship with Him will have definite consequences. He will be unable to bear fruit ("cast out as a branch" instead of abiding in Christ and bearing fruit), and he will retrogress spiritually ("is withered") so that he is like, in a figurative sense, a worthless branch (no fruit and no testimony) that people throw into the fire.[3] The fire must be interpreted as physical, earthly fire that men burn branches in, since "men" cannot cast anyone into eternal hell.

3.   1 Corinthians 9:24-27 and becoming "disqualified."

In the context of this passage, Paul addresses this carnal local church (1 Cor. 3:1-4) about the proper use of their Christian liberty in serving Christ and winning others to Him (9:19-23). He writes,

> Do you not know that those who run in a race all run, but one receives *the prize*? Run in such a way that *you may obtain it.* And everyone who competes for *the prize* is temperate in all things. Now they do it to obtain a perishable crown, but we for *an imperishable crown.* Therefore I run thus: not with uncertainty. Thus I fight: not as one who beats the air. But I discipline my body and bring it into subjection, lest, when I have preached to others, I myself should become *disqualified.*

Paul is writing to believers about the possibility of obtaining the prize or reward of an imperishable crown for persevering in the Christian life (likened to a race) and not being "disqualified" from receiving a

---

[2] Lewis Sperry Chafer, *Systematic Theology* (Dallas: Dallas Seminary Press, 1948; reprint, Grand Rapids: Kregel, 1993), 3:298-99.

[3] Ibid., 300.

future reward when the Lord returns (1 Cor. 3:11-15; 4:5). Salvation is a gift (not a reward) and a present possession for the believer that can never be lost (Eph. 2:8-9), whereas rewards are given to faithful believers at the Judgment Seat of Christ (2 Cor. 5:10-11) when He returns at the Rapture (1 Cor. 4:5). This passage is a prize-or-reward passage for the believer in Christ, not a salvation-from-Hell passage.

4. Galatians 5:4 and having "fallen from grace."

Galatians is Paul's defense of the Gospel of grace against the attacks of legalistic false teachers. In Galatians, the apostle teaches that the Law cannot justify the sinner (2:16), nor sanctify the saint (2:20; 3:1-5). Only God's grace can accomplish these! If the Galatian believers ("you," 5:1) were to embrace these false legalistic teachers that were infiltrating these churches, they would be "estranged from Christ" (loss of fellowship with the Lord, as a husband and wife can be estranged but still married) and will have "fallen from" the principles and teaching of grace. Nowhere does this passage state that they would lose their eternal salvation. Also interesting is the fact that "falling from grace" would not involve living in overt sin, as the phrase is normally used; instead, in the context it means reverting back to a performance-based relationship with God by trying to keep the Law. To turn from grace-based acceptance to a Law-based relationship constitutes quite a fall!

5. Colossians 1:23 and a failure to "continue in the faith."

These believers in Christ (1:2, 4, 5, 6, 13, 14) were completely "reconciled" to God through the sacrificial death of Christ (v. 21) with the desired intent that they would mature spiritually so as to be presented "holy, blameless, and unreprovable" in God's sight (vv. 22, 28) at the Judgment Seat of Christ. But for this to occur they needed to "continue in the faith" (the body of revealed truth), having been "grounded," and remaining "steadfast" in it and "not moved away from the hope of the Gospel" because of the inroads of false teaching at Colosse (Col. 2:8, 16-23). The first-class condition "if" clause (1:23) assumes that they will continue in the faith because either it is true or for the sake of confidently encouraging them to do so. Their ultimate salvation is never in doubt, but their ongoing growth would require perseverance in the faith to reach the desired objective of full spiritual maturity in progressive sanctification.

6. Hebrews 12:14 and "holiness, without which no one will see the Lord."

Many assume that this passage is warning readers that believing in Christ must be accompanied by a holy life; otherwise, a person's faith is not genuine and that person will not go to Heaven in order to see the Lord. This is how one Reformed writer interprets the verse: "The New Testament lays before us a vast array of conditions for final salvation. Not only initial repentance and faith, but perseverance in both, demonstrated in love toward God and neighbor, are part of that holiness without which no one shall see the Lord (Heb. 12:14)."[4] However, the writer of Hebrews does *not* say, "Pursue peace with all people, and holiness, without which *you* will not see the Lord." Rather, when he says, "without which *no one* will see the Lord," it is better to interpret this as a reference to other people seeing the Lord in the believer's life and witness. Nothing in the passage indicates that the expression "see the Lord" means seeing Him only in Heaven. The immediate context deals with the effect of the believer's walk on his relationship to other people: "Pursue peace with all people" (v. 14a); "lest any root of bitterness springing up cause trouble, and by this many become defiled" (v. 15b). Therefore, verse 14 is simply saying that when believers respond by faith to the loving discipline of God, this results in the spiritual fruit of peace, righteousness (v. 11), and holiness (v. 10), so that others may come to see the character of the Lord in the believer's life and witness (v. 14). This is similar to the teaching of other passages such as James 2:14-26; 1 John 2:29; and 2 Peter 1:10. Therefore, Hebrews 12:14 is not requiring a life of practical sanctification and holiness as proof of saving faith.

7. 1 John 2:3 and "by this we know that we know Him, if we keep His commandments."

Many wrongly conclude that the purpose for which John wrote his first epistle was to provide professing believers with tests to judge whether they truly believe in Christ and possess eternal life or whether they are merely false professors. Christopher D. Bass, a Reformed writer, says,

> We must remember that the first letter of John is laden with various sets of criteria or "tests" by which its readers are to evaluate their religious claims in light of

---

[4] Michael Horton, *Introducing Covenant Theology* (Grand Rapids: Baker, 2006), 182.

the way they conduct their lives. The believer's lifestyle therefore serves as either a vital support to his or her assurance or as evidence that he has never really passed over from death to life.[5]

John MacArthur, another popular Reformed writer who advocates Lordship Salvation, claims John wrote this epistle to provide "eleven tests" of genuine saving faith. These include such subjective questions as: "Do you obey God's word?" "Do you reject this evil world?" "Do you eagerly await Christ's return?" and "Do you see a decreasing pattern of sin in your life?"[6] This tests-of-eternal-life view interprets John's purpose statement in 5:13 to be the purpose statement for the entire epistle: "These things I have written to you who believe in the name of the Son of God, that you may know that you have eternal life." But to what does "these things" refer? Does it refer to the entire epistle or to just the verses immediately preceding 1 John 5:13? John's epistle contains other "purpose statements" besides 5:13, and these indicate that John is normally referring to what immediately precedes each "purpose statement." For example, the statement in 2:1 refers back to 1:5-10, while the statement in 2:26 points back to 2:18-25.

The first purpose statement in the epistle occurs in 1:4 where John says that he wrote so that his readers (children of God) might have fellowship with God the Father and His Son Jesus Christ (v. 3) resulting in fullness of joy. This opening statement in 1:3-4 serves as the purpose statement for entire epistle. John's purpose was not to provide criteria by which his readers could determine whether or not they were born again but instead to determine whether they were having fellowship with God. Certain "test" statements in 1 John should be viewed from this perspective, such as, "by this we know that we know Him, if we keep His commandments" (2:3). Free Grace teachers have historically interpreted this as a test of fellowship with God, not as a test of regeneration. Thus the heading for this passage in the original *Scofield Reference Bible* reads, "The Tests of Fellowship: Obedience and Love." Knowing God in an intimate fashion is not necessarily an indication whether one has been born again, for truly regenerate believers sometimes do not know the Lord in a personal way as they should, especially when walking out of fellowship with

---

[5] Christopher D. Bass, *That You May Know: Assurance of Salvation in 1 John* (Nashville: Broadman & Holman, 2008), 182-83.

[6] John MacArthur, Jr., *Saved without a Doubt: How to Be Sure of Your Salvation* (Wheaton, IL: Victor, 1992), 67-91.

the Lord (John 14:7-9; 1 Cor. 15:34; Gal. 4:9; 2 Peter 3:18). To interpret 1 John 2:3 as a test of eternal life ends up making commandment-keeping a requirement for final salvation, which would contradict other clear Scripture passages on salvation by grace apart from keeping the works of the Law (Rom. 3:19-20, 27-28; Gal. 2:16; 3:19-26).

8. Hebrews 3:6 and 14 and "if we hold fast."

These are not admonitions to either stay saved or prove that a person was genuinely saved to begin with because of his perseverance. The recipients are clearly believers in Christ as one would never address an unbeliever by stating, "Therefore, holy brethren, partakers of the heavenly calling, consider the Apostle and High Priest of our confession, Christ Jesus" (Heb. 3:1). Nor, in light of the other passages examined earlier in this book, were these believers somehow in danger of losing their salvation as some allege (Heb. 6 & 10). Instead, these verses serve as encouragements for these persecuted Hebrew Christians to persevere in faithfulness to the Lord amidst their sufferings in order to be rewarded for having been "partakers" with Christ who experienced the suffering of the cross before the crown (Heb. 2:9-18).

9. The present participle of *pisteuō* in the salvation verses in John.

It is true that the word "believe" (*pisteuō*) in the book of John occurs often as a present tense participle (*pisteuōn*), such as in John 3:16, 18, 36, 5:24, and other passages. But the present participle does not necessarily indicate ongoing, continual belief. This is illustrated by passages such as Mark 6:14 where John the Baptist is named and where the present participle occurs for "Baptist" (*baptizōn*), which is more literally translated, "Baptizer." In the context of Mark 6:14, John is called the "Baptizer" even though he is dead! Obviously, John the Baptist was not continually baptizing people even after his death. The present participle was simply used to describe him.[7] Similarly, true to the descriptive function of a participle when the word "believe" is used in participial form it underscores the condition of a person being "a believing one." But, how many times do you have to fish to be a fisherman? Once! How many times do you have to murder to be a murderer? Once! How many times do you have to believe to be a

---

[7] Ricardo G. Campos, "The Abused Present Participle: *Pisteuōn* (the one who believes) in John," paper presented at the Southern California Grace Evangelical Society Conference, August 27, 2005; Michael Makidon, "Did They Believe?" http://www.scriptureunlocked.com/papers/pisteuo.pdf (accessed July 7, 2011).

believer? Once! This does not preclude ongoing faith, but never does it demand it. Moreover, the book of John also describes believers by verbal forms other than the present participle. One such example is John 8:30-31: "As He spoke these words, many believed [aorist, active indicative] in Him. Then Jesus said to those Jews who believed [perfect active participle] Him . . ." Having just believed in Him, they received eternal life as promised in John 3:16 and other salvation verses, yet they certainly did not yet have ongoing faith in Him.

10. Lucifer and the fallen angels (Isa. 14:12-14; Matt. 25:41).

I have seen these passages used for examples of persons who lost their salvation. Though it is true that these fallen angels lost their right relationship with God and are now His avowed enemies, God never offered salvation to them, nor were they ever "saved" to begin with. Only those who are lost can be saved, and the demons did not begin as lost. Why Jesus Christ came to die for human sinners and not fallen angels is a wonder of God's amazing grace as we did not merit this any more than they did!

11. Adam & Eve (Gen. 2–3).

Only those who are lost need to be saved, and Adam and Eve did not begin in a lost condition but in a state of innocence with an unconfirmed disposition toward God. Thus, they did not "lose their salvation" as some allege. However, their rebellion in the Garden of Eden resulted in spiritual death causing them to need God's gift of salvation. God promised Adam and Eve and the entire human race this salvation through the Redeemer via the seed of the woman (Gen. 3:15), which they accepted by faith as they believed the promise of God (Gen. 3:20). In doing so they then experienced the personal provision of God through the death of an innocent, substitutionary blood sacrifice which God used to clothe these two guilty sinners with tunics of skin (Gen. 3:21). What a wonderful picture of Calvary and 2 Corinthians 5:21: "For He made Him who knew no sin to be sin for us, that we might become the righteousness of God in Him!"

12. Nadab and Abihu (Lev. 10:1-2).

Their punishment for violating the Old Testament law by offering profane incense on the altar resulted in swift and sudden divine punishment via death. This passage does not indicate whether they were genuine believers or not, nor does it comment on their eternal destiny or any alleged loss of salvation. But what a stark reminder that you must do God's will God's way!

13. Korah, Dathan, and Abiram (Num. 16).

In keeping with Old Testament law, and highlighting how God took personally and seriously the people's complaints against His designated spiritual leadership led by these three men, "a fire came out from the LORD and consumed the two hundred and fifty men who were offering incense" (v. 35). Again this passage does not indicate whether they were genuine believers or not, nor does it comment on any alleged loss of salvation. Physical punishment from God cannot be equated with the loss of salvation as this would falsely lead one to believe that all the people who died in the Genesis Flood (Gen. 6-8) were saved and then lost their salvation. That would be absurd!

14. Joshua 24:20.

> If you forsake the LORD and serve foreign gods, then He
> will turn and bring you harm and consume you, after
> He has done you good.

God promised the nation of Israel in Deuteronomy 28–30 that their obedience to God's law would bring upon them many physical blessings from God, while their disobedience would result in various forms of divine discipline. Joshua in his last message to Israel reviews their history and God's past dealings with them and then exhorts them to obedience by simply reiterating these promises to God's chosen nation.

15. King Saul (1 Sam. 16:14; 1 Sam. 28; 1 Chron. 10:13-14).

While Bible teachers disagree regarding Saul's personal salvation, there seem to be several pieces of evidence that indicate he was a genuine believer in the true and living God. He openly declares his faith in the LORD and gives Him the glory for the military victory that was won (1 Sam. 11:13) and has the Spirit of God come upon him (1 Sam. 11:6). However, Saul was prone to take things into his own hands (1 Sam. 13), seek to do God's will his way (1 Sam. 15:1-11), live in self-deception (1 Sam. 15:12-15), and desire to be personally honored instead of the Lord (1 Sam. 15:30). Yet reality is that too many carnal believers have followed Saul's example. Thus, the Spirit of God departed from him (1 Sam. 16:14) as He would do at times in the Old Testament, unlike today (Eph. 1:13). This did not indicate a loss of salvation but of divine power and enablement in one's life (as was true also with Samson), which was certainly true with King Saul. This is what caused Saul to eventually seek out a witch at Endor to summon the prophet Samuel from the grave to find out the outcome of the next day's battle.

> And Saul perceived that it was Samuel, and he stooped with his face to the ground and bowed down. Now Samuel said to Saul, "Why have you disturbed me by bringing me up?" And Saul answered, "I am deeply distressed; for the Philistines make war against me, and God has departed from me and does not answer me anymore, neither by prophets nor by dreams. Therefore I have called you, that you may reveal to me what I should do." Then Samuel said: "Why then do you ask me, seeing the LORD has departed from you and has become your enemy? And the LORD has done for Himself as He spoke by me. For the LORD has torn the kingdom out of your hand and given it to your neighbor, David. Because you did not obey the voice of the LORD nor execute His fierce wrath upon Amalek, therefore the LORD has done this thing to you this day. Moreover the LORD will also deliver Israel with you into the hand of the Philistines. And tomorrow you and your sons will be with me. The LORD will also deliver the army of Israel into the hand of the Philistines." (1 Sam. 28:14-19)

It is interesting to note that Samuel precisely communicated that "tomorrow you and your sons will be with me." Where was Samuel? As a believer in the Lord who had died, he was enjoying the presence of the Lord (Ps. 23:6). So where would Saul and his sons be the next day upon their deaths? They would be in the presence of the Lord with Samuel. So why did King Saul die? Was it due to his faithfulness to the Lord as was true of Uriah (2 Sam. 11:17)? No. It was due to maximum divine discipline because of his unfaithfulness to the Lord as was true of Ananias and Sapphira (Acts 5).

So Saul died for his unfaithfulness which he had committed against the LORD, because he did not keep the
word of the LORD, and also because he consulted a
medium for guidance. But he did not inquire of the
LORD; therefore He killed him, and turned the kingdom
over to David the son of Jesse. (1 Chron. 10:13-14)

King Saul does not exemplify a believer in the LORD who lost his
salvation due to unfaithfulness. Instead, he lived as a carnal believer
who lost his fellowship with the Lord, along with his divine guidance, ultimately experiencing maximum divine discipline like the
Corinthian believers (1 Cor. 11:30-32).

16. King Solomon who went apostate (1 Kings 11).

Though Solomon began his reign well as Israel's third king, he did
not finish well. He began his kingship by seeking and receiving
wisdom from the Lord to do God's will (1 Kings 3), but then ended
it with open disobedience to the Lord through idolatry (11:1-2) due
to marrying foreign wives who stole his heart from the Lord (11:3-
5). He "did evil in the sight of the Lord" (11:6) and then was sternly
rebuked by the Lord (11:9-13), promised that his kingdom would
later become divided (11:11-13), and then was divinely chastened by
the Lord through the use of foreign enemies to Israel (11:14ff). What
a sad ending to his life. Yet was Solomon a true believer in the Lord?
Without question! In fact, the Holy Spirit used him to write various
books of the Old Testament. Did he lose his salvation? Nowhere do
the Scriptures indicate this impossibility.

17. Ezekiel 18:20-32; 33:12-18; and "the soul who sins shall die."

"The soul who sins shall die" (Ezek. 18:20). The historical context
of this passage is God using Ezekiel to warn Israel of the physical
blessings or curses that He would render to them based upon their
obedience or disobedience according to Old Testament law. The
death in view is NOT eternal death or separation from God but
physical death for violation and disregard of His law according to
His covenant (Deut. 28–30). That physical life and death are in view
instead of Heaven or Hell is clear upon examining the wording of
the following verses:

> Again, when a wicked man turns away from the wickedness which he committed, and does what is lawful and right, he preserves himself alive. (Ezek. 18:27)

> When I say to the righteous that he shall surely live, but he trusts in his own righteousness and commits iniquity, none of his righteous works shall be remembered; but because of the iniquity that he has committed, he shall die. Again, when I say to the wicked, "You shall surely die," if he turns from his sin and does what is lawful and right, if the wicked restores the pledge, gives back what he has stolen, and walks in the statutes of life without committing iniquity, he shall surely live; he shall not die. (Ezek. 33:13-15)

For one to teach that this passage directed to Old Testament Israel is applicable today or is referring to spiritual life or death is to teach salvation by works, let alone to totally disregard the context and wording of the passage. This would be rank eisegesis and the forcing of one's theology upon the passage instead of paying attention to its historical and doctrinal context.

18. Matthew 6:14-15 and not forgiving others.

> For if you forgive men their trespasses, your heavenly Father will also forgive you. But if you do not forgive men their trespasses, neither will your Father forgive your trespasses. (Matt. 6:14-15)

Jesus Christ spoke these words in His Kingdom teaching during the Sermon on the Mount (Matt. 5–7). This pattern of prayer was given to Christ's disciples in light of His preaching of the Gospel of the Kingdom (Matt. 4:17) and is not an offer of eternal forgiveness or life. Otherwise, salvation would not be by God's grace alone through faith alone in Christ alone (John 3:16; 5:24; Acts 10:43). Instead it would be earned by our own works of righteousness (Isa. 64:6; Titus 3:5), namely our forgiveness of others. Salvation is for forgiven sinners, not forgiving saints. Furthermore, our forgiveness of others under grace is to be motivated by the reality that "God in Christ forgave you" (Eph. 4:32). This verse is in keeping with Christ's answer and parable to Peter in Matthew 18:21-35 regarding God's displeasure with a believer's failure to show compassion and forgiveness to another who has sinned. Again, this verse says nothing about the loss of salvation.

19. Matthew 8:11-12 and outer darkness.

> When Jesus heard it, He marveled, and said to those who followed, "Assuredly, I say to you, I have not found such great faith, not even in Israel! And I say to you that many will come from east and west, and sit down with Abraham, Isaac, and Jacob in the kingdom of heaven. But the sons of the kingdom will be cast out into outer darkness. There will be weeping and gnashing of teeth."

In this context, our Lord is commenting on the faith of a Roman centurion who believed that Jesus is Lord and could heal his son from afar (8:5-9). This Gentile would not be alone in the Kingdom to come, as many other Gentiles who were saved through simple faith would sit down with the patriarchs in the Kingdom of Heaven. However, Jesus' disciples would be startled to hear that fellow Jews ("sons of the kingdom") who never trusted in Christ alone would be cast into outer darkness with weeping and gnashing of teeth.[8] One's ethnic heritage, including being a Jew, does not automatically make one a child of God (John 1:13; 8:36-40). The new birth is appropriated only by receiving Jesus Christ when a person believes on His name (John 1:12). When correctly understood, this passage gives no indication of a believer losing his salvation.

20. Matthew 10:32-33 and being denied before the Father.

> Therefore whoever confesses Me before men, him I will also confess before My Father who is in heaven. But whoever denies Me before men, him I will also deny before My Father who is in heaven.

Matthew 10 explains Jesus Christ's selection of His apostles (10:1-4), their targeted audience—Jews only (10:5-6), their message of the Gospel of the Kingdom (10:7), their demonstration of Christ's power

---

[8] A similar expression and outcome is the result of the unbelieving unprofitable servant in Matthew 25:30.

(10:8), and their physical provisions (10:9-10). Christ anticipates that some would receive their message and others would reject it (10:11-15) and that they will experience much persecution due to their Kingdom message (10:16-23). Our Lord then explains to them not the cost of *salvation* (which Christ fully paid at Calvary) but the cost of *discipleship* in being a devoted and faithful follower of Jesus Christ amidst anticipated persecution and rejection (10:24-42). It is in this context that Jesus Christ declares verses 32-33. What is at stake for these believers whom Christ challenged to follow after Him in discipleship (10:38)? Is it their eternal salvation? No, they were already saved (except for Judas). It is Christ's positive confession to the Father regarding the disciples' faithful service resulting in them receiving a reward or Christ denying them a reward they could have obtained had they been faithful to Him.

> He who receives a prophet in the name of a prophet *shall receive* a prophet's *reward*. And he who receives a righteous man in the name of a righteous man *shall receive* a righteous man's *reward*. And whoever gives one of these little ones only a cup of cold water in the name of a disciple, assuredly, I say to you, *he shall by no means lose his reward*. (Matt. 10:41-42)

This passage does not teach that eternal salvation can be lost as it is a gift from God (Eph. 2:8; Rom. 6:23), not a reward (Rom. 4:4-5). But what Christ's disciples could lose was a potential reward they would have received for faithful service to the Lord. This echoes the same basic truth that Paul later taught Church-age believers in Christ in 1 Corinthians 3:14-15.

21. John 6:66 and Christ's disciples walking away.

> From that time many of His disciples went back and walked with Him no more.

Though many today who count heads would consider Christ's discourse on the Bread of Life as a miserable failure, the Lord intentionally used to separate His disciples. Keep in mind that depending on the context, the term "disciple" referred generically to both saved and unsaved students or pupils under Jesus' teaching as is the case here, while at other times Christ targeted believers only (John 8:30-

31). This underscores the importance of context. Many in this crowd may have never been genuinely saved. On the other hand, some who stayed had believed in Jesus as the Christ, but not all.

> Then Jesus said to the twelve, "Do you also want to go away?" But Simon Peter answered Him, "Lord, to whom shall we go? *You have the words of eternal life.* Also *we have come to believe and know that You are the Christ, the Son of the living God.*" Jesus answered them, "Did I not choose you, the twelve, and one of you is a devil?" He spoke of Judas Iscariot, the son of Simon, for it was he who would betray Him, being one of the twelve. (John 6:67-71)

Once again there is no mention of the loss of eternal salvation. Instead, we observe a positive affirmation that these remaining disciples (except Judas) *believed* and were *assured* that Jesus was the Christ who had the words of eternal life.

22. Ananias and Sapphira and their physical deaths (Acts 5:1-11).

This believing couple intentionally lied to God the Holy Spirit and to the apostles about the sale of some land and experienced maximum divine discipline by God, for both physically died. What a reminder that "for whom the LORD loves He chastens, and scourges every son whom He receives. If you endure chastening, God deals with you as with sons; for what son is there whom a father does not chasten? But if you are without chastening, of which all have become partakers, then you are illegitimate and not sons" (Heb. 12:6-8).

23. Simon the Sorcerer and how he could "perish" (Acts 8:5-25).

Philip's ministry of preaching the Gospel impacted many in Samaria including a man named Simon who "previously practiced sorcery" and made his name famous as "the great power of God" (8:5-11). Yet a great many of the Samaritans "believed" Philip's preaching and were then "baptized" as a public proclamation of their identification and faith in Jesus Christ (8:12). When the Scriptures said they "believed," is it not best to take God at His Word and agree that they believed? Acts 8:13 goes on to state, "Simon himself *believed* and was *baptized.* And he followed Philip everywhere, astonished by the great signs and miracles he saw." When the Scriptures said Simon "believed," is it not best to take God at His Word and agree that he believed? In fact, apparently others agreed that he believed as he was then baptized as well. But later Simon coveted after the power he saw demonstrated through the ministry of the apostle Peter (8:14-20). But I ask you, is Simon the only believer you know who has desired that his name be in the limelight or who coveted after another man's ministry? Frankly, the evangelical woods are filled with many glory seekers, some of whom are believers in Jesus Christ but who are walking after the flesh. What was Peter's response to Simon?

> But Peter said to him, "Your money perish with you, because you thought that the gift of God could be purchased with money! You have neither part nor portion in this matter, for your heart is not right in the sight of God. Repent therefore of this your wickedness, and pray God if perhaps the thought of your heart may be forgiven you. For I see that you are poisoned by bitterness and bound by iniquity." (Acts 8:20-23)

The phrase, "your money perish with you," is not a declaration of the loss of salvation as one's money cannot actually go to Hell. The word "perish" in this context does not refer to eternal Hell as in John 3:16, but to physically die and perish (like what happened to Ananias and Sapphira in Acts 8). The problem was that Simon's heart was not right with God (8:21), and he needed to "repent . . . of this wickedness," which is the right response to revealed sin in a believer's life. This is not an invitation to eternal salvation, for the passage states that Simon had already "believed." This is an invitation to have restored fellowship with God (1 John 1:9) and the need to pray that he would not experience the divine discipline that was possibly forthcoming unless God graciously rescinded it (8:22). Thus, this passage does not threaten believers with the possibility of the loss of eternal salvation; instead, it teaches how bitterness (8:23) and covetousness (8:19) have poisoned many a believer's fellowship with God, brought on His divine discipline, and ruined their testimony to others.

24. Romans 8:13 and how living according to the flesh leads to death.

> For if you live according to the flesh you will die; but if by the Spirit you put to death the deeds of the body, you will live.

In Paul's great treatise of the book of Romans, he has explained the great truths of man's condemnation (1:18–3:20); then God's justification of the sinner who believes in Jesus Christ alone apart from works, law, or ritual (3:21–4:25); followed by the blessings of justification, including eternal security and assurance (5:1-11); the truths of identification due to Adam and Jesus Christ (5:12-21); positional sanctification in Christ (6:1-10); practical sanctification by faith and yieldedness to the Lord (6:11-23); powerless sanctification through living by law (7); and powerful sanctification via the Holy Spirit (8:1-15). Romans 8:13 in its context has nothing to do with a believer's justification or glorification. The "death" in view contextually is not spiritual or eternal death (the loss of salvation) as a result of living according to the flesh rather than living according to the Spirit. This passage refers to the reality of a death-like existence of being temporarily separated from the joys and blessings of walking in fellowship with the Lord. (See also James 1:15, 5:20; 1 Tim. 5:6; and Luke 15:24 for other examples of the child of God's temporary death as a result of being separated from God's fellowship.) So the context argues against viewing this verse as teaching a loss of salvation, as does Paul's previous explanation of eternal security in Romans 5:6-11. In addition, the latter half of Romans 8:28-39 will speak loudly again for the eternal security of the believer and his absolute guarantee of glorification. Thus, as the Bible correctly understood never contradicts itself, nor does a correct understanding of Romans 8:13 contradict the eternal security of the believer's salvation.

25. 1 Corinthians 8:11 and the weak brother "perishing."

> And because of your knowledge shall the weak brother perish, for whom Christ died?

1 Corinthians 8 is about the right use and misuse of Christian liberty as it relates to the eating of meats offered to idols. Paul argues that while the meat is not unclean in itself in spite of its past association with idols (8:1-8), if a Christian fails to act out of love in his liberty, and his eating becomes a stumbling block to others whose conscience is weak, this is not good and should be avoided (8:9-14). The word "perished" in this context does not mean condemned to Hell, for another's misuse of his liberty cannot ultimately decide others' final destiny; only their faith or unbelief in Jesus Christ can (John 3:16-18). Robert Gromacki catches the essence of this word in this context

when he writes, "The weak Christian 'perished' in that he suffered spiritual loss, a sense of sin that affected his fellowship with God. This reckless use of liberty actually violates the purpose for which Christ died (8:11b)."[9] No one loses eternal salvation in this verse, but it warns how the indulgent and insensitive use of a believer's freedom under grace is dishonoring to the Lord and destructive to the walk and growth of other immature Christians.

26. 1 Corinthians 15:2 and having "believed in vain."

> Moreover, brethren, I declare to you the gospel which I preached to you, which also you received and in which you stand, by which also you are saved, if you hold fast that word which I preached to you—unless you believed in vain. (15:1-2)

In this great resurrection chapter, Paul begins by reviewing his past evangelistic preaching to the people at Corinth and how it resulted in them receiving the Gospel and standing for its truth (15:1, 12). Because of the false teaching of the resurrection assailing this church (15:12), he then adds in verse 2 that they could only enjoy salvation from sin's power in their lives (progressive sanctification) in the present ("you are saved"—present tense) "if" they held fast or firm to the Gospel he had preached to them when they came to Christ (which he then explains in verses 3-4). Otherwise, they had "believed in vain." This is another piece of evidence that they had genuinely believed and embraced the Gospel by faith. However, they also needed to hold fast to that same Gospel of Jesus Christ's person, work, and accomplishment (15:3-4) that brought them eternal salvation because it formed the foundation for their progressive and practical sanctification. Apart from fidelity and faithfulness to the saving message of the Gospel of grace, the believers at Corinth would not realize God's intended target or purpose of personal holiness and spiritual maturity ("believed in vain").[10] This is the very same flow of thought as Colossians 1:22-25 which teaches that perseverance in the faith is necessary for progressive sanctification in the life of the believer in Christ, but it is not required for initial justification or ultimate glorification.

---

[9] Robert G. Gromacki, *Called to Be Saints: An Exposition of 1 Corinthians* (Grand Rapids: Baker, 1977), 107.

[10] For an excellent and thorough explanation of this passage, see Thomas L. Stegall, *The Gospel of the Christ* (Milwaukee: Grace Gospel Press, 2009), 479-528.

27. 1 Timothy 5:15 and turning aside to Satan.

> For some have already turned aside after Satan.

The first half of 1 Timothy 5 is about a significant problem in the early Church, namely the care of widows (5:3-16). After commenting on the care of older widows, Paul addresses the younger widows' personal problems and some practical solutions for them.

> But refuse the younger widows; for when they have begun to grow wanton against Christ, they desire to marry, having condemnation because they have cast off their first faith. And besides they learn to be idle, wandering about from house to house, and not only idle but also gossips and busybodies, saying things which they ought not. Therefore I desire that the younger widows marry, bear children, manage the house, give no opportunity to the adversary to speak reproachfully. For some have already turned aside after Satan. (5:11-15)

Some of these younger Christian widows "have already turned aside after Satan" in the sense that they were following after or pursuing the pleasures of sin in the world system whose prince or ruler is Satan (John 12:31; Eph. 2:2). Because of the close relationship between the Devil and his diabolical system, the writers of Scripture occasionally refer to the world system by referring to simply its ruler—namely, Satan (1 Cor. 5:5; 1 Tim. 1:20) as is the case also in 1 Timothy 5:15. This connection between Satan and the world system is another reason why believers are not to love the world (1 John 2:15-17); otherwise, they become spiritual adulterers who whore after the things of the world and become practical enemies of God (James 4:4). 1 Timothy 5:11-15 does not teach the loss of eternal salvation, but it does give a clear warning regarding the consequences of carnality in a Christian's life and the need to resist "the passing pleasures of sin" (Heb. 11:25) by God's Word and Spirit.

28. Hebrews 5:9 and obeying Jesus Christ.

> And having been perfected, He became the author of eternal salvation to all who obey Him.

As was established when commenting on Hebrews 3:6, 14 and 12:14, the recipients of this epistle are clearly believers in Christ as you would never address an unbeliever by stating, "Therefore, holy brethren, partakers of the heavenly calling, consider the Apostle and High Priest of our confession, Christ Jesus" (Heb. 3:1). Nor in light of the other passages examined earlier in this book were these Hebrew believers somehow in danger of losing their eternal salvation as some falsely allege (see Hebrews 6 and 10) but were actually assured that they were "perfected forever" because of the once-and-for-all sacrifice of Jesus Christ (Heb. 10:10-14). Gromacki accurately explains, "The provision of salvation was achieved through the obedience of the Son to the Father at the cross, and the appropriation of salvation is accomplished through the obedience of the repentant sinner toward Christ. In this passage, obedience is synonymous with faith (Acts 6:7; Rom. 6:17; 10:16)."[11]

Warren Wiersbe adds, "Does the phrase, 'them that obey Him' (5:9) suggest that, if we do not obey Him, we may lose that eternal salvation? To 'obey God' is the same as 'to trust God,' as 'them that obey Him' is a description of those who have put their faith in Jesus Christ... Once we have put our faith in Jesus Christ, and thus obeyed His call, we experience His eternal salvation."[12]

The obedience that Jesus Christ in the Gospel requires is simply to believe in the person and finished work of Jesus Christ alone for one's eternal salvation (Rom.1:5, 16; 3:24-28; 5:1; 6:17; 10:16-17; 2 Thess. 1:8-10; 1 Peter 1:22-25). Salvation is not by our works of obedience; otherwise, it would be by law, not grace (Gal. 2:20); and it would be a reward, not a gift (Rom. 4:5). Since the merit-law-works approach to salvation requires of the sinner 100 percent obedience to the Law 100 percent of the time (Gal. 3:10), the Law is clearly stated to be "not of faith" (Gal. 3:11),[13] whereas eternal salvation is clearly by faith alone in Christ alone and "not of works lest anyone should boast" (Eph. 2:8-9). While all believers should be motivated based on their position in Christ to "present your members as slaves of righteousness for holiness" (Rom. 6:19), this is for progressive sanctification in their lives to honor their Savior, not to be saved or be kept saved.

---

[11] Robert G. Gromacki, *Stand Bold in Grace: An Exposition of Hebrews* (reprint, The Woodlands, TX: Kress Christian Publications, 2001), 96.

[12] Warren W. Wiersbe, *Be Confident: An Expository Study of the Epistle to the Hebrews* (Wheaton, IL: Victor Books, 1982), 56.

[13] For a classic study on the subject of law and grace, see Roy L. Aldrich, *Holding Fast to Grace* (Milwaukee: Grace Gospel Press, 2011).

Instead of this passage making eternal salvation conditioned upon ongoing obedience to Christ in one's life and thus capable of being lost or forfeited due to disobedience, it actually teaches that the believer in Christ has received "eternal salvation," which by its definition must last forever. That's eternal security!

29. 1 John 3:15 and no murderer has eternal life abiding in him.

Whoever hates his brother is a murderer, and you know that no murderer has eternal life abiding in him.

This verse at first glance is a perplexing verse indeed that is subject to various interpretations—some doctrinally allowable, and others doctrinally wrong. I would again ask that you be like the Bereans (Acts 17:10-11) and consider what I have written and search the Scriptures to make sure these things are so. As explained in chapter 30, this epistle addresses the believer's fellowship with God (1:3-4) and related truths, not the condition or tests of salvation. This is communicated as John teaches in light of the incipient Gnostic teachers infiltrating the early Church with their false teaching. As a result, John begins this epistle by describing the humanity of Jesus Christ in empirical terms, bookended by the reality that He is "from the beginning" (v. 1) and "eternal life" that was "with the Father" (v. 2), which both emphasize His deity.

That which was *from the beginning,* which we have *heard,* which we have *seen* with our eyes, which we have *looked upon,* and our *hands have handled,* concerning the Word of life—*the life was manifested,* and we have *seen,* and bear witness, and declare to you that *eternal life* which was *with the Father* and was manifested to us. (1 John 1:1-2)

Also it was previously mentioned that one of the key terms in 1 John is the concept of "abiding" in Christ taken from John 15 which describes a believer's fellowship and fruitfulness by and for Jesus Christ.

In contrast to loving a fellow believer, which is a reflection of abiding in Christ and a test of fellowship, we observe in 3:15 that "whoever hates his brother is a murderer." Notice that this person hates "his brother," which indicates he himself is a believer and is failing to love another believer. Therefore, he is not abiding in Christ. God likens this hating of one's brother to being a "murderer." Why? It is because God does not need to see the action of murder to discern the attitude of hatred that underlies the sinful action which is its consequence. This is similar to the statements of our Lord about the sinful attitudes of unrighteous anger and unrestrained lust that God considers "murder" and "adultery" (Matt. 5:22-28).

But this raises the question, what does it mean that "you know that no murderer has eternal life abiding in him"? Does it mean that if you murder, you cannot be saved? No, for Saul was the chief of sinners yet He was given eternal life by God's grace and mercy when he trusted in the Savior (1 Tim. 1:15-16).

Does it mean that if you ever murder, it proves you were never saved? To arrive at this erroneous interpretation would cause you to conclude that both Moses and David were never saved since both were guilty of murder. And if that was the right conclusion, why would Peter exhort believers to not suffer as a murderer if that would be an oxymoron and impossibility (1 Peter 4:12-16)?

Does it mean that genuine believers never "practice" hatred though it can occur on occasions? This creates the problem of how many times you can sin before it is constituted a "practice," especially as it relates to "murder" in the context. And what about the sin of bitterness that oftentimes is a bed partner with hatred that believers are also certainly guilty of (Heb. 12:15).

Or does it mean that you could have been saved, but now you have forfeited it and lost your eternal salvation due to committing murder? If this was possible, how did this sin somehow fail to be paid in full by the blood of Christ? And how could this specific sin have escaped the forgiveness of all sins a sinner receives (past, present, and future) when he comes by faith to Christ (Col. 2:13)?

The solution to this problem is wrapped up in the phrase "eternal life abiding in him." The phrase "eternal life" is a reference to Jesus Christ as introduced at the beginning of this epistle (1:2), and He is referred to again as "eternal life" at the end of John's letter (5:12, 20).

The phrase "abiding in him" hearkens back to the words of our Lord in the Upper Room Discourse (John 13–17) that John repeatedly draws upon in this epistle when Christ clearly stated, "Abide in Me and *I in you*" (John 15:4) in the context of a mutual personal fellowship with Christ and vice-versa. Just a few verses earlier in 1 John 3, the aged apostle dogmatically wrote, "Whoever *abides in Him* does not sin" at the same time because of the purpose and person of Jesus

Christ (3:6). Thus, 1 John 3:15 is simply reiterating this same truth from the opposite angle that, "Whoever [a believer] hates [a failure to love] his brother [a fellow-believer] is a murderer [as God perceives the heart], and you know that no murderer [the believer who is hating his brother] has eternal life [Jesus Christ] abiding in him [by way of Christ's fellowship]. In other words, when a believer hates a fellow-believer, he is not at the same time abiding and having fellowship with Christ, nor is Christ abiding and having fellowship with him. The two are mutually exclusive. Once again John is destroying the incipient Gnostic's false teaching that could adversely affect these believers that light and darkness co-exist with God [1:5], and so can the believer's sin and fellowship with God [1:6-7].

Thus, tremendous light is shed on this verse by again examining the general and specific *context* of 1 John 3, followed by observing the *content* of verse 15 as it relates to the key words "eternal life" and "abiding in him," along with *comparing Scripture with Scripture* such as John 15, 1 John 3:6, and other passages that clearly indicate what this verse cannot be stating. First John 3:15 is a verse consistent with the overall thrust of 1 John that teaches that a believer who is walking in the light abides in Christ and has sweet fellowship with Him (who is love) which results in loving and not hating your fellow-believers. Conversely, when you know that a believer hates his brother, you know that he is not abiding in Christ's fellowship nor is Jesus Christ [eternal life] having fellowship with Him.

Once again let's hear three cheers for examining the context, observing the content, and comparing Scripture with Scripture to arrive at correct conclusions consistent with the message of God's grace and the balance of the Bible! There is no loss of eternal salvation taught in this verse, but did you really expect to find it as the Bible correctly understood never contradicts itself? Perhaps not, but you may have wondered like I did for years, "What exactly is 1 John 3:15 teaching?" Hopefully now you know.

30. 1 John 5:16-17 and the sin leading to death.

> If anyone sees his brother sinning a sin which does not lead to death, he will ask, and He will give him life for those who commit sin not leading to death. There is sin leading to death. I do not say that he should pray about that. All unrighteousness is sin, and there is sin not leading to death.

Are these verses indicating that a believer can commit a sin that leads to spiritual or eternal death, and therefore the loss of eternal salvation? We have already laid out the *general context* of 1 John in chapter 30, along with several previous comments on 1 John 3:15. In addition, the *immediate context* in 1 John 5:14-15 gives divine assurances to answered prayer when asked according to God's will. With these truths in mind, verses 16 and 17 now give a tangible illustration of this.

So let's begin to analyze this passage by observing the *content* of these verses which is fraught with exegetical difficulties and differences among Bible commentators due to John's loose Greek constructions, obscure meanings, and theological imports. Let me add my conclusions to the mix for your studied and prayerful consideration. The word "if" (*ean* + subjunctive = third class condition) indicates that the following event is a possibility. The phrase, "if anyone sees his brother sinning a sin" reveals that the apostle John is talking about one believer ("if anyone" — as intercessory prayer is available to all) observing ("seeing") another believer ("brother") "sinning" (present tense — present active participle of *hamartanō*, indicating that this sinning is deliberate and it appears externally as overt sin, not just a suspicion). When John refers to "a sin" that a believer observes another believer sinning, the nature or description of any particular sin is not given; nor is there a definite article before the word "sin" which indicates that John is not singling out a specific sin but probably the quality of a state of rebellion (see 1 John 3:4). This phrase clearly indicates that believers still sin, sometimes with no regard to whether they are seen or not by others (reflecting hard-hearted carnality) and that some of their sins are clearly observed by other believers (and it should be probably assumed by unbelievers as well). What are the results of this believer "sinning a sin"? Two possible consequences are stated. First, it could be that the sin "does not lead to death." This is best understood to be a reference to "physical" death? Why? It is because...

- there are several cases in Scripture where God disciplined His children via physical death, such as Ananias and Sapphira (Acts 5), many of the Corinthian Christians (1 Cor. 11:30), and others. Thus physical death is a viable option for "death" in this verse.

- the sinner who believes the record of God concerning Jesus Christ has "passed from death into life" spiritually (John 5:24). Thus "spiritual" death (Eph. 2:1) is eliminated as an option.

- the believer has "eternal life" and shall not come into condemnation later (John 5:24) so that he can "know" that he "has eternal life" (1 John 5:13). Thus "eternal" death is removed as an option.

- while the believer can still experience "temporal" death and a loss of fellowship with God because of carnality (Rom. 8:6, 13; 1 Tim. 5:6; James 1:15), this verse says that this sin "does not lead to death." However, James 1:15 is clear that "when desire has conceived, it gives birth to sin; and sin, when it is full-grown, brings forth death." Sin always leads to a breakage of fellowship with the Father for the believer, but this sin in 1 John 5:16 "does not lead to death." Thus, physical death is the only good option exegetically and doctrinally.

The second possible consequence when a believer sins a sin is that it does lead to physical death via divine chastening as "there is a sin resulting in death" (5:16b).

How should a believer respond when he sees a brother sinning a sin that doesn't lead to physical death and the apparent early home going of this rebellious child of God? He should specifically intercede for him in prayer (he should "ask"). What specifically should he ask for? He should ask for his spiritual restoration to fellowship with God ("life" in contrast to temporal "death," for how can God answer his prayer and give the sinning believer "life" unless he is dead in some sense though not physically?) If the believer will pray for the sinning believer this way, the verse promises, "and He" (God) "will give him life" (an answer to his prayer for other believers) "for those who commit sin not leading to [physical] death." Earlier in this epistle 1 John 1:9 made it abundantly clear that when we as believers sin, we need to "confess our sins" and appropriate God's fellowship forgiveness. And 1 John 2:1-2 indicates that while God does not desire for His children to sin, yet they do and Jesus Christ ever lives to make intercession for them as their righteous advocate.

THE SEVEN DEATHS OF SCRIPTURE

		WHEN	CAUSE	WHAT	VERSES	REMEDY
1	SPIRITUAL	At conception	Born in Adam	Separation from a right relationship w/God	Gen. 2:17 Eph. 2:1	Salvation: being "born again" (John 3:3-18)
2	PHYSICAL	When you die	The fall, the curse, and being in Adam	Separation of your soul and spirit from your body	Gen. 35:18 Heb. 9:27 James 2:26	Only "sleep" for a believer, then bodily resurrection (1 Thess. 4:13-18)
3	ETERNAL	Begins when you die physically; lasts forever	Physical death apart from faith in Christ	Separation of your body, soul, and spirit from God forever	Rev. 20:14 Matt. 25:46	Salvation with eternal life (John 5:24)
4	POSITIONAL	At the moment you get saved	Born again in Christ; Identification with Christ's death	Separation from your old unregenerate self as a new creation in Christ	Rom. 6:3-6 Gal. 2:20	It is a remedy!
5	TEMPORAL	During your life, after salvation	Personal sin's of the believer	Separation from a right fellowship w/God	Rom. 8:13 Luke 15:24 James 1:15 1 Tim. 5:6	Walking in the light and confession of sin as needed (1 John 1:3-10)
6	OPERATIONAL	During your life, after salvation	Not truly walking by faith in sanctification	Separation from a right divine production of good works and a right testimony before man	James 2:14-26	Confession of sin and dependence on God (James 1:19-25)
7	SEXUAL	During old age	Physical limitation	Separation from physical ability to reproduce	Rom. 4:17-19	Miracle from God

1 John 5:16 now highlights for us how we as believers are to respond when observing another believer sinning a sin that doesn't result in physical death. The answer is to engage in intercessory prayer for other believers who are sinning which would be consistent with praying according to God's will (vv. 14-15) and genuine love for the brethren (a key concept throughout 1 John as found in 3:11, 23; 4:7, 11-12). What then can we anticipate resulting from our intercession for the sinning believer? The answer at the end of verse 16 is "and He" (God) "will give him" (the sinning believer) "life" (restoration to fellowship due to his temporal death and access to an abundant life; see Luke 15:24) "for those" (this anticipates other sinning believers are also in view and prayed for) "who commit sin not leading to [physical] death." Yes, there is tremendous value in praying out of love for fellow believers, even the sinning ones. This also means that you need to be humble enough to recognize that at times others should also pray for you!

Having explained the right loving response when observing a believer sinning a sin in rebellion towards God, John explains what the believer's response should *not* be toward his fellow believer. He states, "There is sin leading to [physical] death. I do not say that he should pray about that." The New American Standard Bible translates this sentence, "There is a sin leading to death; I do not say that he should make request for this." In other words, when we observe a fellow believer sinning a sin, do not pray that God would divinely discipline him with physical death (though we may be tempted to do so).

Like a good expositor and teacher, the apostle John next anticipated the reactions of his audience to his previous comments and seeks to clarify any misconceptions that could result. Next John anticipates that some people will make light of sin as inconsequential since it does not result in physical death. Thus, he adds, "all unrighteousness is sin" in God's eyes, which is probably another rap against the Gnostic's false teaching which downplayed the significance of sin in the believer's life. He then ends by underscoring that "there is a sin not leading to [physical] death," though it still results in a death-like existence of broken fellowship with God unless the believer confesses it as sin to God and his fellowship with God is restored (1 John 1:9). Hiebert accurately writes, "All sin is serious but not all is hopeless and beyond the reach of Christian intercession; this leaves a standing challenge to brotherly intercession."[14]

---

[14] D. Edmond Hiebert, *The Epistles of John* (Greenville, SC: Bob Jones University

Whether one agrees with all my interpretative conclusions on these two verses or not, one thing is strikingly clear. This passage does not indicate that a brother (believer) who sins a sin (whether leading to physical death or not) ceases to be a "brother" in the forever and forgiven family of God. His eternal salvation is never in jeopardy of loss or forfeiture. And what else would we expect from an epistle like 1 John that is devoted to explaining the truths of fellowship with God as a believer against the backdrop of the false teaching of the Gnostics.

Thus all believers, whether immature or mature, walking in the light or in darkness, are repeatedly addressed in 1 John by such terms as those who are "born" of God (2:29; 3:9 [2x]; 4:7; 5:1, 18 [2x]), or as "little children" (*teknia*—a term used of all believers in 2:1, 12, 28; 3:7, 18; 4:4; 5:21-22) or as "beloved" (*agapētoi*—a term used of all believers who are especially loved by God in 2:7; 3:2, 21; 4:1, 7, and 11).

John is not calling into question the standing of these believers before God as born-again children of God, but on the contrary he repeatedly affirms it. Yet John is challenging and instructing these believers in this epistle with the parent-child motif and its appropriate language about their daily fellowship with their heavenly Father and His Son, Jesus Christ, which results in obedience to God's will and love for fellow believers. Once you have been born into a family are you not the child of your parents forever whether you obey them or not? That parent-child relationship is forever settled and unchangeable. Yet it remains to be seen if you will walk in daily fellowship with your parents or not. A failure to do so never jeopardizes your once-and-for-all physical birth, but it does affect the quality and consistency of the fellowship you will enjoy with them, or the loving discipline they may need to exercise in your life. Did not the Holy Spirit so direct the writers of Scripture, and in particular the apostle John, to utilize the concepts of the never-to-be-repeated new birth that can never be lost or forfeited versus daily, repeated fellowship with God that can be lost or forfeited so as to keep clear these important scriptural truths? I believe the biblical evidence overwhelmingly supports this conclusion. And all God's people said, AMEN!

Dear readers, when you let the Scriptures speak for themselves, they harmonize wonderfully. You need not force or manipulate verses to reconcile them since you don't need to reconcile friends.

Press, 1991), 263.

And once again we observe the Word of God exalting the Son of God and the grace of God which is ever flowing to you and me!

Grace is flowing like a river
From the mount of Calvary.
Look to Jesus Christ the Giver;
He from sin can set you free.

Heaven's fountain ever floweth;
All our need has been supplied.
Still it flows as fresh as ever
From the Savior's wounded side.

Through the blood of Christ forgiven,
Dry the tears from ev'ry face.
Through His cross an heir of Heaven,
Evermore a child of grace.

Come to Jesus, weary sinner;
Calv'ry's river flows today.
All who plunge beneath that fountain
Wash their guilty stains away.

Grace is flowing like a river;
Millions there have been supplied.
Still it flows as fresh as ever
From the Savior's wounded side.[15]

---

[15] Ron Hamilton, *Grace Is Flowing*.

CHAPTER 32

A Conclusion and Closing Invitation

I offer to you my sincere thanks if you have taken the time to read through this entire book. By God's grace and to His glory, I have attempted in this volume to explain the Gospel clearly, define what eternal security is and is not teaching, scripturally support the wonderful truth that the believer in Christ is saved and secure forever, highlight the absolute assurance of eternal salvation that God wants all to have and believers to be established in, interact with the reasons why people don't have absolute assurance of eternal salvation and why they reject eternal security, clarify what a believer can and cannot lose through prolonged carnality if he can never lose eternal salvation, and exegetically engage with numerous "perplexing passages" that are appealed to in an effort to deny eternal security or confuse believers who do believe in it.

This is no secondary issue but involves important scriptural truths related to the "helmet of salvation" (Eph. 6:17) that must be taken and put on to be victorious in the real, invisible, spiritual battle that believers are daily engaged in against the "wiles of the devil" (Eph. 6:11). Since God commands believers to "take" (imperative mood) the "helmet of salvation" and "the sword of the Spirit which is the Word of God," this indicates to us that the truths of the Gospel, eternal security, and the absolute assurance of eternal salvation are crucial areas of doctrine where Satan attacks the believer.

Christian, do you have your helmet on? You need not ever take it off but instead revel and rejoice in the reality and assurance of the present and personal possession of your free and forever gift of salvation, totally offered on the basis of God's grace, paid in full by the shed blood of Jesus Christ, and received by you through simple childlike faith in Him alone. God is saying to you,

> These things I have written to you who believe in the name of the Son of God, that you may know that you have eternal life, and that you may continue to believe in the name of the Son of God. (1 John 5:13)

Believer in Christ, will you now seek, out of gratitude for God's grace and love, to live by faith for and in the Son of God who died for you and rose again in light of your incredible identification with Jesus Christ?

> For the love of Christ compels us, because we judge thus: that if One died for all, then all died; and He died for all, that those who live should live no longer for themselves, but for Him who died for them and rose again. (2 Cor. 5:14-15)

> I have been crucified with Christ; it is no longer I who live, but Christ lives in me; and the life which I now live in the flesh I live by faith in the Son of God, who loved me and gave Himself for me. (Gal. 2:20)

If you have never trusted solely in Jesus Christ for your eternal salvation, and therefore have never possessed the assurance of salvation based upon the Word of God, it is not a matter of walking an aisle, praying the sinner's prayer, asking Jesus into your heart, giving your life to Christ, surrendering to His daily mastery of your life, getting baptized, making a commitment to Christ, or any other good works that you might do to attempt to get God to save you. Why? It is because God has already been propitiated or satisfied with Jesus Christ's (God who became a man) substitutionary death for you and your sins on Calvary's cross and is waiting and willing to save you from a Hell you deserve to a Heaven you don't.

You might ask, "What is the proof that Christ's work on the cross was not only necessary but is enough to save a hopeless, helpless, sinner like me?" Jesus Christ answered when He cried out from the cross and uttered "IT IS FINISHED" (John 19:30)! And what is the proof that God accepted Christ's payment for all of your sins? On the third day, God raised Him from the dead (Rom. 4:25)! Thus, eternal salvation is not a reward for good works or allegedly good people, but it is a free gift for undeserving sinners like you and me!

> Being justified freely by his grace through the redemption that is in Christ Jesus: Whom God hath set forth to be a propitiation through faith in his blood. (Rom. 3:24-25)

Since God has been forever satisfied with what Jesus Christ accomplished on the cross for you, the only question that remains is: "Are you satisfied with the person and finished work of Jesus Christ? Have you by faith staked your eternal destiny on Jesus Christ alone and His finished work rather than your own works so as to receive His promised and guaranteed salvation?" Why not settle this issue of your eternal destiny right now and know beyond the shadow of a doubt that you SHALL NEVER PERISH FOREVER?

> And he brought them out and said, "Sirs, what must I do to be saved?" So they said, "Believe on the Lord Jesus Christ, and you will be saved." (Acts 16:30-31)

> Jesus Christ promised that, "My sheep hear My voice, and I know them, and they follow Me. And I give them eternal life, and they shall never perish; neither shall anyone snatch them out of My hand. My Father, who has given them to Me, is greater than all; and no one is able to snatch them out of My Father's hand. I and My Father are one." (John 10:27-30)

I am not worthy the least of His favor,
But Jesus left heaven for me;
The Word became flesh and He died as my Savior,
Forsaken on dark Calvary.

I am not worthy the least of His favor,
But "in the Beloved" I stand;
Now I'm an heir with my wonderful Savior,
And all things are mine at His hand.

I am not worthy the least of His favor,
But He is preparing a place

Where I shall dwell with my glorified Savior,
For ever to look on His face.

I am not worthy! This dull tongue repeats it;
I am not worthy! This heart gladly beats it.
Jesus left heaven to die in my place—
What mercy, what love and what grace![1]

---

[1] Beatrice Bixler, *I Am Not Worthy*.

Subject Index

abiding in Christ, 108, 206, 212, 215, 279-80, 289, 308
Abihu, 295
Abimelech, 48
Abiram, 296
Abraham, 138, 166, 279
Adam, 120, 122, 295
adokimos, 239
adultery, 204, 279, 309; spiritual, 306
Ahithophel, 47
Alexander, 109, 218
altar call, 84, 318
Ananias, 146, 297, 302
angels, 42, 48, 65, 237
anger, 279
Antichrist, 195
anxiety, 162
aorist tense, 166, 262
apostasy, 55, 90, 108, 114, 166, 244
Arminianism, 21, 28, 106, 108, 134, 175, 191, 208, 257, 259, 261, 269
ascension of Christ. *See under* Christ
asking Jesus into one's heart, 15, 208, 318
assurance of salvation, 7, 21; absolute, 5, 9n, 16-17, 28, 36, 66, 108, 130, 157-69, 278; based on God's promises and Christ's work, 25, 43, 46, 50, 61, 73, 75, 86, 134-42, 200; birthright of every believer, 140; essence of faith, 140-41; examples of, 152-54; false, 147, 158, 221; lack of, 131; loss of, 163-64

baptism: 15, 302, 318
baptismal regeneration, 84
Baptist, 219
Bathsheba, 204
bearing vs. producing spiritual fruit, 206, 214, 290
Beelzebub, 228
Bereans, 9, 223, 308
Bible. *See* Scripture
birth certificate, 143
bitterness, 309
blasphemy against the Holy Spirit, 227-35
blood of Christ, 57, 59-60, 309
Book of Life, 273
born again. *See* regeneration
branch, spiritual, 290
bread of life, 84, 301
Brookes, James H., 150

Calvinism, 21, 28, 106, 108, 134, 146, 161, 175, 178, 191, 208, 257, 260, 261, 269
carnality, 21, 35, 48, 55, 144, 146, 163, 187-88, 215, 298
Catholicism. *See* Roman Catholicism
Chafer, Lewis Sperry, 80, 106, 116, 144, 290
Chapman, J. Wilbur, 148-49
charis, 41
chastening. *See* discipline
childhood salvation, 129, 164

Scripture Index

Other Books by Grace Gospel Press

Available at amazon.com
and barnesandnoble.com

Freely by His Grace: Classical Free Grace Theology. Edited by J. B. Hixson, Rick Whitmire, and Roy B. Zuck. This book contains a wealth of biblical, theological, and practical insight into the theme of God's amazing and free grace. Includes 17 chapters by 14 different authors and leaders presenting a classical Free Grace view on a variety of topics related to salvation, sanctification, and dispensationalism. 634 pp. hardcover

The Gospel of the Christ by Thomas L. Stegall. Does a person have to believe the gospel to be saved forever? This book provides an in-depth, exegetical reply to this question and many related doctrinal issues as it addresses the recent aberration of the gospel within Free Grace evangelicalism known as the crossless gospel. An excellent resource and reference book on what a person must believe to be saved. 828 pp. hardcover

Holding Fast to Grace by Roy L. Aldrich. A classic treatment of the contrast between law and grace demonstrating that the believer in this present dispensation is under a higher standard of grace and is not under the Law of Moses, including the Ten Commandments, as the rule of life. This book is a useful tool to help all believers grow in the grace and knowledge of Jesus Christ (2 Peter 3:18). 110 pp. softcover

The Judgment Seat of Christ by Samuel L. Hoyt. The coming of Christ to rapture believers is an imminent prophetic event. But are you ready for the judgment seat of Christ to follow? This book explains what this great event involves and what you can expect, in a thorough yet easily readable sytle that is biblically balanced and grace-oriented. 228 pp. softcover

Repentance: The Most Misunderstood Word in the Bible by G. Michael Cocoris. This book shows how the words "repent" and "repentance" are used in the Bible and what they mean in their contexts. It demonstrates very clearly that repentance is a change of mind that occurs whenever a person believes, rather than the traditional, religious meaning of turning from sin or changing one's behavior. 100 pp. softcover

Truthspeak by Michael D. Halsey. This book explains the true biblical meaning of five key Christian words that have been distorted by religious "newspeak": grace, finished, repentance, believe, and justified. This book is ideal for showing people the difference between religion and true biblical Christianity. 100 pp. softcover

CPSIA information can be obtained at www.ICGtesting.com
Printed in the USA
BVOW010715071112

304909BV00006B/87/P